MOVEME
ENGLISH LI
1900–1

MOVEMENTS IN ENGLISH LITERATURE 1900 —1940

CHRISTOPHER GILLIE

College Lecturer, Trinity Hall, University of Cambridge

CAMBRIDGE UNIVERSITY PRESS

Published by the Syndics of the Cambridge University Press
Bentley House, 200 Euston Road, London NW1 2DB
American Branch 32 East 57th Street, New York, N.Y.10022

© Cambridge University Press 1975

Library of Congress Catalogue Card Number: 74–16993

ISBNs 0 521 20655 3 hard covers
0 521 09922 6 paperback

First published 1975

Typesetting by Linocomp Ltd,
Marcham, Oxon.

Printed in Great Britain
at the University Printing House, Cambridge
(Euan Phillips, University Printer)

Acknowledgements

Lines from 'A Bride in the 30's' and 'The Watershed' from *Collected Shorter Poems 1927–1957* by W. H. Auden are reprinted by permission of Faber and Faber Ltd and Random House, Inc., copyright Randon House Inc.

'An Irish Airman Foresees his Death' reprinted with permission of M. B. Yeats, Miss Anne Yeats, Macmillan of London and Basingstoke, The Macmillan Company of Canada Ltd and Macmillan Publishing Co. Inc. from *Collected Poems* by W. B. Yeats. Copyright 1919 by Macmillan Publishing Co., Inc., renewed 1947 by Bertha Georgie Yeats; 26 lines from 'Among School Children' reprinted with permission of M. B. Yeats, Miss Anne Yeats, Macmillan of London and Basingstoke, The Macmillan Company of Canada Ltd and Macmillan Publishing Co. Inc. from *Collected Poems* by W. B. Yeats. Copyright 1928 by Macmillan Publishing Co., Inc., renewed 1956 by Georgie Yeats; 'The Second Yeats, Macmillan of London and Basingstoke, The Macmillan Company of Canada Ltd and Macmillan Publishing Co. Inc. from *Collected Poems* by W. B. Yeats. Copyright 1924 by Macmillan

Publishing Co., Inc., renewed 1952 by Bertha Georgie Yeats; 'Who Goes with Fergus' reprinted with permission of M. B. Yeats, Miss Anne Yeats, Macmillan of London and Basingstoke, The Macmillan Company of Canada Ltd and Macmillan Publishing Co. Inc. from *Collected Poems* by W. B. Yeats. Copyright 1906 by Macmillan Publishing Co. Inc., renewed 1934 by William Butler Yeats.

The extracts from *A Passage to India* by E. M. Forster are reprinted by permission of Edward Arnold Ltd.

'Drummer Hodge' and 'The Self-Unseeing' from *The Collected Poems of Thomas Hardy* (Copyright 1925 by Macmillan Publishing Co., Inc.) are reprinted by permission of the Trustees of the Hardy Estate and Macmillan London and Basingstoke, The Macmillan Company of Canada Ltd and Macmillan Publishing Co. Inc.

'On the Idle Hill of Summer' from *A Shropshire Lad* – Authorised Edition – from *The Collected Poems of A. E. Housman*. Copyright 1935, 1940 © 1965 by Holt, Rinehart and Winston, Inc. Copyright © 1967, 1698 by Robert E. Symons. Reprinted by permission of Holt, Rinehart and Winston Inc., The Society of Authors as the literary representative of the Estate of A. E. Housman, and Jonathan Cape Ltd, English publishers of A. E. Housman's *Collected Poems*.

'Preludes' I and IV and the lines from 'Gerontion' and 'Marina' from *Collected Poems 1909–1962* by T. S. Eliot are printed by permission of Faber and Faber Ltd and Harcourt Brace Jovanovich, Inc., copyright 1936 by Harcourt Brace Jovanovich, Inc., copyright © 1963, 1964, by T. S. Eliot.

Contents

1

Introduction:
The world of art and art in the world:
twentieth-century differences

To you literature like painting is an end, to me literature like architecture is a means, it has a use . . . I had rather be called a journalist than an artist, that is the essence of it.

H. G. Wells to Henry James (1915)

Meanwhile . . . I hold your distinction between a form that is (like) a painting and a form that is (like) architecture for wholly null and void. There is no sense in which architecture is essentially 'for use' that doesn't leave any other art exactly as much so . . . It is art that *makes* life, makes interest, makes importance . . . and I know of no substitute whatever for the force and beauty of its process.

Henry James to H. G. Wells (1915)

James and Wells were novelists, and they were friends, but as these quotations from their letters show, they disagreed about the practice of their art. James longed for a wide readership, but it was unthinkable to him that he should acquire one by compromising in the least degree between the exactingness of his art, which was as demanding as he could conceive it to be, and whatever the public might desire in the way of relaxing amusement. Wells was a novelist almost by accident: he wrote novels because he wanted to speak to as large an audience as he could reach, and novels reached a larger one than any other form of entertainment.

Their dispute makes a useful opening for a study of literature in this century for four reasons. First, it was representative of a deep disagreement near the beginning of the century about the nature and purpose of all art, including literature. Secondly, this disagreement was not merely personal and local in time, but in a degree has continued to divide writers till the present day: in short, it differentiates writers in a typically twentieth-century way. Thirdly, it illustrates something important about the character of English literature, not merely in this century, but in much of its history at least as far back as the beginning of the English novel. Finally, in ways which I will try to explain at the end of the chapter,

1

the points of view are worth distinguishing because they help the reader to respond to individual writers who invite the one approach or the other to their work.

It may seem extravagant to base so much on a disagreement between two men who, though they were friends, seem to have been designed by nature for mutual misunderstanding, and who, moreover, had quite different artistic statures. One must begin at least by acknowledging these personal differences, before going on to explore the more impersonal issues.

James was an American from New England; his father had been an abstruse philosopher of great rhetorical power, and his brother, William, was one of the most eminent philosophers of his day. Born to leisure, but imbued with their father's ideals for a lifetime of spiritually lofty and intellectually spacious education of their minds, the brothers were sent to school in America, France, Germany and Switzerland, and Henry then went on a personal exploration of European culture. He admired intensely the most fastidious literary artists of France and Russia – Flaubert and Turgeniev – but he never lost his sense of quite a different criterion: the personal moral integrity which his native country set above any other cultural integrity. In the end he settled in London, moving in sophisticated circles, despising the provinciality of English (as compared to Parisian) taste, but deeply sympathetic to the moral insights of the English (in distinction from the French) fictional tradition.

Wells, an Englishman, was a younger man – born in 1866, some twenty-three years later than James. He was the son of a small trader, became a science teacher in a school, and acquired a science degree at London University. Then, after a discouraging beginning, he achieved a major success in science fiction (*The Time Machine*, 1895) and went on to write a large number of works: more science fiction, novels with a strong autobiographical element set in the lower middle class, huge experiments in popular education (*The Outline of History*, 1920), and polemical works – he joined the socialist Fabian Society in 1903. In fact all his writing might be described as polemical, or at least educational; Wells believed that society must be socially reformed, and that technology would be the great instrument of its reform – an optimism he altogether abandoned at the end of his life. In so far as adjectives can sum up personalities, Wells was extroverted, versatile, bumptious, high-

2

spirited, assertive and credulous; James was introverted, dedicated, urbane, sombre, tortuous and sceptical. They shared a deep concern about the human condition, but even that resemblance concealed an enormous disparity. James's material was the human psyche – its elusiveness, rapacity and vulnerability; Wells's interest in human nature was far more physical and environmental. No wonder, as Wells came to see after James's death, they argued at cross-purposes, but the argument was not merely futile. It was on the contrary fertile in that it concerned not the subject of fiction but the treatment of the subject, and beyond that it raised the question of the purpose and nature of art.

For the sake of intelligibility, it is worth outlining how it all began. In 1912 Wells published a novel called *Marriage*, which opens with a young man named Trafford crashing an aeroplane in a garden where, among others, there is a girl named Marjorie Pope. 'Thereupon', recounts Wells in his *Autobiography* (1934) –

there is bandaging, ambulance work and much coming and going and Marjorie . . . falls deeply in love with Trafford. She drives into the village in a donkey cart to do some shopping and meets the lamed Trafford, and their wheels interlock and they fall talking. All that – except for the writing – was tolerable according to James. But then, in order to avoid the traffic in the high road the two young people take their respective donkey carts into a side lane and remain there talking for three hours. And this is where James's objection came in. Of the three hours of intercourse in the lane the novel tells nothing, except that the young people emerged in open and declared love with each other. This, said James, wasn't playing the game. I had cut out the essential after a feast of irrelevant particulars. Gently but firmly he insisted that I did not know myself what had happened . . . that I had not thought out the individualities concerned with sufficient care and thoroughness . . . Henry James was quite right in saying that I had not thought out these two people to the pitch of saturation and that they did not behave unconsciously and naturally. But my defence is that that did not matter, or at least that for the purposes of the book it did not matter very much.

What were 'the purposes of the book'? Wells has already explained that his original assumption as a novelist had been that 'problems of adjustment were the essential matter for novel-writing'. In other words, he seems to have felt that people wanted to read novels, or could profitably read them, in order to receive enlightenment about the complications of their personal lives.

Now there is little doubt that James, so far, was right in the argument. For how can a novelist present 'problems of adjustment' when he admits that the characters whose problems are to be adjusted have not been fully thought out? Leaving aside the huge questions whether any significant personal problem can ever be 'adjusted', and whether, if it can, there is not an even greater problem in deciding the implications for general living of such a delicate process, Wells is clearly failing to understand that unthought-out characters cannot realistically *have* problems. This is where we come against the difficulty that James and Wells were, as novelists, not merely of different kinds but of different statures. The argument is between James, a major novelist, and Wells, a very talented minor novelist: between a professional who understands his job very well indeed, and an amateur who doesn't fully understand it. But the argument has a deeper level, which is suggested by Wells's complaint, in his autobiography, that James had no idea that a novel could be an aid to conduct. This raises a disagreement which had been maturing between schools of thought over the previous half century, though irregularly, without a consistent front between the parties.

Hebraism and hellenism: conscience and consciousness

In 1869, the critic Matthew Arnold published his influential book *Culture and Anarchy*. In this he distinguished two basic attitudes of mind, one of which sought to pursue morally effective action, disregarding enlightenment of the mind, and the other sought intellectual enlightenment, in indifference to practical conduct. Because the former is ethical and nourished by Bible-inspired protestantism, he related it to the ancient Hebrews and called it hebraism; because the latter is cultural, he derived it from the aesthetic and philosophical achievements of ancient Greece and called it hellenism. A healthy society requires both, for if concern for ideas without concern for practice is plainly absurd, it is equally true that a nation guided merely by its conscience will not be in a position to know whether its conscience is properly educated. This he considered to be the case with the British. If he was right, they were clearly in a serious case, for he typified their cultural attitudes as those of 'barbarians' (upper classes) who preferred the culture of the body to that of the mind, the 'philistines' (the middle classes) who were indifferent to either, and the 'populace' (all the rest)

4

who were ignorant of both. What the British, in Arnold's opinion, needed was education in that nobility of spirit whose embodiment was high art, and especially the art of poetry at its greatest – in Homer, Dante, Shakespeare and Milton. Poetry, he predicted, would replace religion as the source of those spiritual qualities without which any civilisation must lapse into squalor. In his essay 'The Study of Poetry' (1888) he maintained that the best poetry operates as a touchstone of truth and hence as 'a criticism of life' – a test by which the truthfulness and depth of the emotions governing conduct can be judged.

It is plain that Arnold never contemplated the divorce of art from life; quite on the contrary, he complained that high art did not have the centrality which it ought to have in the life of society. All the same, he makes a special claim for poetry as offering an unique function, and recommends a conscious reverence for the poetic medium:

For in poetry the distinction between excellent and inferior, sound and unsound or only half-sound, true and untrue or only half true, is of paramount importance. It is of paramount importance because of the high destinies of poetry. In poetry, as a criticism of life under the conditions fixed for such a criticism by the laws of poetic truth and poetic beauty, the spirit of our race will find, we have said, as time goes on and as other helps fail, its consolation and stay.

Such reverence for an artistic medium tends to make the artists who practise it into a kind of priestly castle, and a 'priesthood' of art is just what one does find emerging among a number of artistic cults in the second half of the century. Arnold did not father them; it was his intention to change the attitude of society towards art rather than to change that of artists towards society. Nevertheless, his was among a number of influences tending in the same direction: the writings of Ruskin the art critic and of Pater the scholar of the Renaissance were others. The tendency had already shown itself in the mid-century group of poets and painters, together with those affiliated to them, who called themselves Pre-Raphaelites. At the end of the century, more extremely and wantonly, it was evident in the Aesthetic Movement whose leader was Oscar Wilde. He wrote in *The Decay of Lying* (1889): 'Art never expresses anything but itself. It has an independent life, just as thought has, and develops purely on its own lines.' This was not what Arnold meant at all, and yet Wilde also was defying the philistines.

5

It was just the priestliness of the artist, this extreme reverence for the medium in which he worked, which Wells disliked in James. In his autobiography Wells explained it thus:

He had no possible use of the novel as a help to conduct. His mind was turned away from any such idea. From his point of view there were not so much novels as The Novel, and it was a very high and important achievement. He thought of it as an Art Form and of novelists as artists of a very special and exalted type. He was concerned with their greatness and repute. He saw us all as Masters or would-be Masters, little Masters and great Masters, and he was plainly sorry that 'Cher Maître' was not an English expression. One could not be in a room with him for ten minutes without realising the importance he attached to this dignity of his. I was by nature and education unsympathetic with this mental disposition. But I was disposed to regard a novel as about as much an art form as a market place or a boulevard. It had not even necessarily to get anywhere. You went by it on your various occasions.

There is some justice in these remarks, but we would be misled and unjust to James if we suppose Wells to mean that James cared nothing for moral insights. Far from this, James, the New Englander with a long puritan tradition behind him, continued to believe that moral insight is central to art as to life. But James would have thought it presumptuous to offer a novel 'as a help to conduct'. He believed in the art of the novel as Arnold believed in the art of poetry: as a touchstone of truth and a 'criticism of life', and he believed that it could be this just because it is separate from life, for 'Literature is an objective, a projected result; it is life that is the unconscious, the agitated, the struggling, floundering cause' (essay on Balzac). Wells, on the other hand, rejected this separation of art from life, although he did come to feel that his argument with James presented him with a real dilemma. It is a dilemma which his contemporary Bernard Shaw summed up in connection with the drama. Writing of Ibsen's controversial play about the status of woman in marriage and society, Shaw said: '*A Doll's House* will be as flat as ditchwater when *A Midsummer Night's Dream* is as fresh as paint; but it will have done more work in the world; and that is enough for the highest genius.'

With these three writers in mind, it is tempting to distinguish their approaches as those of the artist and the journalist. James, certainly, insisted on the title of artist, just as Wells preferred that of journalist, and Shaw recovered English drama from its long apathy by making it into a new kind of journalistic vehicle. The

6

distinction, however, between art and journalism is much more treacherous than it is often taken to be, and some discussion of their relationship is relevant to our subject. For not only has the English novel in its past history commonly been associated with journalism, but the two kinds of writing were closely connected in their very origins.

The English novel: a special case

A strange feature of Arnold's campaign for cultural revival was that he ignored – or almost ignored – the novel. That he should have ignored contemporary drama was understandable: there had been no major English drama since the early part of the seventeenth century; but when we now look back at the literature of Victorian England, it is the novels of Dickens and George Eliot, not to mention important lesser figures, which impress us as its major achievement. Yet he was not alone in this obliviousness; the philosopher, John Stuart Mill, for instance, whose life had been changed by the poetry of Wordsworth, despised prose fiction, and no major critic gave the art of the novel serious attention until Henry James himself, in his essay 'The Art of Fiction' (1884).

The explanation for this neglect seems to lie in the history of English culture as far back as the impact on it of the Renaissance in the sixteenth century. The word 'renaissance' means rebirth, and it was used by men of that century themselves to express their conviction that they had recovered the very spirit of ancient Greece and Rome in their own art and scholarship. But the Renaissance really meant more than this: the men of the period really believed – or acted as if they believed – that they had discovered the meaning of 'civilisation'. In their feeling, the long centuries that lay between themselves and ancient Rome were a protracted interlude, the 'Middle Ages' as they were the first to call them. From the sixteenth to the nineteenth centuries, western Europeans lived in this faith that what the ancient Greeks and Romans and the men of the Renaissance believed to be civilisation was civilisation indeed; that loss of that particular vision meant relapse into barbarism. It is true that by the second quarter of the nineteenth century the English underwent a partial change of heart: gothic, not classicism, gave them imaginative excitement. But this was a change which chiefly affected the visual arts, especially architecture. Although

7

medieval subjects had a strong appeal for nineteenth-century poets, the spirit of intellectual culture was still classical.

However the Renaissance spirit, although it spread widely among western nations, was primarily a scholarly and an aristocratic movement; as C. S. Lewis has said, it caused education to spread *upwards* through society. The literary arts cultivated by the Greeks and Romans – above all rhetoric, poetry and the poetic drama – became the culture of these upper classes and of the more learned of the middle classes. On the other hand the commercial middle classes (and those below them) were far less penetrated by the Renaissance spirit, and far more influenced by the religious movement of the Reformation which reached Britain at about the same time. Thus that large section of society was much more affected by the translated Bible than it was by Virgil and Seneca; indeed a strong section of them was suspicious of all secular forms of literature, especially any sort of fiction.

Nevertheless it was from these classes that English prose fiction, what we nowadays recognise as the novel, took its rise. They were inclined at first to distrust even the religious allegories of John Bunyan (1628–88), and still more the secular tales of Daniel Defoe (1660–1731) – both men from the middle class – but they came to treasure them, for the first dealt in true doctrine as they understood it, and the second with the workaday facts of minute texture such as composed the web of their lives. These proto-novelists were succeeded by a writer from the same class, who has often been designated the first true novelist – Samuel Richardson (1689–1761), who used fiction to preach the kind of morality which his class deeply approved. Certainly there were other kinds of novelist, for instance Henry Fielding (1707–54) who would have nothing to do with Richardson's ethics; but novels, although their readership quickly extended far outside any particular social periphery, basically retained their strongly middle-class characteristics of truth to daily fact and affirmation of middle-class (not necessarily mean, illiberal, or superficial) human and ethical values.

And yet, to nineteenth-century men of culture – the culture of the Renaissance through the 'public' schools – the novel was still felt to be an intruder on the cultural scene. Its matter and manner were tainted with what seemed to be the ephemerality of current events. To suppose that journalism is necessarily ephemeral is a mistake, but to see a connection between the novel and journalism was correct. Defoe, one of the earliest novelists in the modern sense, was also one of the first modern journalists, and in his work the two kinds of writing overlap. Some of his best fictions, for instance *A Journal of the Plague Year*, were reconstructions made to resemble a journalistic account by an eye-witness. Thereafter, although there were many different sorts of novel and some of them improbable and even fantastic narrations, the conscience of the best novelists had resembled the conscience of the best journalists, dictating an imaginative image of current social fact. When Arnold sought for his touchstones of truth, he did not think of looking for them in novels, for no novelist could, or even desired to, epitomise the permanent truths of human experience disentangled from specific social predicaments, as great poets had done.

How, then, did it come about that, by the end of the century, Henry James could make such exalted claims for the novel as high art? A clue to the understanding of this paradox is that James did not consider *English* novels, as they existed up to his time, to exemplify the disciplines and the scope which he considered due to high art. In a lecture delivered in 1905, he deprecates English novelistic indiscipline to his American audience in the following terms:

I do not propose for a moment to invite you to blink the fact that our huge Anglo-Saxon array of producers and readers . . . presents production uncontrolled, production untouched by criticism, unguided, unlighted, uninstructed, unashamed, on a scale that is really a new thing in the world.

James makes these remarks by way of introducing his subject, the French novelist Balzac, and it was to the French school that James had apprenticed himself in his youth. It is at least arguable that James greatly exaggerated the superiority of French novelists over British ones in their care for artistic form; if he did so, it was because the French tradition, more aristocratic in its origins than the English tradition had been, had cultivated a form that was closer to the Renaissance ideal, the ideal of western European culture which fascinated him so strongly.

James turned away from the French for a reason that he gives in his review of Zola's *Nana*:

This is what saves us in England, in spite of our artistic levity and the presence of the young ladies – this fact that we are by disposition better psychologists, that we have, as a general thing, a deeper, more delicate perception of the play of character and the state of the soul.

9

But it seems that he never fully considered what it was in the form of the English novel (since it had one of some sort) that gave it this greater freedom. The English novelist began with 'a something to say' – a theme more or less strongly felt according to his seriousness and capacity – and then allowed the theme to generate its own growth. The result, if his imagination was too weak or the theme too casually felt, might be triviality or confusion – just the sort of confusion which James thought characteristic of life and alien to art, and which he found in Bennett's *Clayhanger* (1910) and *Hilda Lessways* (1911): 'A huge and in its way a varied aggregation, without traceable lines, divinable direction, effect of composition . . .' But if the novelist were a genius and fully engaged, the novel might achieve its own consistency while unfolding into great amplitude. One might call this – to evoke one of its finest practitioners – the Dickens method. The James method – and he remained aesthetically a disciple of the French – began with contemplation of a selected theme and proceeded by exclusion of irrelevancies and concentration on essentials. The Dickens method was from the spontaneous emergence of the theme to its fullest amplification by a generous welcome to contingent material.

I have called this 'the Dickens method' and not 'the Wells method', because Wells is too small a novelist to set up against James. But a younger novelist than either was beginning to establish himself when the Wells–James dispute was at its height: this was D. H. Lawrence (1885–1930). He is now seen to have been one of the greatest English novelists, and he belonged to the English tradition in the sense that James deplored as well as in the sense which he admired.

D. H. Lawrence and the book of life

Lawrence, the miner's son, belonged to the great Nonconformist tradition of English literature; the tradition which had from the start been suspicious of the classical Renaissance and its civilisation, who did not attend the great public schools to receive a classical education, who were the spiritual core of Arnold's philistines, although often much less uncultured than he made them out to be. Although lately they had read much else, for generations their chief literature had been the English Bible, which for them had been 'the Book of Life'. But in his essay 'Why the Novel Matters', unpublished in his lifetime, Lawrence wrote:

The novel is the book of life. In this sense, the Bible is a great confused novel. You may say it is about God. But it is really about man alive. Adam, Eve, Sarai, Abraham, Isaac, Jacob, Samuel, David, Bath-Sheba, Ruth, Esther, Solomon, Job, Isaiah, Jesus, Mark, Judas, Paul, Peter: what is it but man alive, from start to finish? Man alive, not mere bits. Even the Lord is another man alive, in a burning bush, throwing the tablets of stone at Moses's head.

No doubt the old-fashioned Nonconformist would have thought Lawrence's way of putting it blasphemous, but Nonconformists had indeed read the Bible in the spirit he suggests, right back to that great proto-novelist, John Bunyan himself. It was not merely the supreme book of moral and spiritual guidance, but of dramatised guidance; moreover the strict Nonconformist believed that beside it all other kinds of instruction – by poetry, philosophy and science – were frivolous and vain. Bunyan, and in their ways even Defoe and Richardson, were extending the functions of the Bible in their fictions by presenting as wide as possible a range of types in as full as possible particularity and in factually convincing predicaments. In this tradition, Lawrence believed that the novel and only the novel (though he uses the term so loosely as to include Shakespeare and Homer as well as the Bible) envisaged human nature in its entirety, and not selectively:

For this reason I am a novelist. And being a novelist, I consider myself superior to the saint, the scientist, the philosopher, and the poet, who are all great masters of different bits of man alive, but never get the whole hog.

In his beliefs, Lawrence can only be described as a religious man. He was far from being an orthodox Christian in any shape. He was religious because he believed that the final truth about human nature was a mystery. It was not a mystery in the sense in which some philosophers would understand the word: a centre of darkness only awaiting sufficiently penetrating shafts of light from the disciplines of philosophy, science and psychology to become fully clarified, but in the sense that human nature cannot be rationally understood (as a computer can be) but can only be known in communion with itself, through relationship with others. In this belief, Lawrence considered that our society has given far too much attention to the education of the reason at the expense of education of the feelings. 'Educated!' he exclaims in his essay, 'The Novel and the Feelings', 'We are not even *born*, as far as our feelings are concerned.' And he believed that the novel was the great educator of the feelings because

In the novel you see one man becoming a corpse, because of his so-called goodness, another going dead because of his so-called wickedness. Right and wrong is an instinct: but an instinct of the whole consciousness in a man, bodily, mental, spiritual at once. And only in the novel are *all* things given full play, or at least they may be given full play, when we realise that life itself, and not inert safety, is the reason for living.

('Why the Novel Matters')

There are resemblances in all this to Arnold's doctrine that great poetry can provide the touchstone for a true 'criticism of life'. But Arnold feared above all the changefulness of his age, and his appeal to poetry was to a resource of permanent truth which transcend flux. Lawrence would have none of this; permanence was for him fixity, and fixity was death:

'The grass withereth, the flower fadeth, but the Word of the Lord shall stand for ever.' That's the kind of stuff we've drugged ourselves with. As a matter of fact, the grass withereth, but comes up all the greener for that reason, after the rains.

He was more in tune with William Blake, another great figure in the Nonconformist tradition, for instance in Blake's Proverbs of Hell: 'Drive your cart and your plow over the bones of the dead.' (One could quote much else from Blake to show his kinship with Lawrence.) But in style Lawrence's writings have kinship with those of H. G. Wells and Wells's friend Arnold Bennett. He was not a journalist in the sense that Wells was, of seeking to influence 'opinion', for Lawrence had no interest in opinion of the kind that can be made or unmade by a newspaper; nor was he a journalist in the sense that Bennett was, that he ever wrote merely to sell. But he was a journalist in his essays in the colloquiality of his style, which was as different as it could be from James's, and aimed to achieve communication with the reader as directly and expeditiously as possible. His novels, too, have that seeming discursiveness – or form within what appears to be formlessness – which resembles the journalist's licence rather than the artist's exclusiveness. Lawrence was indeed as consistently serious as James was, as a novelist. The difference between them was that while for James the novel was 'the great art and the great form', and he recommended aspirants to 'do something with life' (*Letter to the Deer-field Summer School*), for Lawrence it was a mere 'tremulation on the ether' unless it *brought* life and vitalised the consciousness.

The two kinds of fiction

'It is art that *makes* life', declared James in his last letter to Wells, meaning that it makes life significant. For Wells, art, or specifically the novel, was just one of many kinds of communication which life makes use of. For Lawrence, 'the novel as a tremulation can make the whole man alive tremble' – it was the life-bringer. In so far as James laid his emphasis on 'the world of art' while Wells and Lawrence both emphasised 'art in the world', it seems fair to say that Lawrence was on Wells's side of the question, although in his seriousness and importance as a novelist he was closer to James.

It is difficult to find adequate terms with which to distinguish these two kinds of writer. If we choose to call James an artist and Wells and Lawrence journalists, this is misleading, for even Wells was an artist some of the time and Lawrence was one all the time, though both were different kinds of artist from James. Both Wells and Lawrence have been designated 'prophets', but this is also a misleading term to ascribe to them, for it has two meanings. One sense (which the poet William Blake had not been afraid to apply to himself a hundred years before) is appropriate to Lawrence, and implies one who sees more and reveals more about his world than other men do; the other sense, appropriate to Wells in much of his science fiction, implies an unusual capacity to predict a course of events. The two senses are distinct, for a visionary may make no attempt to predict events (though Lawrence occasionally did), and the predictor may have no sense of the inner meaning of what he predicts. The term prophet is also unsatisfactory inasmuch as it cannot be extended to include a writer like the novelist Arnold Bennett, whose work is in many ways comparable to that of Wells, but who lacked Wells's sense of mission and was in neither sense of the word a prophet.

I offer instead the word 'interpreter' for writers like Lawrence, Wells and Bennett in order to distinguish them from writers such as James, since it begs fewest questions and comes closest to expressing what they have in common. An interpreter conveys meanings from one language into another, but he may have a more mysterious function like that of the Interpreter in Bunyan's *Pilgrim's Progress* who 'showeth the things of the Lord': that is to say, he transmits meanings through imaginative symbols in order to enlighten the pilgrims on their journey. Bunyan was himself such an interpreter, and the word fittingly expresses the work of many English novelists who have pursued his aims of psychological understanding and his desire to direct their readers to a fuller life.

This word, too, is not fully satisfactory (and must be regarded as strictly provisional), for when James claimed that 'art makes life' he was also, in his way, proclaiming himself an interpreter. But when Wells protested that James turned his back on the novel 'as a help to conduct', he was, if rather crudely, making a genuine point. To appreciate a writer like James, the reader – especially of the later novels – has to subject himself to the Jamesian 'world or art', whereas Lawrence, Wells and Bennett do their best to remain in the reader's world, so as to act directly on his conduct, attitude and feelings. James found himself becoming more and more abstruse in his art, because he was concerned to exploit its resources to the full for the sake of realising its scope, and he made this his concern, because he felt that the novel as an art had been unduly neglected in England. It flourished, however, as an entertainment, which was why Wells and Lawrence chose to communicate through it.

But what of a medium which, as an art in James's sense, had been fully cultivated over a long period, but had lost its popularity? This was the very different predicament in which the poets found themselves at the beginning of the century.

Poetry and communication

Poetry in the second half of the nineteenth century did not fulfil the high expectations which Arnold, among many others, thought due from it. Few poets of any age have combined so sensitive an ear for the music of language with such earnestness of purpose as Tennyson, few have proposed more strenuous thinking in verse than Robert Browning; few have been more intelligent than Matthew Arnold, have had a more intense feeling for beauty than Rossetti and Swinburne, or have been more serious in social endeavour than William Morris. Moreover all these were men of high talent, if not genius. And yet poets and poetry remained peripheral to the mind of the age. The confidence of the great Romantics at the beginning of the century – of Wordsworth who believed that poetry could regenerate society by renewing in it the purest and deepest human responses, of Blake who believed that poetry could enlarge the shrivelled minds of the age, of Shelley who preached that poets are 'the unacknowledged legislators of mankind' – such confidence forsook the Victorians.

Part of the explanation may be that the poets, daunted by the vigour and success of the scientists and their philosophic disciples, felt, without fully recognising their misgiving, that they had been robbed of all the powerful weapons of thought, and that this had reduced them to a province of emotion which – increasingly like the English countryside – many enjoyed visiting but few used for their working hours. 'As civilisation advances', wrote the historian Macaulay, 'poetry necessarily declines', and he was not the only one or the first to think so. In the first fourteen years of the twentieth century, most of the poets I have mentioned were dead, and of the best Victorians, only Thomas Hardy, who had returned to poetry after many years as a novelist, was still producing vital work. Hardy wrote of the English countryside, which circumscribed the work of so many of his contemporaries, better than they did, because he had grown out of it, an offspring of its peasantry, and because he combined a naive and poignant peasant's vision of the world with an instructed, sad acceptance of the destruction by the rationalists of the old poetic idealisms and religious faiths. But Hardy was inimitable, because the unique life of his verse was contributed by his idiosyncratic temperament to conservative forms.

There were of course many younger poets, and a substantial, if relatively small, reading public; in 1912 there was even a self-conscious poetic revival – the Georgian poets, so-called because George V succeeded Edward VII in 1910. These, however, did little more than ripple the surface of the dim poetic waters. Poetry was dim because no one could see the purpose it served any more: no one wanted from it the great epics and verse-dramas which the Victorians had still aspired to produce, and no one expected from it anything much better than the occasional pleasant tune.

And yet the decade 1910–20 was to turn out the most interesting one in poetic development for a hundred years. There were two especial reasons for this: one was the influence of drastic events – the wars in Europe and in Ireland – and the other, a change in thinking about the medium of poetry. The events of course influenced the thinking, but it happened that the thinking was chiefly done by three poets – Pound, Eliot and Yeats – who were not directly engaged in the events.

The chief event, the war of 1914–18, did throw up a group of poets whom the war made into a legend, giving them a kind of importance independent of their actual achievement. These were the so-called War Poets. Wilfred Owen, Siegfried Sassoon, Rupert Brooke, Edward Thomas, Edmund Blunden, Charles Sorley, Julian Grenfell, Robert Graves, Isaac Rosenberg – all these were soldiers, and only three (Sassoon, Blunden and Graves) survived; the rest (except Brooke, who died before he saw fighting) were killed in action. Owen and Sassoon are the best known, although good critics have thought Rosenberg the most original, and Thomas (who wrote little directly about the war) the finest in achievement.

Larger numbers of the population were engaged in the fighting than in any previous war, but the fighting men were divided from the civilians not only by the Channel but by the screen of war propaganda, so that there were (to borrow Benjamin Disraeli's phrase about the rich and the poor in the 1840s) 'two nations'. The squalor and horror of the front-line did not in consequence impress the home public, who were encouraged to glorify their own troops and hate the enemy. But for Sassoon and Owen the war was tragedy, the sufferers of which were on *both* sides of the battle line. For them, it was not their poetry that mattered, but the anger and compassion they could communicate through it. In a note to his poems, Owen wrote:

> Above all I am not concerned with Poetry.
> My subject is War, and the pity of War.
> The Poetry is in the pity.

Yet these elegies are to this generation in no sense consolatory. They may be to the next. All a poet can do to-day is warn. That is why the true Poets must be truthful.

He could not have expressed better the effect his poems were to have: in revulsion of horror and disgust after the exultation of victory, readers learned from them what war 'and the pity of war' really was. The War Poets were interpreters who had found a new

16

'use' for poetry. Yet none of them wrote major poetry; very possibly it was impossible to write it in their physical and psychological conditions. That is not important. What is important is that they broke barriers, although only the temporary barriers erected by the evil of war. They were able to do this because they used familiar forms with deep sincerity, and just because these forms had become associated with the communication of emotion and little else, the war poems were effective in communicating with private emotions at a time when these had become screened or hardened or distorted by public hysteria and official perversion.

But there were more permanent, less easily discernible barriers to be broken if contemporary poetry were ever again to become reading for intelligent and busy people. One was the barrier of language: the poets had come to assume that only certain words with certain emotional connotations were fit for 'poetic diction', and only certain rhythms (the artificial ones known as 'metrical') were musical enough for poetry. There were indeed exceptions: Hardy did not avoid 'unpoetic' diction, and Kipling used a popular ballad idiom, but these did not alter the current of assumption. Another barrier was that of thought: here the assumption had come to be that thinking is separate from feeling, and what the poet considered to be thinking was what he supposed the philosophers and scientists to do. Since he believed that he could not compete with them, he assumed that thinking was not his business, unless indeed he engaged in a rarefied emotional thinking such as the philosopher could not reach because for him it was not thought at all. A third barrier was that of 'realism': the poet and the great public had come to believe that what is 'real', what a human being has to contend with in the facts of his daily life, belongs to life's surface; a photograph was considered real whereas an oil painting was to some degree untrustworthy. It seemed not to be the poet's function to do with this surface – the surface of the environment in which most people live, that is to say the towns – but to provide holidays in the country by providing only pleasing surfaces, or escaping from surfaces by engaging in fantasy. But these barriers were only the evidence of a deeper one, which was not in the nature of a wall but of a gulf. It divided the minds of men from the unifying spiritual tradition which had animated Chaucer and Shakespeare. There was no longer a community of thought and feeling which all men and women shared, even in wretchedness, and the War displayed the fragmentation for all to see. Pound wrote in *Hugh Selwyn Mauberley* (1920):

> There died a myriad,
> And of the best, among them,
> For an old bitch gone in the teeth,
> For a botched civilization,
>
> Charm, smiling at the good mouth,
> Quick eyes gone under earth's lid,
>
> For two gross of broken statues,
> For a few thousand battered books.

Eliot and Pound were, like James, Americans; Pound made his home in Britain from 1908 till 1920; Eliot came here at the beginning of the war and, again like James, he stayed. Americans, perhaps because they inhabit a country of continental dimensions and look across to the small continent of Europe from the whole of which America has drawn its population, are often less insular than the British in their cultural purview. For James, Pound and Eliot, the cultural capital of Europe was not London but Paris, and though their native language was English, they were much more inclined than an English writer might be to see their culture as belonging to a European, not merely an English tradition. Just as James was drawn to the French novel, so Pound and Eliot were attracted to the Mediterranean cultures, and, so far as recent literature went, to French rather than English poets.

The French poets of the late romantic and symbolist movements – Baudelaire, Mallarmé, Laforgue, Rimbaud, Verlaine – were much more central to their era than the English Victorian poets, more adventurous in exploring their consciousness, more ruthless in facing the sombre and little understood regions of experience, more exploratory and uncompromising in their handling of language. Thus Eliot's and Pound's intelligent assimilation of the French influences swamped the banks of English poetic prejudice. English verse had come to resemble little streams and pools, easily identifiable in their scope and pleasant for a refreshing dip although offering little to the adventurous swimmer. The two Americans gave poetry a new panorama, bewildering and alarming in its depth and seeming boundlessness.

Such at least was the feeling of many readers of Pound's and Eliot's early work which appeared at the end of the war. However

18

these writers also demanded – although not so as to counteract the readers' dismay – a new strictness from poets in the critical handling of language. In the programme of the Imagist movement (a rival to the Georgians in 1912) Pound advocated that poets should use common speech as their medium, but use it exactly; that rhythms should obey no standardising rules, but should be sensitively adapted to moods; that images should be hard and clear, and that the poet should above all aim at concentration. Eliot's early critical essays (*The Sacred Wood*, 1920) drew attention to long-neglected areas of English poetry, the later Jacobean drama and the Metaphysical School contemporary with it, in which the division between thought and feeling did not hinder the poet. In an essay on the Metaphysicals (1921), Eliot epitomised the difference between them and the Victorians thus:

Tennyson and Browning are poets, and they think; but they do not feel their thought as immediately as the odour of a rose. A thought to Donne was an experience; it modified his sensibility. When a poet's mind is perfectly equipped for its work, it is constantly amalgamating disparate experience; the ordinary man's experience is chaotic, irregular, fragmentary. The latter falls in love, or reads Spinoza, and these two experiences have nothing to do with each other, or with the noise of the typewriter or the smell of cooking; in the mind of the poet these experiences are always forming new wholes.

The effects of Pound and Eliot in their poetic practice and criticism on the barriers which had hemmed in poetry were rather different. Pound bulldozed them away, by showing that many of them were based on tired conventions, timidity and lazy thinking. Eliot was more positive and philosophic. He was able to enlarge poetic scope not so much by flattening barriers as by showing that some of them were real but had been misunderstood. Thus on the question of thought and feeling, he acknowledged that the philosopher (his academic training had been in philosophy) thought in a way that poets didn't and shouldn't attempt; however this did not mean that poets should not think. Their poetry should be what he called 'the emotional equivalent of thought' ('Shakespeare and Seneca', 1927), thereby recovering 'the unification of the sensibility', for

Our civilization comprehends great variety and complexity, and this variety and complexity, playing upon a refined sensibility, must produce various and complex results. The poet must become more and more comprehensive, more allusive, more indirect, in order to force, to dislocate if necessary, language into his meaning. ('The Metaphysical Poets')

Poetic meaning thus became different from prose meaning, and based on associative rather than on logical connections; but the poet who was incapable of logical thinking, and was thus not qualified to recognise the difference, would not be capable of achieving this independence.

The Irishman, W. B. Yeats, offers a different case. An older man (Eliot was born in 1888, Pound in 1885, and Yeats in 1865) he began his poetic carer much earlier, and in the 1890s was already a leader of the decadent romantics of that decade. Between 1900 and 1910 he had tried to establish a distinctively Irish theatre in Dublin – and in a way succeeded – but the experience disillusioned him, and his two volumes between 1910 and 1914 have a deliberate meagreness of expression, a discarding of all romantic effects. The European war, which helped Eliot and Pound to persuade the public away from the debris of romanticism, did not influence Yeats : as a patriotic Irishman, hoping for his country's independence, he considered that it did not concern him. But the tragic Dublin rebellion of 1916 moved him deeply; that and the Irish rebellion of 1919–21 became themes of a new, far more forceful kind of verse; he went on to write his greatest poetry at the age of sixty.

In the meantime, in the pre-war years, he too made acquaintance with the French symbolists and came under the influence of Ezra Pound, although he felt that Pound's and Eliot's poetry was antithetic to his own. In overt respects, he was the most conservative of the three : his verse is highly formal in the traditional sense of the word, and mostly sequential in its syntax, and strongly marked in its metrical rhythms. And yet Yeats carried symbolism farther than either, making it into a language of his own which can best be learned by reading his poems in sequence.

Together, Eliot, Yeats and Pound enormously increased the scope of the poetic medium, but to do so they had to reconstitute it, and in its reconstitution they made their work much more difficult for the general reader. They were artists in the sense in which I have tried to use the word, and they were great interpreters, but they had to be the first, to dedicate themselves to the medium, before they could be the second. They made poetry respected by an educated élite, but they could not, and scarcely tried to, make it popular in the sense in which some of the great romantics had succeeded in doing.

Artists, interpreters, and the reader

The classification of writers – classical or romantic, symbolist or realist, artist or journalist – is always to some extent misleading. Writers are rarely consistent in their own theories when they adopt any, and when a critic imposes a distinction – for instance 'artist or interpreter' – he is running a grave risk of oversimplifying literature. For no imaginative writer who is not to some extent an artist will have value as an interpreter: if the fictional world does not contain its own self-consistent reality, the reader will reject it as an interpretation of the world he knows or of any other sort of world. Equally, it is difficult to conceive how a work of fictional art could have substance if it were not in some sense an interpretation of reality. But it is still true that some writers think of themselves as dedicated first of all to the medium in which they have chosen to work, whereas other writers will devote themselves much less to theoretical attention to the medium, and more to the effect of it on their public. The reasons for this difference of emphasis will vary much: James considered that critical neglect of the medium of the novel in England had unduly limited its scope as an interpretive art; Lawrence, on the other hand, saw that the novel, good or bad, had a flourishing public, and he was chiefly fascinated with its potentiality for communication. Eliot thought that English verse was worn so threadbare that it was no longer capable of interpreting experience significantly until it was reconstituted; Owen, on the other hand, felt that the forms available to him sufficed to express what he needed to communicate in his special circumstances. Our task is now to discern why and how the artist–interpreter distinction between twentieth-century writers may be of use to the twentieth-century reader.

The obvious use for the distinction is that it may help us to understand why some writers seem almost to cultivate obscurity in their work. James in his later novels, Eliot and Pound, Yeats in some of his greatest poems, not to mention writers we have not yet glanced at, have all exasperated readers by the difficulties they present. Sometimes this exasperation is excusable and even justifiable: the artist may occasionally (to use Eliot's phrase) so dislocate language, or (to use Pound's) attempt such concentration of language that the effort of understanding is not in fact repaid by what is communicated. It is not a problem encountered only in twentieth-century writings: Blake in parts of his prophetic poems seems to have been struggling with meanings beyond the reach of the images through which he tried to transmit them; Browning sometimes tied his language into knots which reveal little when they are untied. All the same, difficult writing is commoner in the twentieth-century than in past centuries, and most of it is difficult for good reasons.

The reader seeks meaning. 'Meaning' is whatever gives shape and therefore brings comprehension; 'comprehension' can mean both 'understanding' and 'inclusion'. In the twentieth century we have immensely extended our field of knowledge, but our sense of being able to relate this knowledge to a centre within ourselves has diminished; we know more, but what meaning – what shape and comprehensibility – has our knowledge?

The imaginative artist shows us ways in which the shapelessness of experience can have form and therefore meaning. If he chooses the way of the artist, he will show us how *in his medium* (the novel or the poem) it is possible to relate what is disparate, but he will not attempt to show us how his medium relates to other ways of thinking and feeling, or to the conduct of our lives. If, on the other hand, he chooses the way of the interpreter, he will be explicitly challenging, even assaulting, our usual assumptions and judgements. Neither way of writing is in itself superior to the other (though we have seen that the one or the other may seem the only possible course) but it is likely that the artist may present more difficulty than the interpreter. He often suffers, and even cultivates, isolation, preferring the discriminating appreciation of a small circle to a mass of half attentive readers. The interpreter, on the other hand, is likely to consder isolation as failure or defeat : Wells and Bennett would probably have abandoned novel-writing, as Shaw did before them, if they had not achieved large publics. Lawrence, who did suffer isolation, was deeply affronted and discouraged by it. Moreover, Lawrence's isolation had different causes from those that isolated James, who would have preferred popularity if only he could have achieved it without compromising his own high standards. Lawrence, too, had high standards, but of a different sort; whereas James felt loyalty to the truthfulness of his art, Lawrence felt loyalty to the truthfulness of his vision of life. He knew that art had its own truthfulness – 'Never trust the teller, trust the tale' was one of his dicta – but the truthfulness due to art was for him secondary to life-truth; and it was because his 'message', his life-truths, were seriously misunderstood that he felt himself isolated.

Ultimately all works of literature demand judgement of one kind: they are valid contributions to the life of the mind, or they are not. But before we can make a judgement of a writer, we have to appreciate him, and there are always obstacles to appreciation; they vary from writer to writer, and sometimes with different works by the same writer. I offer my distinction between artists and interpreters because it indicates two main obstacles to appreciation. A reader may feel that, for instance, a poem by T. S. Eliot offers a difficulty resembling that of a cryptogram: he may decide that it is his business to crack the code, or to leave the poem alone, and having perhaps no inclination for codes, he may choose to do the latter. But if he attempts the first procedure, he will be making a mistake, for a good poem is never a mere code which will yield a prose translation. It is a medium in which our minds can learn to live, and only when we have learned to live in it can we know whether it is good for us. Or a reader may feel about a novel by Lawrence that the author is 'making a case' about the way to live, and he may hastily decide to reject the novel because, in advance, he rejects the case. But this would be premature, because first he should discover whether Lawrence has done his work as an artist – whether the novel 'stands up' on its own terms; then, even if he still rejects the case, he will do so on terms which will have enriched his own capacity for judgement.

In the chapters that follow I shall not attempt to classify every writer as 'artist' or 'interpreter'; to do so would often be arbitrary and unhelpful. If the reader bears the difference in mind, however, he may find it easier to understand the directions of our literature in the first forty years of this century, and why certain writers have developed in ways that may at first seem surprising and unpredictable.

2

The early twentieth-century novel:
James, Wells and Conrad

Henry James

If experience consists of impressions, it may be said that impressions *are* experience, just as . . . they are the very air we breathe. Therefore, if I should say to a novice, 'Write from experience and experience only,' I should feel this was rather a tantalizing monition if I were not careful immediately to add, 'Try to be one of the people on whom nothing is lost!'

. . . the deepest quality of a work of art will always be the quality of the mind of the producer.

Henry James: *The Art of Fiction*

In the early 1900s Henry James was an elderly, magisterial figure with over twenty-five years of writing life behind him, during which he had acquired prestige, but little popularity. By 1900 he had published fourteen novels and eighteen volumes of stories, as well as criticism, travel books and plays; by his death in 1916 he was to complete only four more novels and to publish two more collections of stories, though others were published posthumously. His style in these late novels (*The Sacred Fount*, 1901; *The Wings of the Dove*, 1902; *The Ambassadors*, 1903; *The Golden Bowl*, 1904) had become notoriously abstruse, but his predominant theme remained constant.

He has been called 'the historian of fine consciousnesses'. His theme was the developing experience of the human consciousness in its most ample and sensitive reaches into the complexities of relationship with other human beings, and this meant for him an exploration of the moral life of the consciousness – the working of the conscience. His heritage from the Atlantic coast of America, the seat of those English colonies which had originated from the Puritan moral revolt against the English establishment, was the intense cultivation of the conscience; but, like many highly educated nineteenth-century Americans, he felt a poverty of experience upon which the conscience would work. It was high civilisation

24

which contributed dense and opulent experience for the mind, and high civilisation was not to be found in the American colonies projected from Europe, but in Europe itself. The mind had to be educated before the conscience could mature, and so it was in Europe that James settled.

But the civilisation of Europe presented James with a double dilemma, upon which he worked all his life. If the conscience proves uncongenial to civilisation, which has to be sacrificed? And if a conscience without civilisation denotes an impoverished consciousness, what in the end can a civilisation offer if it ignores conscience? The double dilemma was complicated by James's recognition of two sorts of conscience. The American conscience was apt to dictate that a life is justified only by dedication to economically profitable work, even when the work is narrowing to the mind and coarsening to the manners. From this tyranny, civilisation could release the mind by enhancing the free life of the tastes and the appetites. But this freedom may itself become a tyranny to the other sort of conscience, the sort that is not subservient to a rigid framework, but itself an aspect of the consciousness – a moral fastidiousness about human relationships, a sensitive revulsion from using people for one's personal advantage. Against this sort of conscience, the free life of the tastes and the appetites may be merely the gracious exterior of a brutal egotism.

The theme of civilisation against this finer sort of conscience is most nobly expressed in the novel which many critics consider James's masterpiece – *The Portrait of a Lady* (1881). Isabel Archer is a poor American girl who comes to Europe with a fine ardour for the enlargement of her experience. Her cousin, Ralph Touchett, persuades his father to leave her his share of his inheritance:

'I should like to make her rich.'
'What do you mean by rich?'
'I call people rich when they're able to meet the requirements of their imagination. Isabel has a great deal of imagination.'

The money, however, is a burden to Isabel. She has been free, with no obligation except the enlargement (in the sense of enrichment) of her freedom, but now her freedom is shadowed by the conscience of responsibility. She is aware of herself as ignorant, unformed, unworthy of a great fortune; she feels that somehow the money must be passed on to another whose worthiness and need are both greater.

She meets Madame Merle, an American expatriate of immaculate sophistication but no scruples, and Madame Merle exploits Isabel's morbidity by inveigling her into marriage with another American expatriate, Gilbert Osmond – a fairly poor dilettante artist, collector, 'man of taste', who is in fact cold, mean, loveless and unlovable. Madame Merle's secret motive is that she has once been Osmond's mistress, and though they have been long separated, they share a daughter (who is ignorant of her maternity) just approaching marriageable age, if only she can be found a dowry. Isabel supposes that she is endowing a man of talent and 'beautiful mind', hitherto crippled in his potentiality by poverty. Only after marriage does she realise the moral bleakness and darkness of his mind, and of her marriage which his mind encloses:

It was the house of darkness, the house of dumbness, the house of suffocation. Osmond's beautiful mind gave it neither light nor air; Osmond's beautiful mind seemed to peep down from a small high window and mock her.

She has yet to learn the worst: the full tale of the conspiracy by which Madame Merle has 'trapped' her; the way in which her husband intends to use her money to sacrifice his daughter Pansy – convent bred into a human *objet d'art* – to another mercenary marriage. Yet at the end of the book, Isabel does not escape her marriage when she has the chance: her responsibility to her stepdaughter, still more the responsibility of accepting the consequences of her choice – her own, after all, however deceitfully she has been betrayed – drives her back to her husband when she could have recovered freedom with an American of far less culture but far richer generosity of heart. James evades the happy ending because it would have reduced his heroine. Civilisation, as he saw it in the Europe of his day, cultivated the tastes and appetites and thereby afforded happiness, but through Isabel (and her cousin Ralph) he points to a higher ideal, a truer civilisation, which entails the possibility of sacrificing happiness for the sake of the dignity of the conscience. But the happiness has to be understood before the sacrifice of it can become real.

James's own choice of what he thought was perhaps the best of his novels was one of the latest – *The Ambassadors*. In this he portrays both sides of the double dilemma of the choice between conscience and civilisation, although it is the tyranny of the rigid, aesthetically insensible conscience that the novel exposes first and most forcefully. The central character is a middle-aged man, Lewis Lambert Strether, who has been sent to Europe by the woman to whom he is virtually engaged to marry, a rich New England widow, to bring back her son, Chad Newsome, to work on advertising the family business. (What the business manufactures is never specified, but it appears to be a familiar object of low esteem – perhaps chamber pots or lavatory pans.) It is understood between Strether and Mrs Newsome that the success of his mission will settle their marriage. Failure would be unfortunate, for Strether is a poor man and Mrs Newsome, whom he genuinely admires but does not love, is rich. Disgraceful failure would be unthinkable, for she is patroness of the review which he edits, and withdrawal of her patronage would entail the loss of his only employment. And fail disgracefully, in the eyes of Mrs Newsome, is just what Strether does.

For New Englanders such as Mrs Newsome, Europe (and especially Paris) was like the combination of a rather dangerous finishing-school and a highly sophisticated fairground; in so far as it was not serious, it could confer on young American rough diamonds a polish which gave them an advantage over their unpolished competitors, but in so far as it was serious, it was wicked. Chad has been sent to acquire the polish, but he has given up writing letters and shows no sign of returning. Mrs. Newsome will not herself come to Europe – she does not have to, for she 'knows' Europe already, and if she came, what she saw would only confirm what she already 'knew', as happens in the case of Strether's friend Waymarsh who accompanies him, and in that of Chad's sister, Sarah Pocock, who is sent out as Mrs Newsome's second ambassador, when (on the information of Waymarsh) Strether has clearly failed as the first one.

Strether's problem (from the point of view of his mission) is that he cannot reject Europe; he not only accepts it, but falls in love with it, is enlarged by it, is matured by it, and finds Chad enlarged and matured too. His impression is immensely deepened when he meets Madame de Vionnet, the 'bad woman' from whom Mrs Newsome wants her son rescued. Marie de Vionnet is thirty-eight and married, with an exquisite nearly grown daughter, but separated from her husband. She is herself exquisite; moreover she has not only shaped Chad lovingly into the gracious being that he has become, but her attachment to him (so Strether is explicitly

27

informed by a common friend) is virtuous. Strether idealises them, and crowns their European perfection of civilisation with a New England halo of moral beauty. No wonder Sarah Pocock, when she arrives, is outraged: she can see none of it, not even the semblance of perfection, but only the fleshpots.

Only at this point, when his own future has been sacrificed, does Strether reach the final stage of his European education. The reality is that Chad and Madame de Vionnet are indeed lovers, and the latter has been using Strether to keep Chad in France for the sad but vulgarly commonplace reason that she is a middle-aging woman terrified of losing a lover who is too young for her. Not only has she cheated Strether, but Chad has as well, and so (for mixed motives) have all their friends. Worse follows, for when Strether, now out of deep compassion, tries to make Chad swear loyalty to his mistress, he perceives beneath the solemn promises that the young man is by now much more in love with advertising than he is with Marie de Vionnet – that he *will* return to the family business which Strether had come to see as too base for him. Strether has ruined himself in vain.

Distinguished critics have not always agreed with James in his own valuation of *The Ambassadors.* F. R. Leavis, for instance, writes in *The Great Tradition* that the novel

produces an effect of disproportionate 'doing' – of a technique the subtleties and elaborations of which are not sufficiently controlled by a feeling for value and significance in living. What, we ask, is this, symbolized by Paris, that Strether feels himself to have missed in his own life? Has James sufficiently inquired? Is it anything realized? If we are to take the elaboration of the theme in the spirit in which we are meant to take it, haven't we to take the symbol too much at the glamorous face value it has for Strether? Isn't, that is, the energy of the 'doing' (and the energy demanded for reading) disproportionate to the issues – to any issues that are concretely held and presented?

It is true that James's late style is demanding. His sentences are often ponderously long, as though he is tiptoeing round a point which is too fine for plain statement; the dialogue, similarly, often proceeds by inferences, as though indirection were the only method by which the characters feel able to treat their delicate topics. Moreover it is easy to feel – especially after a very simplified summary such as mine – that Strether is far too ingenuous: ingenuous, almost boyish, in his enthusiasm for Paris; ingenuous (one might almost say girlish) in his interpretation of the central relationship. But there is an important clue, pointed out by James's biographer Leon Edel, about how James may have meant the novel to be read. In the garden of the sculptor Gloriani, Strether urges a young friend, the American painter Bilham, to 'live'—

'Live all you can; it's a mistake not to. It doesn't much matter what you do in particular, so long as you've had your life. If you haven't had that, what *have* you had?'

In Book VI, chapter 3, Bilham reminds Strether of this—

'Didn't you adjure me, in accents I shall never forget, to see, while I have a chance, everything I can? – and *really* to see, for it must have been that only you meant.'

'Live' – 'see': the change apparently passes unnoticed by Strether. So 'seeing' is 'living'? Perhaps it can be, if we understand 'seeing' as James understood it. For how often do we 'really see' the people and happenings that surround us? How often do we even try to?

Seeing takes three forms in the novel: the first is the act of perceiving harmony or disharmony; the second is seeing in depth; the third, and most important, is seeing with imagination.

The first experience that Strether has of Europe is of harmony, of the rightness of the relationship of parts. It is his experience above all of Chad and Marie de Vionnet, but it is also his first impression of Mary Gostrey, who is his guide into the European scene – 'features – not freshly young, not markedly fine, but on happy terms with each other . . .'

Since the season is an important accent in the expressive tone of the novel (which begins in early spring, proceeds through the unfolding of the season, and ends in dry hot dusty summer) a similar expression is much later used of the weather:

The early summer had brushed the picture over and blurred everything but the near; it made a vast warm fragrant medium in which the elements floated together on the best of terms, in which rewards were immediate and reckonings postponed.

Correspondingly, the Americans who represent Mrs Newcome's side of the question, who are unable to see Europe and Paris and the transformed Chad in this way, are shown out of harmony, discordant, or ill at ease. Thus the first we see of Waymarsh is his sitting awkwardly on a hotel bed – 'It represented the angle at which poor Waymarsh was to sit through the ordeal of Europe' –

and Sarah at Chad's grandest party is 'dressed in a splendour of crimson which affected Strether as the sound of a fall through a skylight'. This kind of seeing, the perception of the quality of relationships, is a characteristic that marks civilisation.

But it is in character with the second kind of seeing in the novel – seeing in depth – that Strether receives his final, illusion-shattering glimpse of Chad and Marie de Vionnet when he is serenely in pursuit of the first kind: he is attempting to identify a particular colouring of landscape which he has admired in one of the French painters. He catches sight of them in a boat, and realises that they are trying to avoid him – trying to avoid, that is, betraying to him their true relationship. The first kind of seeing is the recognition of harmonies, but seeing in depth is dramatic: the constant unscreening of the truth, no matter whether harmony is thereby deepened or disrupted. The characters in the novel are constantly talking about this second kind of seeing. As one turns the pages, the phrases catch one's eye:

> 'Ah it was but too visible!'
> '. . . but if the more I see the better he seems?'
> 'See?' he echoed with a groan, 'Haven't we seen enough?'
> 'You'll see for your self. One does see.'

Very near the end, Strether says of Mrs Newcome: 'She's the same. She's more than ever the same. But I do what I didn't before – I see her.' Quite at the end, Mary Gostrey tries to prevent Strether from returning to America, but he (like Isabel Archer) insists that he must face the consequences of his actions. She has to acknowledge that he is right—

> 'But why should you be so dreadfully right?'
> 'That's the way that – if I must go – you yourself would be the first to want me. And I can't do anything else.'
> So then she had to take it, though still with her defeated protest. 'It isn't so much your *being* "right" – it's your horrible sharp eye for what makes you so.'

It is Strether's 'horrible sharp eye' – his eye for the truth of his conscience – which is the price he has to pay for seeing both harmoniously and incorruptibility. The fine assessment of appearances is otherwise corrupting because it becomes superficial – an overvaluation of what merely seems to be beautiful. And this is in fact Chad's true condition; presumably it is why he contemplates so enthusiastically a career in advertising.

Both Mary Gostrey and Chad commend Strether for his imagination (just as Ralph commends Isabel for the same faculty in the *Portrait*) although Chad surely does so with a hidden irony, or even a hidden contempt. Strether's imagination consists in seeing the best that lies beyond the good. On the surface, the painful irony of the book is that Mrs Newsome's faction appears to be right in their certainty that Marie de Vionnet is a mere seductress, doing all she can to keep Chad in her clutches. But, unlike Strether, they are incapable of his ability to appreciate the surface graciousness and charm of the couple, and when this has been exposed, they lack his compassion, which causes him to attempt the salvage of a loyal relationship out of the ruins of what seemed to be a noble one. Just in being right, Mrs Newsome's party are all the more exposed as wrong – as rigid, obtuse, insensitive, and life-denying.

The Ambassadors is surely not as fine a novel as *The Portrait of a Lady*, but in one respect it is more interesting. The latter is, in regard to the relationship of the author with his material, a typically nineteenth-century novel, in so far as in it the author plays God to his characters: we assume that he has not only created them, but knows all about them; that it is up to him to tell us about them just what we need to know. In *The Ambassadors*, on the other hand, James identifies himself as closely as possible with his central character: James assumes no omniscient privilege, but is content to make Strether grope, and the reader grope with him. Much of the difficult indirection of the style is due to this, and other twentieth-century novelists were to follow the way which James is here opening. In their relationship to the reader, such novelists seem arrogant, by the demands they make, in comparison with nineteenth-century ones; but in relationship to their characters, with the conception of what constitutes a human consciousness, they are humbler.

H. G. Wells

If the world does not please you, *you can change it.*
H. G. Wells: Mr Polly, Chapter 9

Henry James, as an American, was an outsider to the British scene, and he never forgot it. H. G. Wells began life far too much inside it, subject to its oppressions, and equally he never forgot it. His father ran a small hardware shop in Bromley, then a small country town outside London, but already in Wells's childhood becoming a suburb. The shop was a failure; his father was indifferent to it, preferring cricket; his mother was a slave to it, but did not make it the more successful. His father, though lazy and egotistical, was lively-minded; his mother's mind was constricted by the deadening kind of religious and social piety which William Blake had heaped with scorn a century before. She worked herself to exhaustion for her three sons, but her one ambition for them was that they should stand, angularly correct and clothed in accordance with the pieties, behind a draper's counter. But Herbert Wells was his father's son without his father's indolence. His autobiography wittily and poignantly describes his struggles. Some of the chapter headings bear witness: 'First Start in Life'; 'Second Start in Life'; 'Third . . .'; 'Fourth . . . '; 'Fifth . . .'; 'Sixth Start in Life or Thereabouts'. By the mid-eighties, he was nonetheless a very promising young science student in London, nagged by a neglect which extended from indifference on the part of the authorities to a poor student's welfare, to contempt on the part of the establishment for the kind of studies that did not make a gentleman.

What James saw was the decadence of the higher reaches of European culture; what Wells saw was struggle. He saw the struggle of such young men as himself – physically and culturally under-nourished, gracelessly pathetic, yet warmly admirable in their indefatigable refusal of defeat. But his scientific training and enthusiasm also enabled him to see the struggle which was to engage his complacent society as it was dragged, blindfold and protesting, into a century dominated by technological powers undreamt of for their power to bring prosperity or destruction. His novels and tales portray both sorts of struggle and just as, in scope, the two sorts were immensely contrasted, so were his two sorts of fiction. It is probably true that his best fiction was all written before 1914. The sort that was autobiographical, treating of men of his type and class, included *Love and Mr Lewisham* (1900); *Kipps* (1905); *Tono-Bungay* (1909); *The History of Mr Polly* (1910); and *The New Machiavelli* (1911). His second kind of fiction was the scientific romance: *The Time Machine* (1895); *The Island of Dr Moreau* (1896); *The War of the Worlds* (1898); *When the Sleeper Awakes* (1899); *The First Men in the Moon* (1901). The lists show the science fiction stopping when the social fiction begins. This is not quite a true picture, but it is true that it was as a science fiction writer that he first achieved his immense popularity, and it seems that only when he had achieved the peak of success and a safe income could he turn back with some pity and confidence to the history of his own struggles.

As a journalist of technological prediction, Wells is famous for his foresight, though his success in this respect has sometimes been exaggerated. It is not, in any case, as a technological predictor that he is really interesting, but as a prophet of scientific drama and doom. He was the first imaginative writer to awaken the general public to the perspectives opened up by technological science, and though he was immensely optimistic about the prospects if the public took control of technology, he was correspondingly sombre about them if technology were left in the hands of men who wanted only power, or in those of scientists whose moral concern was limited to a belief in their right to pursue research regardless of the consequences. He saw those consequences as merely brutal.

An example is *The Island of Dr Moreau.* The narrator, named Prendick, is a castaway on an island whose sole inhabitants are a scientist, Dr Moreau, and his assistant, Montgomery. They are, that is, the sole inhabitants who are indubitably human, for the island is also inhabited by grotesque beings who seem partly human and partly animal. A stock of animals is landed at the time of Prendick's own arrival, and he is presently distressed by the sounds from behind a locked door of a creature in acute and incessant pain; it is a puma, undergoing vivisection. Eventually Dr Moreau is persuaded to explain. He is following up the logical consequences of European vivisectional experiments, which had made plain that it is possible not merely to transfer parts of an organism to another position on the body, and thus to heal a wound for example, but to transfer organs from one animal to another – to alter an organism into a monster. It dawns on Prendick that 'The creatures I had seen were not men, had never been men. They were animals – humanised animals – triumphs of vivisection.' It is in fact Moreau's ambition to use vivisection to 'create' human beings. So far he has failed: 'First one animal trait, then another, creeps to the surface and stares at me' ... 'And they revert' ... – but he has great hopes of the puma. The puma, however, escapes:

I heard a sharp cry behind me, a fall, and turning, saw an awful face rushing upon me, not human, not animal, but hellish, brown, seamed with red branching scars, red drops starting out upon it, and the lidless

33

eyes ablaze. I flung up my arm to defend myself from the blow that flung me headlong with a broken forearm, and the great monster, swathed in lint and red-stained bandages fluttering about, leaped over me and passed.

The monster – not yet human, no longer a puma – kills Moreau, and dies itself. Moreau's death breaks a spell. So far the semi-humans on the island have lived under his dictatorship, practising a ritual and a code (which forbids them, among other things, to eat flesh, so as to inhibit their carnivorous instincts) but now that they have seen their god die, they are no longer sure whether their law exists. Prendick half persuades them that Moreau is not dead, that he still watches over them although he is invisible – an obvious attempt by Wells to parody and satirise the role of religion in society. Eventually Montgomery also perishes, half animalised himself by his alcoholism, and Prendick is left alone to watch Moreau's monsters reverting to their fully animal condition. He gets back to England, but there he lives in suspicious dread of every human being he sees. For are not humans, according to Darwinian biology, known to have evolved from beasts? Moreau has only attempted to abridge the evolutionary process. 'I see faces keen and bright, others dull or dangerous, others unsteady and insincere; none that have the calm authority of a reasonable soul.' It might be Gulliver speaking, after his voyage to the Land of the Houy-hnhnms, but Swift subjects Gulliver himself to his irony, whereas Prendick is a mere lay figure.

And if Wells thought that 'the calm authority of a reasonable soul' is what distinguishes what is fully human, then Moreau is calm, authoritative, and even reasonable (in the sense of ruled by reasoning) enough to constitute a criterion, but he is certainly not meant to be one. On the contrary, Wells unmistakably intends the reader to be disgusted by Moreau's moral narrowness and ruthlessness and the pervertedness of his single-minded reasoning. Then what did Wells have in mind as a criterion of true humanity? The answer seems to be that he was as powerless to embody the idea imaginatively as Moreau was by his surgery. It is as though, for Wells, what is 'human' in us is a thin ice on which we are ever-lastingly skating.

If Wells never created a richly complex character, at least in his social, autobiographical novels he wrote graphically of two prevalent kinds of human condition. The first kind is that of people dominated by things, by institutions, by the habits of old beliefs from which the life has departed; the second is of people asserting themselves against oppression and danger, by the force of their own distinctive vitality. *The History of Mr Polly*, not the most ambitious of his social novels but for that reason all the freer from his characteristic faults, has some notable examples of both.

Alfred Polly's origins and beginnings in life are like those of Wells himself, and there is nothing to differentiate him from thousands of other young men in similar circumstances except a romantic sensibility, a large appetite for books, and a faculty for humorous verbal invention which he uses to keep up his head against the grey oppressiveness of the conventions that exert their authority over his existence. His father, who never greatly cared for him, dies, and his cousin Johnson, a ticket-collector on the railway, takes charge of the funeral arrangements. The death means little to Polly, though he feels some personal sadness, beyond the fact that it has left him with a small legacy, and it means nothing at all to Johnson, for whom, however, funerals mean a great deal.

'Where'll you get your mourning?' asked Johnson abruptly.
Mr Polly had not yet thought of this by-product of his sorrow.
'Haven't thought of it yet, O'Man.'
A disagreeable feeling spread over his body, as though he was blackening as he sat. He hated black garments.
'I suppose I must *have* mourning,' he said.
'Well!' said Johnson with a solemn smile.
'Got to see it through,' said Mr. Polly, indistinctly.
'If I were you,' said Johnson, 'I should get ready-made trousers. That's all you really want. And a black satin tie, and a top hat with a deep mourning band. And gloves.'
'Jet cuff-links he ought to have – as chief mourner,' said Mrs Johnson.
'Not obligatory,' said Johnson.
'It shows respect,' said Mrs Johnson.
'It shows respect, of course,' said Johnson.

Under the Johnsons' unswerving supervision, the ceremony is conducted with immaculate respectability; and these decencies accomplished, the indispensable collation that follows them, to which Polly is obliged to invite all his relatives, passes hilariously, the more so because his relatives include his three Larkin girl cousins, each of whom is rapacious for a marriage, without which they can scarcely be said to have a socially presentable future.

To his own surprise, he finds himself duly married to the most serious of the three, unaware that the process of courtship, even the proposal itself, has never been in his control. Mrs Larkin mourns, as she is obliged to, the loss of a daughter whom she is in reality only too glad to get off her hands – ' "Such a goo-goo'-goo' girl," she sobbed.' One of Wells's distinctive talents was his remarkable mimicry by orthography of the special speech-idiom of types and classes. No doubt he owed it partly to the fact that an unprivileged young man had to acquire a socially correct accent with care, and this involved noticing aberrancies and idiosyncrasies as well as the 'right' social forms. Thus the ritual of the wedding is travestied by the blurring of its beautiful language by the bored priest:

The officiating clergy sighed deeply, began, and married them wearily without any hitch.

'D'bloved we gath'd gether sighto 'Gard 'nface this con'gation join gather Man Woom Ho Mat-mony whichis on'bl state stooted by Gard in times mans in'sency . . .'

Mr Polly's thoughts wandered wide and far and once again something like a cold hand touched his heart, and he saw a sweet face in sunshine under the shadow of trees. Some one was nudging him. It was Johnson's finger diverting his eyes to the crucial place in the Prayer Book to which they had come.

'Wiltou lover, comfer, onerkeeper sickness and health . . .'

'Say, "I will".'

Mr Polly moistened his lips. 'I will', he said hoarsely.

At the end the ceremony was 'like the momentary vision of a very beautiful thing seen through the smoke of a passing train . . .'

Mr Polly, like Wells's father, now becomes a bad shopkeeper in an unpromising neighbourhood. His wife almost at once turns weary and sullen – it was in any case the status of marriage she wanted, not the man – and his irrepressible hatred of routine and apathy causes him to quarrel with his shopkeeping neighbours. In his despair, he decides to burn down his shop while his wife is at church, and take his life. He sets alight to the building with efficiency, but in the act of putting his razor to his throat, he realises that he will incidentally cause the death of the old lady who lives in the attic of the shop next door. Instead of committing suicide, he sets out to rescue her.

In this episode, Wells displays his other great talent for characterisation – his depiction of the elation and comedy of vital human beings enjoying crisis. The old lady is almost stone-deaf and very stiff in the joints; she has to be got away over the roof, and she enjoys every minute of it:

'I've never been out on a roof before,' said the old lady.
'I'm all disconnected. It's very bumpy. Especially that last bit. Can't we sit here for a bit and rest? I'm not the girl I used to be.'
'You sit here ten minutes,' shouted Mr Polly, 'and you'll pop like a roast chestnut. Don't understand me? *Roast Chestnut!* ROAST CHESTNUT! POP! There ought to be a limit to deafness. Come on round to the front and see if we can find an attic window. Look at this smoke!'
'Nasty!' said the old lady, her eyes following his gesture, puckering her face into an expression of distaste.
'Come on!'
'Can't hear a word you say.'
He pulled her arm. 'Come on!'
She paused for a moment to relieve herself of a series of entirely unexpected chuckles. 'Sich goings on!' she said. 'I never did! Where's he going now?' and came along the parapet to the front of the drapery establishment.

Mr. Polly is greeted as a hero for the rescue, and he loses nothing, for he is insured. His neighbours, with whom he has been on such bad terms, are now cordial: they have only lost unsalable stock, and are also insured. But he is back where he started, loaded with his loveless marriage, and an employment which is unprofiting and pleasureless. He decides, now, not to commit suicide but to simulate death by drowning, and to vanish. The ploy is successful, and the book ends with a charming idyll which has the same relation to reality as pastoral usually has. Only one episode has the distinct ring of truth; out of curiosity, he makes an expedition back to the village to see how his 'widow' is getting on. He is greatly altered in appearance, but she (now keeping a teashop with a sister) identifies him, and is dismayed. Obligingly, he vanishes again.

Unlike James, Wells was no artistic innovator; what he had to communicate could best be told by the old methods. In his social novels, they are the methods of the earlier Dickens, but even Dickens did not know the lower middle classes with the sharp inwardness of Wells. In his science fiction, however conservative his narrative methods, Wells probably remains an unequalled master. Like a narrow but brilliant spotlight, he alerted his public to two of what have become the principal preoccupations of our society – alerted them for action.

Joseph Conrad

> My task . . . is by the power of the written word to make you hear, to
> make you feel – it is above all to make you *see*.
>
> Joseph Conrad: *A Personal Record*

Joseph Conrad's full name was Teodor Josef Korzeniowski. The
change from the Polish to the English epitomises a strange career.
The child of a Polish patriot took to the sea in foreign ships, and
then became a great novelist in his third language, for he knew
French before he learned English. Wells accomplished one leap
from his native element into a strange one, and this is more than
most accomplish; Conrad accomplished two.

His early passion for the sea was an unlikely one for a boy of his
background, descended as he was from inland families whose traditions were estate-owning. But his father had literary devotions as
well as his patriotic one. He was a man of letters and translator of
French and English literature, and it seems to have been his translation of Victor Hugo's *Travailleurs de la mer* which first inspired
his son seawards. Moreover, Conrad's early life was physically un-
settled, although emotionally well rooted. The part of Poland to
which he belonged was ruled by Russia, and when the boy was only
five, the Russian government regarded his father as sufficiently
dangerous to compel the family to remove to Russia, where the
father could be kept under surveillance. Conrad's mother died in
this exile, and his father died a few years later, after returning to
Poland. An only child, he was left at twelve an orphan, under the
guardianship of his maternal uncle.

Conrad never lost his patriotism, his desire for a strongly knit
community, but he also never lost his sense of loneliness – his early
experience of exile and of the loss of close family ties. The contrast
between the fact of loneliness and the need for community seems
to have become his dominant preoccupation; they are the themes
of his work; they are also reflected in the two phases of his career.
At sea, from 1875 till 1894, he lived in the close ties of a ship's crew,
but this was balanced against what is an emblem of loneliness – a
ship on the great oceans on a long voyage. For the rest of his career,
his life as a writer, with a conception of his art as austere as that
of his friend and master Henry James, was one of lonely dedication without popular appreciation (until the success of *Chance* in
1914), though this again was counterbalanced by the loyalty and

admiration of his literary friends, who included James and (at first) H. G. Wells.

Two other qualities distinguish him, the first of which is his cosmopolitan awareness. The three novelists discussed in this chapter show very different degrees in this respect. Wells is clearly the most insular; James, with his intimate knowledge of French culture and his fascination by transatlantic contrasts, was essentially cosmopolitan. But Conrad was more cosmopolitan still. As a seaman, he learned to know men of many nations in Asia as well as Europe; as a writer he was a European rather than a Pole or an Englishman, although it was to English traditions that he eventually gave his deepest loyalties. When Conrad introduces a Russian, a Swede, an Englishman or a Frenchman, into his fiction, it is always to make strong inferences from their origins; we learn why the character is a Russian and not a Scandinavian, a Frenchman and not an Englishman. Nor is the distinction made by the kind of crude typology often used to distinguish national characteristics; Conrad uses nationality with deep understanding of how a national tradition, for good or ill, disposes leading characteristics in individuals.

Conrad's other distinguishing mark is his intentness. This word is meant to signify something different from the quality of concentration so often found in the work of great novelists. In Conrad indeed we may feel less of that concentration of art that we find, for instance, in James, in the sense that he gives us less consistent minuteness of observation of human behaviour. What he gives us instead is the sensation of unremitting watchfulness. The difference of effect on the reader is that between the kind of attention a fine actor commands, and the kind exacted by a fine acrobat: both instil in us the tension of drama, but whereas the actor is communicating drama, the acrobat is enacting it; we do not believe that the actor really falls dead on the stage, but we do believe that the acrobat may break his neck. Yet Conrad's characters are as fictional as those of any other novelist; the fact that he drew more than most novelists do on his personal experience and the experience of real people does not make them less so. What makes them different is Conrad's constant preoccupation with moral ordeal.

This preoccupation shows itself in Conrad's treatment of character. He does not use the analytic method of James, whose characters unfold in a process of discovery, nor does he exhibit the rich gallery of types of a Dickens or a Balzac. Conrad deals in styles rather than types, the style denoting the individual's behaviour in the face of the ordeal. An early story, *The Nigger of the Narcissus* (1897), exemplifies his method.

The story is about the near-disintegration of the corporate unity of a ship's crew by two of the seamen – a dying negro, named Jim Waite, and a mutinous Englishman whose name is Donkin. Until the recruitment of these two at Bombay, all has been well with *Narcissus*. She is a beautiful merchant sailing vessel, the pride of her captain and her crew, although she is known to have certain weaknesses in her design: her behaviour under stress, in a storm, is unreliable. Her weaknesses, however, are regarded with affection by those who sail her; they are loyal to her as to a person; correspondingly, the bond that holds the officers and the crew is impersonal – a mutual respect for a communally acknowledged discipline which loyalty to the ship requires. Thus, the crew, officers, and ship together make a kind of compound personality; each individual has his idiosyncrasies like any other individual, is personally more or less liked and respected, but their peculiarities are submerged in the communal way of life which the ship's routine imposes.

Waite and Donkin disrupt this unity by their diverse egotisms. When it becomes clear that there is something deeply wrong with Waite – though whether he is really dying or merely an extraordinarily skilful shirker remains long in doubt – the other seamen become magnetised to him, in uneasy awe of his arrogant assumption that all considerations should give way to the solemnity of his predicament. But a mysterious alliance develops between the negro and Donkin, who, himself openly resentful and rebellious, alone regards Waite derisively as a like-minded man playing the same role, but with deep cunning and dissimulation. Such an attitude, instead of outraging Waite, cheers him, for he is really dying and really afraid of death; he uses his sickness as a means partly of self-admiration and partly of commanding respect or at least consideration from the rest of the ship's company, but he would much rather believe himself a shirker with a future than a sick man doomed. Since no one respects Donkin, no one believes his opinion of Waite, but their association forces the rest of the crew to listen to his cunning, subversive talk, against the officers, against the ship, and against their lot of hard labour with small reward.

Two other characters stand out. One is the quarrelsome, soft-hearted Irish seaman, nicknamed Belfast, who leads the rescue of Jim Waite in a storm, and whose attitude to the negro is positively maternal. The other is the oldest seaman on board, Singleton, a simple-minded, silent man of great experience, wholly dedicated to his way of life. He is the only member of the crew to remain untouched by the sinister alliance between Waite and Donkin:

One day, however, at dinner, as we sat on our boxes round a tin dish that stood on the deck within the circle of our feet, Jimmy expressed his general disgust with men and things in words that were particularly disgusting. Singleton lifted his head. We became mute. The old man, addressing Jimmy, asked: 'Are you dying?' Thus interrogated, James Waite appeared horribly startled and confused. We all were startled. Mouths remained open; hearts thumped, eyes blinked; a dropped tin fork rattled in the dish; a man rose as if to go out, and stood still. In less than a minute Jimmy pulled himself together: 'Why? Can't you see I am?' he answered shakily. Singleton lifted a piece of soaked biscuit ('his teeth' – he declared – 'had no edge on them now') to his lips. – 'Well, get on with your dying', he said with venerable mildness; 'don't raise a blamed fuss with us over that job. We can't help you.'

Singleton remains an embodiment of truth; the other seamen become entangled in a confused web of half-truths and (sometimes charitable) lies. The feat of Jim's rescue during the storm magnetises the crew still closer to the nucleus of Jim and Donkin, and mutiny is only prevented by the coolness of the captain, who calls Donkin's bluff. The negro dies, within sight of land in accordance with Singleton's superstitious prediction, and Donkin gloats over him during his last hours, robbing him of his money in his final minutes.

The Nigger of the Narcissus is a work which meant much to Conrad. It was the third of his writings (preceded by *Almayer's Folly*, 1895, and *An Outcast of the Islands*, 1896) and with it he felt that his art had come to maturity. Although it remains one of his best-known tales, not all critics assign to it much importance, but it is still a fine achievement, and, regarded as a kind of fable, it tells us much of his distinctive vision. Conrad did not invent the name 'Narcissus' for the ship; he had sailed in one so called; yet it suits his artistic purpose. In accordance with the myth, it expresses the idea of man looking at himself, admiring himself, and not so much ignoring his weaknesses as mollifying them with self-pity, just as the crew admire the ship and fondly pity her defects. However, although their attitude to the ship may seem sentimental and absurd, it unites them in an emotion the effects of which are to make them disinterested and disciplined; James Wait's genuine narcissism, on the other hand, rots and divides them from their corporate loyalty, which is then further corrupted by Donkin's self-interested bitterness. The ship, with her inherent weaknesses, undergoes the ordeal of the storm and barely survives; the crew undergo their still more dangerous, because insidious, moral ordeal, and they too barely survive it. Wait, himself a character of pathos if not of tragedy, predisposes the conditions for this ordeal, but it is Donkin who makes it actual.

Donkin, the base and destructive man who cannot rise to the meanest level of moral disinterest, becomes a familiar style of character in Conrad; so does Singleton – the man who is so simple-minded and simple-hearted that his integrity is unshakable. But Singleton is a specialised man: his moral significance may be universal, but his human capacity is limited to his sea-going vocation. One of Conrad's convictions seems to have been that integrity is rare enough within specific functions; outside these – in the complex activities we all perform on land as social animals – human egotism, expressing itself in self-preservation, in ambition, or merely in the desire for a quiet life, is almost universal and universally predatory. The only defence against it is self-knowledge.

The man of imagination, who has or achieves self-knowledge, is the third of the three main styles of character in Conrad's work, Donkin and Singleton being representative of the other two. He is the chief protagonist of most of the finest stories and novels: *Lord Jim* (1900), *Heart of Darkness* (1902), *The Secret Agent* (1907), *Under Western Eyes* (1911), *The Secret Sharer* (1912), *Victory* (1915), *The Shadow-Line* (1917). In three of these (*Heart of Darkness, The Secret Sharer, The Shadow-Line*) he is the first-person narrator of the tale. Conrad was strongly inclined to the method of first-person narration – a method which James despised. Their difference in this respect illuminates the difference between their writing temperaments. James valued the role of the disinterested historian, whose detachment from his fictions enables him to present them with the effect of things authentically uncovered, revealed. Conrad, with his sense of experience as ordeal, felt that his fictions gained authenticity by the presence of a character who can show the effect of the ordeal on his own pulses, either by being himself the protagonist undergoing the ordeal, or by his role as a close observer. Yet Conrad valued as much as James did his independence as an artist who does not contaminate his work by his personal feelings, lest by doing so he should destroy the work's sufficiency to itself. Thus he was faced by the dilemma of either losing the sort of immediacy which his particular narratives required, by emulating James's authorial detachment, or of sacrificing objectivity by the use of the autobiographical form. The solution he used was the invention of a particular fictional narrator – a retired English sailor named Marlow – who resembles Conrad himself in the quality of much of his experience and in the temperament on which that experience worked, but is distinguished from Conrad both by the Englishness of his character and by the way in which he is himself characterised through the eyes of other observers. The method is evident in *Heart of Darkness*. This tale, like *The Nigger of the Narcissus*, had special personal importance for Conrad, since it is based on an experience of his own, when he commanded a river steamer in the Congo in 1890. It is an experience which, so he told his friend Edward Garnett, transformed him from an animal into a man.

The story begins on the deck of a yacht at the mouth of the River Thames; the crew are friends, waiting for the tide to turn so that they can take to the open sea. Marlow is one of their number, and it is he who tells the tale to fill in time, but he, his circumstances, his method of narrating, are first sketched by an introductory narrator, supposedly present in his audience. Thus the ordeal described in the story, although it was Conrad's own, is set at a distance from the reader because Marlow himself is given distance; at the same time, it has immediacy by the narration of it in Marlow's own tones, with his personal inflections, hesitations and particular emphases. At first it seems that he is telling a candid adventure story: the 'heart of darkness' is merely unexplored Africa, to which Marlow as a young man (like Conrad himself) had been drawn by its mystery. But as Marlow draws his listeners more and more into the adventure, it changes its nature from physical exploration to moral exploration: the search for the heart of darkness becomes a search into the human heart, represented by Marlow's search for trader Kurz, who is like a shadow counterpart of himself. Kurz, with 'all Europe' in his heredity, had come to Africa with the highest motives for the enlightenment of its benighted natives, and has ended there as one of the dark deities of the very people he had hoped to redeem. The power of the story issues from its method of narration – Conrad's method, naturally – but described in the opening paragraph as Marlow's:

The yarns of seamen have a direct simplicity, the whole meaning of which lies within the shell of a cracked nut. But Marlow was not typical (if his propensity to spin yarns be excepted), and to him the meaning of an episode was not inside like a kernel but outside, enveloping the tale which brought it out as a glow brings out a haze, in the likeness of one of those misty halos that sometimes are made visible by the spectral illumination of moonshine.

The method is characteristic of the greatest of Conrad's works, his novel *Nostromo* (1904). This, by far the most spacious of his novels, and indeed one of the most spacious in English fiction, cannot be described in such simple terms as *The Nigger* or *Heart of Darkness*. It is not told by one narrator, though first-person narration from time to time occurs in it, nor can its subject be summarised in terms of Conrad's three basic 'styles' of character – the base man, the man of simple integrity, the imaginative man of self-knowledge – though all three are included in its large cast. Its theme is the creation, and then, through the self-centredness of its members, the moral disintegration, of a fictional South American state. Their styles of egotism extend from the fiery devotion to the republican ideal of the Italian immigrant, Viola, to the self-absorption in his personal reputation of the title character – a nickname which, translated, means 'Our Man'; from the identification of the Englishman, Charles Gould, with the silver mine on which the society's wealth is based, to the identification with the social scene and the girl of his desire of the French-educated Martin Decoud, who dies when he finds himself condemned to isolation on a deserted island. The man of self-knowledge is Dr Monygham, the Irishman who can never forgive himself for betraying his political associates under torture; the man of simple character is the harbourmaster, Captain Mitchell, who in crisis acts with imperturbable courage and coolness, but who is quite unable to discern the faintest indications of inner decay in the society he has helped to build up, when the outer danger to it has passed away. The base man, the subverter of ideals, is Sotillo, the commander of the forces sent to crush the state, who is diverted from his purpose by his maniacal greed for the silver which he is deceived into believing has been sunk in the water of the harbour. Upon these and other individuals, each differentiated by their intense, personal motivations, the silver of Mount Higuerota towering above the city acts first as a symbol and the opportunity for united action, and then divisively, destroying deviously and subtly their inner loyalties. It is characteristic of Conrad that the contrast to the corrupting force of the silver is one of the few women of importance in the novel – Charles Gould's wife, who is separated from her husband by his total devotion to the interests of his mine. But she is powerless to influence the downward course of the society whose degeneration is understood only by herself and her devoted admirer, Dr Monygham. Women play a relatively small role in Conrad's novels, but, when they occur, they commonly represent helpless, unused touchstones for disinterested value. Conrad seems to have believed that men, by their inherent egoism, have made a mess of the world, and that women, by their predicament, epitomise the evidence of the mess men have made.

But although Conrad (with the exception of Hardy) is the most pessimistic of English novelists, he is far from undermining normal human inspirations for living. It is not only that his work (in tales like *Youth*, the title story of the volume that includes *Heart of Darkness*) does justice to the exhilaration of living, and (in a tale such as *Typhoon*, 1903) to the triumph of the human spirit over physical danger. These themes are also included in the large fabric of *Nostromo*. But that novel and others heighten and intensify response to life because their intense concern with the moral ordeal gives his characters grandeur even in their defeat. And they are not always defeated; in particular, *The Secret Agent* shows the triumph of the man of self-knowledge (the Assistant Commissioner) over the short-sightedness, corruption, egotism and fanaticism which converge, in that novel, to produce a society governed by police tyranny aund undermined by nihilism. Conrad offers no recipe for the redemption of society; on the other hand, he reinforces our faith in the final and inexorable reality of human beings as preeminently moral beings.

James and Conrad had much in common with each other, and Wells stood over against them. For the American and the Pole, enlargement and clarification of vision was the first requirement of the novelist, and vision, for them, was moral or not worth the name. James was more concerned with the capacity for moral recognition in the human mind; Conrad's preoccupation was more with the kinds of stress that press upon moral assumptions. That was the difference of their personal experience and their artistic temperaments. Beyond this difference is the deeper resemblance: that both of them give the impression of making discoveries which are important first of all for themselves; for them, the work of art has to be a supreme test of the calibre of its author's mind, before it deserves the attention of the public.

For Wells the urgent task was not self-discovery, but public enlightenment. It is this that sets him decisively in opposition to his two colleagues, and it is summed up in a letter to him by Conrad: 'The difference between us, Wells, is fundamental. You don't care for humanity but think they are to be improved. I love humanity but know they are not!'

This is somewhat unfair; it might be truer to say that Wells was not troubled as James and Conrad were by individual humanity, but that he was more troubled than they were by humanity in its social mass. He certainly knew more than either of the two foreigners about the environment of the common man in English society, about what the common man felt about it, and about its prospects. But the standpoints are of course not really antagonistic; they are complementary, for society is composed of individuals, and if it conditions them, it is also conditioned by them. James and Conrad were a godsend to the English novel, which needed them in order not to harden into insularity just when the really strong insular tradition of Dickens and George Eliot had ceased. What the English novel needed, in about 1914, was a novelist who understood the social scene from within as thoroughly as Wells did, but possessed an insight into the human consciousness comparable to that of James or Conrad. Such a novelist was already emerging, in the person of D. H. Lawrence.

3

D. H. Lawrence (1885-1930)

The human individual is a queer animal, always changing. But the fatal change today is the collapse from the psychology of the free human individual into the psychology of the social being, just as the fatal change in the past was a collapse from the freeman's psyche to the psyche of the slave. The free moral and the slave moral, the human moral and the social moral: these are the abiding antitheses.

D. H. Lawrence: John Galsworthy

In 1919 D. H. Lawrence wrote a sketch called 'Adolf', for *The Athenaeum*, a weekly review edited by his friend John Middleton Murry. Murry rejected it as unsuitable, perhaps because it contained a single unmentionable obscenity – the French word 'merde'. But Murry may have had other grounds as well.

The sketch is about a rabbit, which Lawrence's father found in the fields on his morning walk to the coal-pit where he worked as a miner. The rabbit is a baby one, and the children adopt it as their pet, but it refuses domestication. At first it brings them near despair by its refusal to take food or even to stir: 'Love and affection were a trespass upon it. A little wild thing, it became more mute and asphyxiated still in its own arrest, when we approached with love. We must not love it. We must circumvent it, for its own existence.' Their discretion is rewarded; Adolf's existence becomes very positive, but very much his own:

He had cultivated the bad habit of pensively nibbling certain bits of cloth in the hearth-rug. When chased from this pasture he would retreat under the sofa. There he would twinkle in Buddhist meditation until suddenly, no-one knew why, he would go off like an alarm-clock. With a sudden bumping scuffle he would whirl out of the room, going through the doorway with his little ears flying. Then we would hear his thunderbolt hurtling in the parlour, but before we could follow, the wild streak of Adolf would flash past us, on an electric wind that swept him round the scullery and carried him back, a little mad thing, flying possessed like a ball round the parlour. After which ebullition he would sit in a corner composed and distant, twitching his whiskers in abstract meditation. And it was vain we questioned him about his outbursts. He just went off like a gun, and was as calm after it as a gun that smokes placidly.

Adolf delights the children, and dismays their mother for whom the cottage, kept presentable by her own hard efforts, is no place for a wild animal. The father, temperamentally more at ease in the fields than at his wife's domesticating hearth, remains genially aloof. Eventually everyone has to agree that Adolf is too incorrigibly wild for a house to contain him, and the father is instructed to restore him to the fields (' "Best pop him i'th'pot", said my father, who enjoyed raising the wind of indignation.'). Lawrence ends the sketch with some general reflections about rabbithood:

See him running for his life. Oh, how his soul is fanned to an ecstasy of fright, a fugitive whirlwind of panic. Gone mad, he throws the world behind him, with astonishing hindlegs. He puts back his head and lays his ears on his sides and rolls the white of his eyes in sheer ecstatic joy of speed. He knows the awful approach behind him; bullet or stoat. He knows! He knows, his eyes are almost turned back into his head. It is agony. But it is also ecstasy. Ecstasy! See the insolent white flag bobbing. He whirls in the magic wind of terror. All his pent-up soul rushes into electric motion of fear. He flings himself on, like a falling star whooping into extinction. White heat of the agony of fear. And at the same time, bob! bob! bob! goes the white tail, merde! merde! merde! it says to the pursuer. The rabbit can't help it. In his utmost extremity he still flings the insult at the pursuer. He is the unconquerable fugitive, the indomitable meek. No wonder the stoat becomes vindictive.

The sketch, slight as it is, has much of the essence of Lawrence in it, and much that explains the controversy that has centred on him. No doubt, the *Athenaeum* public might have been shocked by the word 'merde', though today its English translation can be used on the radio; even so, if 'shit' conveyed idiomatically what 'merde' does in French, Lawrence might, even in 1919, have used it. One of his disquieting practices was to ignore all conventions of respectability in his language, whether literary conventions or social ones. He was the first major novelist in English to be of working-class origins, and he had the working-man's incorrigible habit of using the language he needed to use, disregarding social and stylistic amenities. He wrote as he talked, and the style of his writing – in essays, fiction, and poetry – is the 'stylelessness' of colloquial speech. This was one of his qualities which disaffected the reading public.

But another cause of disaffection is indicated by his representation of the rabbit itself. Adolf is very much a rabbit, a very convincing portrayal of the animal, but, like the animal in the chapter entitled 'Rabbit' in his novel *Women in Love*, it is not at all according to the traditional literary fashioning of rabbit images. It has none of the cosiness of traditional rabbit meekness, none of the cuddliness which is supposed to make tame-bred rabbits eminently suitable as pets for children that can identify with them in their own need to be loved. This is a wild rabbit, which repels the possessive love of human beings. Its nature is its own or it dies; its terror is itself frightening; its panic is joy as well as agony; its white tail is not (so Lawrence asserts) just a signal to guide its young in danger, but a gesture of contempt in the midst of terror. Whereas convention cherished the rabbit-image as something that elicits the simpler, more sentimental human emotions, Lawrence writes of Adolf as of a beast that evokes confused feelings, and flouts naive attempts to identify with him. Yet in a complex way the writer does invite the reader to identify with the beast: somewhere in the reader there is an Adolf, with the same unaccountable impulses and fits of purposeless energy, and the same invincible sense of identity in the face of obliterating fears. Murry may well have thought that the *Athenaeum* public would not like Lawrence's rabbit, or would not understand him, or would not want to understand him.

It is not that Lawrence's inferences about rabbit feelings are necessarily true; how do we know that the animal's terror in flight is also ecstasy? The distinction of his description is its imaginative consistency and its capacity to convey a life which is purely a life of the senses and at the same time a complete, free life, a 'selfhood' not filtered to our understandings through a mental sieve, in such a way that we receive of it only what accords with our predisposed notions of the animal, rabbit. And if Lawrence gives us the sense of what it is to be a rabbit with this kind of complexity combined with sensuous immediacy, how will he convey human beings to us?

In a well-known but difficult passage of a letter (June 1914) to his friend Edward Garnett, Lawrence wrote:

You mustn't look in my novel [*The Rainbow*] for the old stable *ego* of the character. There is another *ego*, according to whose action the individual is unrecognisable, and passes through, as it were, allotropic states which it needs a deeper sense than any we have been used to exercise, to discover are states of the same single radically unchanged element. (Like as diamond and coal are the same pure single element of carbon. The ordinary novel would trace the history of the diamond – but I say 'Diamond, what! This is carbon.' And my diamond might be coal or soot, and my theme is carbon.)

Lawrence is saying that a human being has an identity (an 'ego') beyond the identity that his ordinary social relationships endow him with. 'Allotropic' is a chemical term which refers to the process by which a material can change its characteristics without any additions to or substitutions for what constitutes its substance. So a character in a novel may differ from another as coal differs from diamond, but Lawrence declares that all the time it is the essential element in both characters, corresponding to carbon, that is his real concern. But does human nature have such a common basis, and can it undergo such a change?

In answer to this question, it is useful to consider the role which social class plays in nineteenth-century novels. It is part of a novelist's task to communicate to his readers the illusion that a character is real: that he may walk bodily into the room as the reader sits in his chair. To achieve this, the novelist is greatly assisted if he can start with a common denominator of understanding with the reader – a starting point for the illusion, on which both can agree. Class, in the nineteenth century, was such a common denominator: class habits, manners, dress and ways of life were defined and distinctive. If Dickens introduces a character as a successful lawyer or a village blacksmith, it is immediately possible for the reader to form a mental outline of the character, within which outline Dickens will delineate the individuality he has in mind. It is true that, by the end of the novel, the character's social class may have become one of the least significant things about him; this will depend on the novelist's seriousness, his talent, and on the role he has made the character play. But the class definition is likely to remain with him, or if it changes (as happens with Pip in Dickens's novel *Great Expectations*) the change is likely to signify the symptom of any deeper change that has occurred within him.

By the beginning of the twentieth century, the class fixities were becoming insubstantial. The divisions, indeed, remained, and class was (still is) an abiding clue to characterisation; but Lawrence's own career, from miner's son to famous novelist, was, like Wells's, an indication of the new social fluidity, owing more to intelligence than to wealth, which was dissolving the old class stereotypes. These were no longer a reliable common denominator of understanding between author and reader. To say so much, however, is to mention a change which might have influenced Lawrence only as an artist, in his novelistic technique. But he was always more than an artist-technician; he was essentially a man of deep religious feeling who believed that art does nothing of value if it does not renew moral vision. Even this might also be said of James and Conrad, but Lawrence further believed it to be his mission to show that the social stereotypes had become a tyranny, denying the life of the spirit of which they had become faint shadows, and ever more oppressive as the old Christian vision faded and faded. Man was fighting a deadly battle with himself in the dark, not recognising the enemy as the false idea of himself, and not perceiving the fatal issues at stake. His approach was influenced by his reading of Nietzsche and also the works of Sigmund Freud, who was beginning to exert his profound influence on the intelligentsia when Lawrence began writing. But Lawrence was antagonistic to what he felt to be the narrowness, negativity and materialism of Freud's teaching: he intended his own exploration of the unconscious to be dramatic and life-enhancing, whereas he believed Freud's to be not only destructively analytic but life-reducing.

The first major work in which Lawrence attempted such exploration was his autobiographical novel, *Sons and Lovers* (1913). It was the third of his novels, succeeding *The White Peacock* (1911) and *The Trespasser* (1912), neither of them works of comparable originality. The originality of *Sons and Lovers* consists in the re-creation of his relationship with his mother (Mrs Morel in the book) who had developed a more than merely maternal passion for him after the death of his elder brother. This is the main theme of the novel, but it is interwoven with his mother's unhappy relationship with his father (to whom, later, he believed he had done injustice), his own relationship with the two women with whom, successively, he was as a young man in love, and the bitter rivalry between the first of these, Miriam, and his mother. The pain, ecstasy, and intensity of these relationships are displayed together with a substantial account of the environment in which they unfold – the semi-industrial, semi-rural surroundings of the mining village, Miriam's purely rural setting of the farm, and the lively intellectual and social life centring on the Nonconformist community to which the Morels belonged. Wells always described working- and lower-middle-class life in negative terms, as the life of deprived individuals; he shows nothing like the positive feelings of the Morel family:

They were not badly off whilst Morel was in the hospital. There were fourteen shillings a week from the pit, ten shillings from the sick club, and five shillings from the Disability Fund; and then every week the butties had something for Mrs Morel – five or seven shillings – so that she was quite well to do. And whilst Morel was progressing favourably in the hospital, the family was extraordinarily happy and peaceful. On Saturdays and Wednesdays Mrs Morel went to Nottingham to see her husband. Then she always brought back some little thing: a small tube of paints for Paul, or some thick paper; a couple of postcards for Annie, that the whole family rejoiced over for days before the girl was allowed to send them away; or a fret-saw for Arthur or a pretty bit of wood. She described her adventures into the big shops with joy. Soon the folk in the picture-shop knew her, and knew about Paul. The girl in the book-shop took a keen interest in her. Mrs Morel was full of information when she got home from Nottingham. The three sat round till bedtime, listening, putting in, arguing.

Hardships are not dwelt on, but there is hardship, for the easy-going father drinks, has no social pride, and flouts the efforts of Mrs Morel (an ex-schoolteacher, proud of her sturdy, middle-class ancestry) to maintain order and decency in the household. His spontaneous charm and instinct for enjoyment accounts for the success of his courtship of her, but their early love is soon blasted by his lax and irresponsible habits to which she responds with a dismay deepening quickly into disgust and anger. However Lawrence is not satisfied to present them at the level of mere bickering and daily estrangement: the mutual antagonism of his parents is still a relationship with implications, not merely for their outward behaviour, but for their own deeper selves, and it is here that his ability to lift nature into active association with the more mysterious levels of human nature again and again distinguishes the art of this novel.

An example is the first violent quarrel between the parents. Morel one night has returned home drunk, and his retort to his wife's remonstrances is to turn her out of doors. The action has a peculiar brutality because Mrs Morel is pregnant.

For a while she could not control her consciousness; mechanically she went over the last scene, then over it again, certain phrases, certain moments coming each time like a brand red-hot down her soul; and each time she enacted again the past hour, each time the brand came down at the same points, till the mark was burnt in, and the pain burnt out, and at last she came to herself . . .

She hurried out of the side garden to the front, where she could stand as if in an immense gulf of white light, the moon streaming high in face of her, the moonlight standing up from the hills in front, and filling the valley where the Bottoms crouched, almost blindingly. There, panting and half weeping in reaction from the stress, she murmured to herself over and over again: 'The nuisance! the nuisance!'

She became aware of something about her. With an effort she roused herself to see what it was that penetrated her consciousness. The tall white lilies were reeling in the moonlight, and the air was charged with their perfume, as with a presence. Mrs Morel gasped slightly in fear. She touched the big, pallid flowers on their petals, then shivered. They seemed to be stretching in the moonlight. She put her hand into one white bin: the gold scarcely showed on her fingers by moonlight. She bent down to look at the binful of yellow pollen; but it appeared only dusky. Then she drank a deep draught of the scent. It almost made her dizzy.

Mrs Morel leaned on the garden gate looking out, and she lost herself awhile. She did not know what she thought. Except for a slight feeling of sickness, and her consciousness of the child, herself melted out like scent into the shiny, pale air. After a time the child, too, melted with her in the mixing-pot of moonlight, and she rested with the hills and lilies and houses, all swum together in a kind of swoon.

Eventually the chilly night arouses her, and she becomes fearful for the child within her. At last she is able to awaken her husband from his stupor; shamefacedly he lets her in. There is no reconciliation:

Mrs Morel knew him too well to look at him. As she unfastened her brooch at the mirror, she smiled faintly to see her face all smeared with the dust of the lilies. She brushed it off, and at last lay down. For some time her mind continued snapping and jetting sparks, but she was asleep before her husband awoke from the first sleep of his drunkenness.

It is important, for the appreciation of Lawrence's art, to understand the effect of this episode. Ostensibly, it makes little difference: the Morels' relationship is not significantly better or worse, though his behaviour to her improves as he becomes more aware of the burden of her pregnancy, and some of his original love and tenderness for her revives. But the episode tells us much more of the strength and depth of Mrs Morel's own nature. She is outwardly puritanical and grim, but her feelings never wither; her emotional stature grows rather than diminishes, and this gives her the force, not merely to outface her husband, but to counteract the emotional demands which Miriam is to make on Paul. The episode in the garden after the quarrel shows the deep resources of her feeling-nature, as it rises in response to the lilies in the moonlight, to break up and dissolve the wreckage of her surface self caused by her husband's injury to her dignity – the dignity to which she is so sensitive. One cannot say that the injuries are healed by this process: 'the mark' of the brand 'was burnt in', and she becomes, if anything, more resolute in her opposition – if not to her husband himself – at least to his habits of which she so deeply disapproves. What we see happening to her in the garden is more subtle than a process of surface healing; it is reconstitution, from a deeper level, of the self, by means of an experience which is more powerful in its positive action than the destructive experience which she has suffered.

This ability to use environment, especially, natural life, to show the workings of that part of the psyche which lies beyond the rational mind gives Lawrence an unprecedented power to present the deeper experience of inarticulate characters. An example is his story *The Fox*, included ten years later in a volume entitled *The Ladybird* (1923). Two girls, nearing thirty, 'known by their surnames, Banford and March', live a kind of simulacrum of married life on a poultry farm. March, as the more robust, plays the role of man about the place, while Banford, nervous and frail, keeps house. But the arrangement is unsatisfactory: March, it is indicated, while genuinely fond and protective of her friend, is uneasy in the role which circumstances have cast her for. The farm, besides, does not thrive, because the young women are not seriously interested in it; they need it to carry on the interests they believe they really care about, such as painting china. Especial harm is done to the fowls by a marauding fox, which is March's function to dispose of. She sees it; she has a gun, but she does not shoot—

She lowered her eyes, and suddenly saw the fox. He was looking up at her. His chin was pressed down, and his eyes were looking up. They met her eyes. And he knew her. She was spellbound – she knew he knew her. So he looked into her eyes, and her soul failed her. He knew her, he was not daunted.

She struggled, confusedly she came to herself, and saw him making off, with slow leaps over some fallen boughs, slow, impudent jumps. Then he glanced over his shoulder, and ran smoothly away. She saw his brush held smooth like a feather, she saw his white buttocks twinkle. And he was gone, softly, soft as the wind.

These two paragraphs tell us something more about Lawrence. The first contains some nebulous language ('She was spellbound . . . her soul failed her') – a quality not uncommon in his fiction when he is seeking to convey a state of mind in direct terms. March, like Banford, is an inarticulate person: she has states of mind like anyone else, and like anyone else's they can be deeply disturbing. But she has no words to explain the state of mind to herself. Indeed, if she had, she would (in Lawrence's opinion, and Freud would have agreed with him) have used language to falsify experience, by simplifying it and explaining it so that it was no longer disturbing but adaptable to her wishes. The second paragraph is quite different: the fox is evoked with delicately exact concreteness. The fox in the story, alive or dead, is always itself except in March's dreams, non-human, perfect in its own nature.

And yet in another sense it is a symbol. March is a divided being: consciously she is a farm worker and the protector of the more vulnerable Banford; unconsciously, she is a woman who feels herself denied by this way of life. The fox is the marauder, the destroyer of the way of life: to March, the protector of her friend, he is the enemy; to March, the woman who is being denied, he is the ally, and their strange interchange of gaze is her recognition that fundamentally she would be more human by acknowledging kinship with the fox than she is by asserting her loyalty to her friend.

In the course of the story, a stranger appears; his name is Henry, and he is the grandson of the previous owner of the farm. He turns up, expecting to find his grandfather still alive, and is allowed to stay, because he is useful in putting the farm to rights. He shoots the fox. But he is himself the human marauder, desiring March as his wife. They do not 'fall in love' in the ordinary sense of the phrase, but it becomes clear that March secretly wants what he does, at the same time refusing either to give Banford up or acknowledge that she wishes her out of the way. The resolution of this dilemma comes when Henry fells a tree:

'Mind yourself, Miss Banford,' he said. And his heart held perfectly still, in the terrible pure will that she should not move.
'Who, me, mind myself?' she cried, her father's jeering tone in her voice. 'Why, do you think you might hit me with the axe?'
'No, it's just possible the tree might, though,' he answered soberly. But the tone of his voice seemed to imply that he was only being falsely solicitous, and trying to make her move because it was his will to move her.

55

'Absolutely impossible,' she said.

He heard her. But he held himself icy still, lest he should lose his power.

'No, it's just possible. You'd better come down this way.'

'Oh, all right. Let us see some crack Canadian tree-felling,' she retorted.

There was a moment of pure, motionless suspense, when the world seemed to stand still. Then suddenly his form seemed to flash up enormously tall and fearful, he gave two swift, flashing blows, in immediate succession, the tree was severed, turning slowly, spinning strangely in the air and coming down like a sudden darkness on the earth. No one saw what was happening except himself. No one heard the strange little cry which Banford gave as the dark end of the bough swooped down, down on her. No one saw her crouch a little and receive the blow on the back of the neck. No one saw her flung outwards and laid, a little twitching heap at the foot of the fence. No one except the boy. And he watched with intense bright eyes, as he would watch a wild goose he had shot. Was it winged, or dead? Dead!

How many ways are there to commit a murder? And how much can the spoken word be belied by the tone of the speaking voice? The triumph of the story is the way in which Lawrence shows the true working of events to be quite otherwise than a witness might suppose from the film of appearances. This was a great advance in the reach of the fictional imagination; no other novelist had articulated so well the wordless operations of human nature.

Critics widely agree that Lawrence's masterpieces are his novels *The Rainbow* (1915) and *Women in Love* (1921). They seem to be sequels, since the heroine of the last half of the former novel, Ursula Brangwen, is also one of the two heroines of the latter, the other being her sister Gudrun. But they are in fact independent books. *The Rainbow* is a kind of historical novel, tracing the relationships of the Brangwen family through three generations from about the middle of the nineteenth century to some date near 1914. *Women in Love* is a post-war novel, in which post-war English culture is dramatised through the experience of four characters. The war itself does not have a place explicitly in either. This was not just because Lawrence was not conscripted for military service owing to his tubercular symptoms, nor is it explained by the fact that he hated the war, both for what it was, and because his position as a civilian was psychologically the worse by his marriage in 1914 to a German woman, Frieda von Richthofen. His hatred of the war would clearly not have justified his exclusion of it from his artistic work. He excluded it because he did not see it as so important in itself, but as the outcome of the psychic conflicts and contradictions which were already his subject. Since the psyche of modern man was, for him, already at war with itself, open war would sooner or later became its natural expression. Here we pick up again his quarrel with the 'social ego', which becomes explicit in the argument between Ursula Brangwen and her lover, Anton Skrebensky, an Englishman of Polish descent who is a young officer in the Royal Engineers:

'. . . I hate soldiers, they are stiff and wooden. What do you fight for, really?'
'I would fight for the nation.'
'For all that, you aren't the nation. What would you do for yourself?'
'I belong to the nation and must do my duty by the nation.'
'But when it didn't need your services in particular – when there *is* no fighting? What would you do then?'
He was irritated.
'I would do what everybody else does.'
'What?'
'Nothing. I would be in readiness for when I was needed.'
The answer came in exasperation.
'It seems to me,' she answered, 'as if you weren't anybody – as if there weren't anybody there, where you are. Are you anybody, really? You seem like nothing to me.'

The argument has point for the novel from Ursula's concluding remarks. What *is* a self, when the categories of nation and class have come to hang too loosely to define it, and when religious categories of church, soul and flesh have lost imaginative conviction? The novel concerns these very questions, and the answer it gives is that the nature of the self can only be discovered through recognition in intimate relationship of otherness, and this, Lawrence believed, is above all the true meaning of sexual union.

This might be described as the theme of the novel, but it manifests itself differently in each generation, and for this reason *The Rainbow* can justifiably be described as a historical novel. To describe it as that is of course different from describing it as the work of a historian. The nature of history can never be fully caught by historians, since the historian must always separate himself from his subject in order to understand it. He can never, by the nature of his discipline, express at first hand what it was to feel in the self the effects of the changes he records, although the fact that, even as he writes, he is undergoing the influence of changes which are the material of future historians will affect his interpretation of the past. Only the novelist (if he is a great novelist) can, by his sympathetic imagination, diagnose and render what it meant to live the history which the historian can only describe. In *The Rainbow*, Lawrence goes a long way to show how the nineteenth century disrupted self-sufficient ways of life, promoted women beyond their subservience to household functions, changed perceptions by extending education – though not quite as the educators meant – revived and then dashed down traditional religious feeling, and hardened social and political attitudes by divorcing them (directly or indirectly through industrialism) from inherited experience, at the same time leaving these attitudes exposed as the only easily accessible frameworks of faith. The influences are mainly (but not wholly) divisive, stultifying, or destructive; yet in the midst of them the individual retains an obstinate sense of indestructible identity. But if he merely yields to the current of the time, he becomes stultified, like Skrebensky; if the individual attempts to compromise with it against hidden convictions, he becomes divided, as Will Brangwen does and Ursula nearly does; if he sides actively with the destructive forces, he will be inwardly destroyed, like her uncle, the colliery manager.

But *The Rainbow* is an affirmative book, concerned with the life-valuing essence of the human being. Its central current is religious for this reason, and moves through the three generations as through three phases of religious feeling. In the first generation the traditional religion is still active, its terminology still expressively available for communication; in the second generation, the traditional religion has become more personal and subjective, showing the precariousness of dubious revival; in the third, Ursula's spiritual affirmation is in terms which seem quite different from the traditional language, and yet she returns to it spontaneously in its most primitive elements. These changes can only be made clear by reference to the book.

First there is the passage in which Tom Brangwen, 'deeply serious and hugely amused at the same time', makes a speech at the wedding party which celebrates the marriage of his stepdaughter, Anna Lensky, with his nephew, Will Brangwen:

'There's very little else, on earth, but marriage. You can talk about money, or saving souls. You can save your own soul seven times over, and you may have a mint of money, but your soul goes gnawin', gnawin', gnawin', and it says there is something it must have. In heaven there is no marriage. But on earth there *is* marriage, else heaven drops out, and there's no bottom to it.'

'Just hark you now,' said Frank's wife.

'Go on, Thomas,' said Alfred sardonically.

'*If* we've got to be Angels,' went on Tom Brangwen, haranguing the company at large, 'and if there is no such thing as a man nor a woman amongst them, then it seems to me as a married couple makes one Angel.'

'It's the brandy,' said Alfred Brangwen wearily.

'For,' said Tom Brangwen, and the company was listening to the conundrum, 'an Angel can't be *less* than a human being. And if it was only the soul of a man *minus* the man, then it would be less than a human being.'

'Decidedly,' said Alfred.

And a laugh went round the table. But Tom Brangwen was inspired. 'An Angel's got to be more than a human being,' he continued.

'So I say, an Angel is the soul of man and woman in one: they rise united at the Judgement Day, as one Angel—'

'Praising the Lord,' said Frank.

'Praising the Lord,' repeated Tom.

'And what about the women left over?' asked Alfred, jeering. The company was getting uneasy.

'That I can't tell. How do I know as there *is* anybody left over at the Judgement Day? Let that be. What I say is, that when a man's soul and a woman's soul unites together – that makes an Angel—'

'I dunno about souls. I know as one plus one makes three, sometimes,' said Frank. But he had the laugh to himself.

'Bodies and souls, it's the same,' said Tom.

'And what about your Missis, who was married afore you knew her?' asked Alfred, set on edge by this discourse.

'That I can't tell you. If I am to become an Angel, it'll be my married soul, and not my single soul. It'll not be the soul of me when I was a lad: for I hadn't a soul as would *make* an Angel then.' (Ch. 5)

It is a passage which might have occurred in one of the more liberal Victorian novelists, such as George Eliot. Tom's handling of the traditional religious vocabulary – bodies, souls, angels, Judgement Day – is humorous and yet serious, easy and yet honestly baffled; he uses it to confess the deepest truth he has ever known, a truth which can only be otherwise expressed by the dramatisation of his courtship and marriage to Lydia Lensky in the first three chapters. His forebears had tilled the soil unreflectingly; he had been the first to receive secondary schooling. Its influence had not been to send him searching for mental enlargement, but to imbue him with a new self-conscious sense of personal incompleteness, a hunger for emotional enlargement. He had achieved this, and a sense of personal wholeness and self-possession, through his marriage with a stranger of alien background. The union has not been a mental one, requiring the exchange of ideas; each remains ignorant and uncomprehending of the other's social and national background. They have been content with their total reliance on what each has found complementary in the other in their feeling responses. It is this that Tom has tried to express in his fable of the married soul becoming an Angel: only by transmutation into relationship of the opposition between subject and object can the self affirm itself. The friendly derision of Tom's audience arises partly from incomprehension, but it is not his language they fail to understand; it is the seriousness of his nature which is deeper in its insights than theirs.

The second passage relates to Will and Anna, on their visit to Lincoln Cathedral. Will's temperament is that of an artist, and he has felt the influence of the nineteenth-century High Church revival which was also one source of much later nineteenth-century aestheticism:

Here in the church, 'before' and 'after' were folded together, all was contained in oneness. Brangwen came to his consummation. Out of the doors of the womb he had come, putting aside the wings of the womb, and proceeding into the light. Through daylight and day-after-day he had come, knowledge after knowledge, and experience, remembering the darkness of the womb, having prescience of the darkness after death. Then between-while he had pushed open the doors of the cathedral, and entered the twilight of both darknesses, the hush of the two-fold silence, where dawn was sunset, and the beginning and the end were one. (Ch. 7)

But Anna is a woman of the new generation—self-reliant and without ties with the past. His religion is not, for her, the same material of experience which Lydia allowed to remain unquestioned in Tom; it possesses his emotions which she alone should possess. Worse, it seeks to possess her:

Her soul too was carried forward to the altar, to the threshold of Eternity, in reverence and fear and joy. But ever she hung back in the transit, mistrusting the culmination of the altar. She was not to be flung forward on the lift and lift of passionate flights, to be cast at last upon the altar steps as upon the shore of the unknown. There was a great joy and verity in it. But even in the dazed swoon of the cathedral, she claimed another right. The altar was barren, its lights gone out. God

60

burned no more in that bush. It was dead matter lying there. She claimed the right to freedom above her, higher than the roof. She had always a sense of being roofed in.

Anna succeeds in upsetting the spell which binds her husband by drawing attention to the grotesque carvings on the capitals of the pillars: ' "However much there is inside here, there's a good deal they haven't got in," the little faces mocked.' One is reminded that the Cathedral was not as it had been in the Middle Ages, when religion had accommodated the little faces quite well; the sombre glory which so enraptured Will was a Victorian mysticism, a special experience which comprehended much less of life. Anna destroys Will's brooding sense of the numinous. In so doing she subjugates him to herself, but she also suppresses the creative artist in him. The marriage becomes a success on her terms, but she too is reduced by her victory.

At the end of the book, Will's and Anna's daughter, Ursula, finds herself driven into isolation by estrangement from her parents, misunderstanding by her friends, and above all the failure of her affair with her lover, Anton Skrebensky – all the consequence of her refusal to abate her demands on life. She concludes that she has been wrong and arrogant, and writes to Skrebensky to tell him so. Then a strange episode occurs: crossing a field at night, she is thrown into a panic by restless horses which seem to be pursuing her. She has tried to deny her instincts for life, but to deny one's instincts is not to abolish them: her fear of the horses was really the fear of her own rebellious instincts projected on to creatures that live by instinct. The shock restores her to self-consistency, but only gradually does real hope for living return to her.

Repeatedly, in an ache of utter weariness she repeated: 'I have no father nor mother nor lover, I have no allocated place in the world of things. I do not belong to Beldover nor to Nottingham nor to England nor to this world, they none of them exist, I am trammelled and entangled in them, but they are all unreal. I must break out of it, like a nut from its shell which is an unreality.'
And again, to her feverish brain, came the vivid reality of acorns in February lying on the floor of a wood with their shells burst and discarded and the kernel issued naked to put itself forth. She was the naked, clear kernel thrusting forth the clear, powerful shoot, and the world was a bygone winter, discarded, her mother and father and Anton, and college and all her friends, all cast off like a year that has gone by, whilst the kernel was free and naked and striving to take new root, to create a new knowledge of Eternity in the flux of Time.

The real hope breaks upon her with her vision of the rainbow – a biblical image of promise – arching itself over 'the old, brittle corruption of houses and factories'; a symbol of the earth's new architecture, 'built up in a living fabric of Truth, fitting to the overarching heaven'. Ursula's hope blossoming with the brightening rainbow is the last of a series of arch symbols which occur through the book: the arch of the union of Tom and Lydia at the end of Chapter 3; the arched roof of Lincoln Cathedral to which Will's spirit soared in ecstasy; the arch of the sky beyond it which Anna's spirit seeks like a bird. The book itself has a structure somewhat resembling an arch, starting from the fertile soil cultivated for generations by the Brangwen ancestors, and returning to the acorn symbol of fertility by which Ursula images the release of her inner life from the constriction of her circumstances.

Women in Love differs from *The Rainbow* most obviously by being spatial in its dimensions rather than temporal; that is to say, it moves over a much wider range of society and environment, from the schoolroom to the country house, from the mining town to the Café Pompadour in London, and its time-span covers months rather than years. Its four central characters are Ursula Brangwen, a schoolteacher; her sister Gudrun, an artist; Gerald Crich, a mine owner and manager, and Rupert Birkin, who begins as a school inspector but is really a portrait of Lawrence himself, presented, however, with some objectivity and even sardonically. Besides these, some characters are prominent in parts of the narrative, such as Lady Hermione Roddice, in the foreground of the opening chapters, and the German sculptor Loerke in the closing ones. In addition, the novel presents 'worlds' of characters: there is, first, the mining world of the Crich family, then the country house world of intellectuals centring on Hermione, the artistic world of the Café Pompadour, and the Tyrolean world with which the book concludes. These worlds relate to one another, so that the book resembles a spectrum of colours, each very distinct in itself, yet merging with its neighbour rather than sharply defined from it. This is partly because each of the four central characters has some affinity with one or another. But the novel is different from its predecessor not merely in being more spacious socially and environmentally. Its characters are also more articulate, so that the dialogue has a keener intellectual force, and even very minor characters (like Gerald's mother, Mrs Crich) contribute vividly, however briefly, to what in the end can be seen as an elaborate design of remarkably varied mental tones. Yet though *Women in Love* is in this respect more intellectual in its components than is *The Rainbow*, it is not more meagre in its poetic and symbolic quality; this kind of imagery is indeed still richer and more disturbing. Some of the symbolic episodes are directly intelligible, like that in Chapter 9 (*Coal-dust*) where Gerald Crich unconsciously dramatises his own personality by forcing his terrified horse to stand at the level-crossing while the goods-train clanks backwards and forwards with unbearable clamour. Some of them are mysterious, like the scene in Chapter 19 (*Moony*), in which Rupert Birkin tries to shatter the reflection in the lake of the moon, image of the goddess Cybele. But direct or oblique in what they communicate, these symbolic episodes form a more distinct and a richer aspect of the novel than equivalent scenes in *The Rainbow*.

For such reasons, *Women in Love* is often considered a greater book. But Lawrence must have felt that he was working in more difficult material. To trace the past in its contribution to the present is difficult enough, and impressive in so far as the novelist succeeds, as Scott's earlier novels and Tolstoy's *War and Peace* testify, but to penetrate to the depths of the writer's own time, and not merely to evaluate its culture but attempt to expose the promise and the perils it holds for the future – this is even harder, and perhaps explains the peculiar greatness of *Anna Karenina*. It seems that Lawrence meant his four principal characters to form a kind of potential nucleus for a modern society of promise. Their qualities seem to be complementary in such a way that they would, in harmony, make for wholeness: Gerald is governed by reason and the will; Rupert by intuition and the imagination, Gudrun by emotion, and Ursula by the senses. However, only the relationship of Ursula and Rupert harmonises; that between Gerald and Gudrun becomes mutually destructive. This mixture of promise and foreboding is somewhat marred, partly by traces of bitterness and disillusionment in Lawrence whose *Rainbow* had been banned for obscenity, and who suffered persecution and suspicion during his writing of *Women in Love* owing to the fact of his German marriage, and partly by a certain indistinctness of vision in consequence of which it is never fully clear what he intended to convey by the deep but unfulfilled friendship between Gerald and Rupert. *Women in Love* does not match *Anna Karenina* in greatness, yet it would be hard to find another novel which tells us so much about our century and is so universal in its import.

Lawrence has been, and still is, greatly misunderstood; and the extent of public misunderstanding is often the measure of the importance of a writer. He has been accused of making a religion of sex, though he repeatedly shows the destructiveness of mere sexuality, for instance in the final stage of the relationship between Will and Anna Brangwen; he has been accused of inaugurating modern permissiveness, though again and again he shows his abomination of promiscuity; it has been said that he despised the intelligence, although by precept and by practice he constantly asserts the necessity of its cultivation and its vigilance. But in extenuation of this public misunderstanding, it must be admitted that he is a very difficult writer. It was inevitable that he should be, because he undertook renewal of the heart of western culture by constant antagonism to the tyranny of its concepts of the head. This compelled him to make a frontal assault on some of the basic terms in our evaluating language – on 'love' for instance, a word often questioned by his characters because it has been diluted and distorted from opposite directions by two kinds of decadence, religious and romantic. To undertake a reading in depth of Lawrence, it is perhaps not enough to study his fiction, for this is part of and also depends upon a critical position which is clarified by his essays, especially those on literature, in the posthumous volumes *Phoenix I* and *Phoenix II*. The fiction itself is best approached though his wonderful stories which display his imaginative power more assimilably than the more spacious work of the novels does, complicated as this work is by the turmoil of his argumentative mind. *Daughters of the Vicar* (1914), *Odour of Chrysanthemums* (1914), *The Fox* (1923), *The Captain's Doll* (1923), and the short novel *St Mawr* (1925), read in that order, make a good introduction. Another reason for suggesting the stories of Lawrence before engagement with the novels is that much that he was trying to do with language was essentially poetic; the short story has more in common with poetry than the novel has, and it is not a coincidence that English poetry was undergoing renewal during the most important decade of Lawrence's fiction – 1913–23.

4

The recovery of poetry 1900-1920

Beginnings: A. E. Housman (1859–1936); Thomas Hardy (1840–1928); Edward Thomas (1878–1917)

When a poet's mind is perfectly equipped for its work, it is constantly amalgamating disparate experience; the ordinary man's experience is chaotic, irregular, fragmentary. The latter falls in love, or reads Spinoza, and these two experiences have nothing to do with each other, or with the noise of the typewriter or the smell of cooking; in the mind of the poet these experiences are always forming new wholes. T. S. Eliot: *The Metaphysical Poets*

This chapter is not intended to begin from a merely negative view of English poetry as it was at the opening of the century. It can be maintained, and has been, that English poetry was then both sick and lost: sick because the strength of the language had gone out of it, and lost because it did not receive much attention from serious minds. But the word 'recover' can mean 'return to', as in the sentence 'The swimmers recovered the shore'. If we say that English poetry 'recovered' in this sense of the word, we mean that the poets returned to a conception of their art which had once been important not only to poets. This happened in a number of ways, so that it might be more accurate to speak of 'recoveries' than of 'recovery'. But our first attention must be for the verse that had not yet undergone, or was only beginning to undergo, the new influences.

In 1896 A. E. Housman published a small volume entitled *A Shropshire Lad*, which is still one of the most famous books of verse produced in the last hundred years. Here is an example:

> On the idle hill of summer
> Sleepy with the flow of streams,
> Far I hear the steady drummer
> Drumming like a noise in dreams.

> Far and near and low and louder
> On the roads of earth go by,

> Dear to friends and food for powder,
> Soldiers marching, all to die.
>
> East and west on fields forgotten
> Bleach the bones of comrades slain,
> Lovely lads and dead and rotten;
> None that go return again.
>
> Far the calling bugles hollo,
> High the screaming fife replies,
> Gay the files of scarlet follow:
> Woman bore me, I will rise.

The feeling is poignant; the language economical, exact for its purposes, and musical. But who is the 'I' that is speaking? Not the poet – a distinguished scholar with no intention of joining up. Supposedly it is the Shropshire lad – the country boy, who would be rustic in speech and barely literate, certainly far from using language of this sort. In fact the poet is concerned to project a mood – about the dreamlike beauty of the countryside, the magnetic glamour and bitter destructiveness of war, the pathos of youth cut down in its flower, and, uniting these, the melancholy and perverseness of human existence. The youth feels that it is in his nature to go ('Woman bore me'), although he knows that 'None return again'. Fact and actuality do not matter to the poet: many soldiers do return from the deadliest wars, and no Shropshire lad seduced by the recruiting sergeant would feel just like this; the countryside does not have 'idle' hills for those who work on them. Yet there is no doubt that the poem moves the reader – once he has surrendered to the spell which it seeks to cast on him. It is representative of Housman; his only other volumes, *Last Poems* (1922) and *More Poems* (1936), have the same themes, treated in the same way.

A Shropshire Lad was published just before the South African War; at the end of it, in 1901, Thomas Hardy published *Poems of the Past and the Present*, which includes 'Drummer Hodge':

> They throw in Drummer Hodge, to rest
> Uncoffined – just as found:
> His landmark is a kopje-crest
> That breaks the veldt around;
> And foreign constellations west
> Each night above his mound.
>
> Younge Hodge the Drummer never knew—
> Fresh from his Wessex home—

> The meaning of the broad Karoo,
>   The Bush, the dusty loam,
> And why uprose to nightly view
>   Strange stars amid the gloam.
>
> Yet portion of that unknown plain
>   Will Hodge for ever be;
> His homely Northern breast and brain
>   Grow to some Southern tree,
> And strange-eyed constellations reign
>   His stars eternally.

The language of this poem is laconic, factual. The rhythms and diction do not draw the reader into a mood, but rather sharpen his attention by their terseness; the use of 'west' as a verb is characteristic of Hardy's practice of condensing his language. And yet, although the poem has none of Housman's overt but vague, cosmic sadness, it is as spacious in its implications, and far more precise. The facts are that Hodge, a real countryman this time, is bundled into a war and into a land he knows nothing about, and becomes a part of it for ever; the implications are again the perverseness of fate, particularly of the poor and ignorant, but this time the perverseness is not merely attributed by the poet – it arises from the evidence.

Some twelve years after the close of the South African War came the Great War which killed so many poets, among them Edward Thomas, who only just had time for the small output of verse which made his reputation. His poems about war are fewer still, among them the single quatrain 'In Memoriam (Easter 1915)':

> The flowers left thick at nightfall in the wood
> This Eastertide call into mind the men,
> Now far from home, who, with their sweethearts, should
> Have gathered them and will do never again.

These lines abstain from direct appeal to the emotions even more than Hardy's poem does. The language is plain, with the plainness of prose, and the rhymes seem casual, almost fortuitous, only heightening the plainness of the speech with faint music. Yet the quatrain shows delicate art in its rhythm, especially in the placing of the natural pauses for the voice. It is the last four words which show this art most, perfectly colloquial as they are, yet condensing the whole feeling into the last two.

Each of these three poets, so briefly exemplified, was individual,

67

and their differences call for attention before we note their resemblances. Housman stood closest to the public standpoint at
the end of the nineteenth century. He was a highly intellectual,
learned man. Yet he stated that 'Meaning is of the intellect, poetry
is not', and in the same lecture (*The Name and Nature of Poetry*,
1933) that 'to transfuse emotion – not to transmit thought but to
set up in the reader's sense a vibration corresponding to what was
felt by the writer – is the peculiar function of poetry'. Hardy wrote
in his diary that 'The Poet takes note of nothing that he cannot
feel emotionally', but he adds: 'a poet should express the emotion
of all the ages and the thought of his own'. Hardy was a reluctant
antagonist to Christian theism, and believed, significantly for the
kind of attention that was given to poetry, that he could express his
heterodox faith in verse without arousing the consternation which
he caused when he expressed it in his novels. Like Housman's, most
of Hardy's verse is melancholy or sombre, but the sombreness
seems to proceed from a different cause. Housman is melancholy
because his temperament was melancholy, but Hardy's sombreness, though no doubt in part explicable by his temperament, proceeds also from his intellectual conviction. In his own words, he
believed it to be an evident truth that 'the Supreme Mover . . .
must be either limited in power, unknowing, or cruel', and that it
was his task as a poet to confront his intellectual despair, without
disguise or qualification.

Thomas, a younger man who started writing poetry late in his
short life, was less influenced than Hardy by consciously held beliefs. In this he was more a child of the new century, for it was characteristic of the Victorians that, when they abandoned traditional
doctrine, they felt the need of a new one, even if it be a philosophy
of despair. But Thomas looks forward, too, in his attitude to verse
technique. Because the familiar stanzaic forms and the diction
concentrated as 'poetic' had so long been used to transmit private
emotion, and so had tended to become facile means of arousing
stock responses, younger poets increasingly sought to break the
moulds, and even to attempt what is more or less accurately called
'free verse'. Thomas, though he did not experiment in free verse,
was moving in that direction. Hardy, on the other hand – and as
we shall see he was not alone in this among the major figures –
seems to have found in the very artificiality of traditional form a
defence against personal indulgence of emotion, but he resisted the

excessive artificiality of its musical effects by employing them with a new fastidiousness and sensitivity.

Two further examples, one from Hardy and one from Thomas, will help to clarify their distinction in these respects. First, 'The Self-Unseeing' by Hardy:

> Here is the ancient floor,
> Footworn and hollowed and thin,
> Here was the former door
> Where the dead feet walked in.
>
> She sat here in her chair,
> Smiling into the fire;
> He who played stood there,
> Bowing it higher and higher.
>
> Childlike, I danced in a dream;
> Blessings emblazoned that day;
> Everything glowed with a gleam;
> Yet we were looking away!

The subject is the happiness that was not recognised in its perfection because it was taken for granted, and is now contrasted with the ruined cottage which embodies in its abandonment the irrecoverability of the past. But characteristically, Hardy does not state his nostalgia, nor does he evoke it by evocative language. He evokes it by the scene itself as it exists in his memory, and implies his sadness in the final line, which states the fact that underlies the feeling. The light dactylic and trochaic metre infuses the lines with wistful gaiety, but the last line of the first stanza contains the heavy spondee 'dead feet', which nails into the past that living moment. The feeling is personal and the form traditional, but the delicate factuality of the poem raises it from the level of private nostalgia to the impersonality of universal experience.

Here is Edward Thomas's 'The New House':

> Now first, as I shut the door,
>   I was alone
> In the new house; and the wind
>   Began to moan.
>
> Old at once was the house,
>   And I was old;
> My ears were teased with the dread
>   Of what was foretold,
>
> Nights of storm, days of mist, without end;

69

> Sad days when the sun
> Shone in vain: old griefs and griefs
> Not yet begun.
>
> All was foretold me; naught
> Could I foresee;
> But I learned how the wind would sound
> After these things should be.

The quatrain form is here used more freely: the line-lengths vary, like the rise and fall of the wind itself. The rhyme music is subdued, by restriction to two line endings in each four. This flexibility – another example of Thomas relaxing the verse medium in the direction of prose – enables the poet to play down the special quality in the experience he is expressing, so that the reader feels that it might be his. It is indeed an emotion which might be felt by anyone alone in a newly-built house, still empty of all its furnishings, and acting as a drum to resonate the wind as it blows around the bare external surfaces and through the gaps under the doors. The mournful experience is presented as the poet's, but the poem does not make the reader feel the mournfulness as due to the poet's temperament, but to the circumstances of the location. This is not Housman's transfusion of emotion, but the re-enactment of a particular occasion for emotion.

Hardy and Thomas, then, stand apart from Housman with his doctrine of the transfusion of emotion, and the extent to which they do so marks them off as poets of the new century. Their distinguishing mark (in Thomas still more than in Hardy) is one kind of impersonality. It is important to understand the sense in which this word can be used of a poet, for there is another sense in which it cannot be used: in so much as all art of importance is individual, it is personal in essence. But it is also true that an artist is distinguished from an ordinary man to the extent that he has what the rest of us are without: a synthesising means of relating himself to his environment and to his experience of it. The reality of our environment is multiform, various and fragmented, and we receive this reality fragmentedly through the variety of our senses and faculties, although we colour the compound with the prevailing qualities of our individual temperaments. But the artist is able to use an element of his experience – his medium, which in the instance of the poet is his language – as though it were an additional faculty uniting the rest. His medium is not only a medium in the sense that all his faculties are at home in it, but also in the sense that it constitutes a form of communication, by means of which the unity of experience which the artist is able to create in it is shared by the public who respond to it. Thus the poet, as any other artist, may be two men. As an ordinary man, he is subject to his temperament, but as a poet his temperament is subject to his medium. It is in this sense that Hardy and Thomas belonged to the new century much more than Housman did, and it is in this sense that they are impersonal. But why should leading poets of the twentieth century have sought impersonality?

The personal poem, centred, as it tends to be, on the personal temperament of the poet, tends also to lack centrality for the public for whom the poet writes. The poem that issues from the mood and the personal temperament of the poet may – if the poet is as gifted as Housman was – have a wide appeal, but it will be a poem of retreat into the self, instead of a placing of the self in the larger circumstance of common humanity. Poetry in 1900 had become a retreat. Even the poetry of Hardy and Thomas took little direct account of the temper of the age by comparison with the work of the novelists; to that extent it was still a poetry of private circumstance. What the leading poets increasingly sought to recover was relationship with contemporary history, which both includes and denies what is private. This makes a study of the War Poets an instructive one.

War Poets: Wilfred Owen (1893–1918); Isaac Rosenberg (1890– 1918)

Here, first is Wilfred Owen's 'Anthem for Doomed Youth':

> What passing-bells for these who die as cattle?
>   Only the monstrous anger of the guns.
> Only the stuttering rifles' rapid rattle
>   Can patter out their hasty orisons.
> No mockeries now for them; no prayers nor bells,
>   Nor any voice of mourning save the choirs,—
> The shrill, demented choirs of wailing shells;
>   And bugles calling for them from sad shires.
>
> What candles may be held to speed them all?
>   Not in the hands of boys, but in their eyes
>   Shall shine the holy glimmers of good-byes.

71

> The pallor of girls' brows shall be their pall;
> Their flowers the tenderness of patient minds,
> And each slow dusk a drawing-down of blinds.

The poem is a sonnet; that is to say, it has a traditional form, which three centuries earlier in western Europe had become widely popular because its intricate and close organisation had enabled poets to use it for concentrated emotional expression. The material for this sonnet is indeed new: war had been used by sonneteers as a symbol for the conflict of emotions, but here war is the subject, and peace provides the sad and ironic symbols. Owen has taken a standpoint midway between the fighting and the home fronts, and he bridges the two, not only by making the one setting evoke the other for the senses but making the one setting counterbalance the other in the emotions by fusing nostalgia with irony. The outrage of war remains and is indeed affirmed by the poem, but the private feelings are afforded breathing space by the neutralisation in a mood of the impersonal and the personal.

Very different is the effect produced by Isaac Rosenberg's 'Break of Day in the Trenches':

> The darkness crumbles away—
> It is the same old druid Time as ever.
> Only a live thing leaps my hand—
> A queer sardonic rat—
> As I pull the parapet's poppy
> To stick behind my ear.
> Droll rat, they would shoot you if they knew
> Your cosmopolitan sympathies.
> Now you have touched this English hand
> You will do the same to a German—
> Soon, no doubt, if it be your pleasure
> To cross the sleeping green between.
> It seems you inwardly grin as you pass
> Strong eyes, fine limbs, haughty athletes
> Less chanced than you for life,
> Bonds to the whims of murder,
> Sprawled in the bowels of the earth,
> The torn fields of France.
> What do you see in our eyes
> At the shrieking iron and flame
> Hurled through still heavens?
> What quaver – what heart aghast?
> Poppies whose roots are in man's veins
> Drop, and are ever dropping;

But mine in my ear is safe,
Just a little white with the dust.

Here there is no traditional pattern; on the contrary, not only is
the poem rhymeless but its rhythm is free. The poet speaks in his
own person and it is his personal predicament that is his subject, but
ostensibly his subject is the rat, about which his mind moves in
detached speculation though with envy for its capacity for survival
– and perhaps for its sanity? His tone, at least, seems to catch some
of the sardonic quality he attributes to the rat, though it is too
light for bitterness. He shares the rat's detachment from the dead
that lie about them, and yet knows he may share their lot at any
time; he is detached from the poppies whose roots are nourished
by the dead, but accepts them as emblems of mortality including
his own. In the last two lines, he seems to identify with the rat itself
in its aptitude for life, and he wears his poppy like a flag. As an
emblem of defiance, perhaps? But also of life, sanity and courage.
He and his poppy are only safe for the living moment, and that,
after all, is the human condition, in war or in peace.

The two poets were different in their attitudes both to poetry and
to war. Owen deliberately chose the vocation of war poet, realising
that the strength and narrowness of the personal communication
that poetry had become made is peculiarly apposite as a means of
reducing the inhumanly massive horror of the war – its worst
feature – to an apprehensibly human compass. Mass horror obliter-
ates the private self, but in his poems Owen resuscitates it by sub-
stituting, for suffering, pity for suffering. This was a fine achievement, but it was a defensive one; neither poetry, the poet, nor the
reader was fundamentally altered by it, though (morally) they
survived by it. Rosenberg did not hate the war less than Owen did,
but he accepted it impersonally as – inhuman as it was – a world of
experience which could be assimilated into his poetic consciousness and enlarge it. Unlike Owen, he did not see a vocation in war
poetry as such, but the war was the fact, and as a fact it had to be
lived through. Writing to an older poet, Laurence Binyon, from
France in 1916, Rosenberg said:

I am determined that this war, with all its powers for devastation, shall
not master my poeting; that is, if I am lucky enough to come through all
right. I will not leave a corner of my consciousness covered up, but
saturate myself with the strange and extraordinary new conditions of
this life, and it will all refine itself into poetry later on.

He did not survive; like Owen, he was killed in 1918. Owen recovered a use for poetry, but Rosenberg was seeking to recover the potentiality of poetry, whose scope, among the great poets of the past, had not felt encompassed by the private temperament. There is of course no guessing what they might have achieved had they survived. And meanwhile other poets not engaged in the war were discovering what demands the age was making on them if poetry was to recover its reach.

W. B. Yeats (1865–1939)

. . . all that is personal soon rots; it must be packed in ice and salt. W. B. Yeats: *A General Introduction to my Work*

The *Introduction* (1937) was written late in his life, at the end of a career at the beginning of which he was a leader of the last phase of late nineteenth-century Romanticism; he had now become one of the two leading poets writing just past the height of the poetic recovery, which he had himself done much to bring about. And yet superficial acquaintance might suggest that the form of his poetry had remained remarkably constant. Throughout his career, Yeats used traditional stanzas with a strong, clear musical form, as sharply distinguished as they could be from the fluidity of prose rhythms. It is this pronounced form that Yeats is referring to when he speaks of the need to pack what is personal in 'ice and salt':

If I wrote of personal love or sorrow in free verse, or in any rhythm that left it unchanged, amid all its accidence, I would be full of self-contempt because of my egotism and indiscretion, and foresee the boredom of my reader. I must choose a traditional stanza, even what I alter must seem traditional. I commit my emotion to shepherds, herdsmen, camel-drivers, learned men, Milton's or Shelley's Platonist, that tower Palmer drew. Talk to me of originality and I will turn on you with rage. I am a crowd, I am a lonely man, I am nothing.
Ancient salt is best packing. (*Introduction*)

Yeats's critical prose is often elliptical: the logical sequence between the second and third sentences in this passage – between his need for a traditional stanza and his need to embody his emotions in 'shepherds, herdsmen . . .' – is not obvious. But for Yeats, both implied dramatisation and detachment from the private temperament.

Although the artifice of traditional form and the dramatic fiction

74

are evident in his work from the first, Yeats writes in his *Introduction* that

It was a long time before I made a language to my liking; I began to make it when I discovered some twenty years ago that I must seek, not as Wordsworth thought, words in common use, but a powerful and passionate syntax, and a complete coincidence between period and stanza.

'Twenty years ago' takes us back to *The Wild Swans at Coole* (1919), a volume which includes one of his best known short poems, 'An Irish Airman Foresees his Death'. Before examining this, it is worth looking at his early style by considering 'Who Goes with Fergus?' from his second volume *The Rose* (1893):

> Who will go drive with Fergus now,
> And pierce the deep wood's woven shade,
> And dance upon the level shore?
> Young man, lift up your russet brow,
> And lift your tender eyelids, maid,
> And brood on hopes and fear no more.
>
> And no more turn aside and brood
> Upon love's bitter mystery;
> For Fergus rules the brazen cars,
> And rules the shadows of the wood,
> And the white breast of the dim sea
> And all dishevelled wandering stars.

The reader needs to know that Fergus is a warrior in ancient Irish mythology, instructor of its great hero, Cuchulain. The young man and maid are to live with godlike passions, renouncing their private griefs. Fergus rules universal nature to which human nature is normally subject; one cannot be sure whether the nature that he rules is thought of as reflected in the confusions of the sad and subjected young man and maid. Nor is it necessary to worry about such a point. The grave, exalted cadence of the poem does its work by its strong accent on the verbs and the evocative adjectives.

'An Irish Airman' was written some twenty-five years later, to commemorate the death of Major Robert Gregory, the son of Yeats's friend Lady Gregory:

> I know that I shall meet my fate
> Somewhere among the clouds above;
> Those that I fight I do not hate,
> Those that I guard I do not love;
> My country is Kiltartan Cross,

My countrymen Kiltartan's poor,
No likely end could bring them loss
Or leave them happier than before.
Nor law nor duty bade me fight,
Nor public men, nor cheering crowds,
A lonely impulse of delight
Drove to this tumult in the clouds;
I balanced all, brought all to mind,
The years to come seemed waste of breath,
A waste of breath the years behind
In balance with this life, this death.

The airman chooses to join Britain's war against Germany, despite his conviction that neither victory nor defeat will help or harm his native country. He fights for the sake of intensifying life and death, and not on the romantic impulse of youth, but after mature reckoning of the consequences. Here is no mythological hero, but a man making a choice which must have been similar to the choice of many Irish in the First World War. The poem then is set amongst the facts of history, not in the timeless zone of mythology, but although this is part of a change that Yeats had undergone, it is not the whole change, nor is it the most significant difference when we compare this with the earlier poem.

When we compare the two poems, we notice, first, a resemblance in their pronounced metre and rhyme. But next, we shall notice that the earlier one makes concessions to a conventional poeticality which is absent from the later. A clue to the difference is in the use of adjectives. Those in 'Who Goes with Fergus?' are mainly emotive rather than functional, and once we see them in this way, we may wonder whether the emotive language is altogether consistent: if 'white breast of the sea' refers to sea-foam fading into indefinite distance, is 'breast' the suitable word? The adjectives in 'An Irish Airman' are functional only, as well as much fewer: 'likely', 'happier', 'public', 'cheering'. Then we find a different relation of metre to syntax. In the first poem, the syntax and the diction are to an extent subordinate to the lyric pattern: each line with its rhyme ending is the significant unit of the poem. Is 'now' introduced mainly for 'brow', and is the puzzle about 'white breast' to be explained by the phrase's metrical service? In the second poem, there is no sense of difference between the syntax and the metrical pattern; the two match, and the metre enhances and enforces the resolution and dignity of the statement. This, then, is what Yeats meant by the 'complete coincidence between period and stanza'.

Some of what has been said about Yeats's strict adherence to traditional verse patterns could also apply to Thomas Hardy. They resemble each other most in the way in which they used traditional forms, not, like Housman, as a means for the direct transfusion of emotion, but as a 'freezing' of personal emotion in the artifice of the pattern. Hardy, however, was naiver in his attitude to verse form; he believed that poetic form had been fully explored, and that it was the business of the modern poet to put the forms made available by the past to the best possible contemporary effect. He was thus a more passive conservative than Yeats, who recognised the validity of his contemporaries' experiments, but believed that they were not for him. As we have seen, Yeats in any case shows an important development in his use of traditional forms, whereas it is unusually difficult to date a Hardy poem by its style. Hardy remained a lively poet in spite of his conservatism because he was a regional poet, owing much through his background as the son of a village mason to the ballad and folksong tradition of the west of England. Yeats was also much concerned with the culture and tradition of his own country, but it was a concern of a different kind with much wider implications.

Yeats was by birth, background, ancestry and loyalty, all Irish, but culturally he was Anglo-Irish. This is to say that he belonged to that succession of Irishmen who accepted English as their language and English literature as their heritage, with just the important difference that they belonged to a country which socially, religiously, economically was not part of England, but in many ways antagonistic, or at least antithetic, to England. Unlike England, Ireland was not an industrial country with a strong middle class, though the Anglo-Irish writers usually were middle class; it was a Catholic country, though the writers were usually Protestant; it was a poor country, exploited by and governed from England until 1921. The Anglo-Irish writers whom Yeats was proud to acknowledge his forebears included Swift, the philosopher Berkeley and all the best dramatists of the eighteenth and nineteenth centuries. However, although a few of them – notably Swift – occasionally stood by Irish as opposed to English interests, they mostly accepted English cultural dominance so fully that it is easy to forget their Irish connection. It was only the rise of the Irish national movement in the nineteenth and early twentieth centuries which made Anglo-Irish writers self-consciously Irish, and even then they were not unanimous. Though John Millington Synge and Yeats strove to establish an indigenous Irish theatre in Dublin, Oscar Wilde and Bernard Shaw remained contributors to the English theatre in London.

The difference lay not in political sympathies so much as in attitudes to the values, uses and purposes of language. Shaw, like Wells, was a Socialist and a propagandist. He saw how a new kind of stage rhetoric, together with a new emphasis on social themes on the example of Ibsen, gave great opportunities for transforming the moribund London theatres into media for social criticism. Wilde saw the London stage as a medium for the revival in a fresh and more sophisticated style of the comedy of manners. Both owed something to a joy in language as rhetoric and as a game of wit which survived in Ireland because language was not so subdued to scientific and commercial purposes there as it was in England. But whereas Shaw and Wilde exploited this gift from their background, Yeats and Synge sought to use it for a renewal of the sources of cultural life.

English in England was the language of an elaborately developed society, and no longer one language so much as many languages, varying according to the social and functional contexts and the special intentions of the user. The language of one class was not that of another; the language of commerce was not that of diplomacy or the church. Such diversity was mainly an advantage to the novelists, especially to those who were acute social observers like Wells, but it was an impediment to a poet who sought a central position in his culture; for poetry, to exert its full resources, seeks the current of a common dominant stock of speech. Ireland, largely a peasant country, still had such a speech. J. M. Synge (1871–1909) demonstrated its availability and force in his plays of Irish peasant life for Yeats's Abbey Theatre in Dublin. His masterpiece was *The Playboy of the Western World* (1907), of which the following is an extract:

Pegeen: And it's that you'd call sport, is it, to be abroad in the darkness with yourself alone.
Christy: I did, God help me, and there I'd be as happy as the sunshine of St Martin's Day, watching the light passing the north or the patches of fog, till I'd hear a rabbit starting to screech and I'd go running in the

furze. Then, when I'd my full share, I'd come walking down where you'd see the ducks and geese stretched sleeping on the highway of the road, and before I'd pass the dunghill, I'd hear himself snoring out – a loud, lonesome snore he'd be making all times, the while he was sleeping; and he a man'd be raging all times, the while he was waking, like a gaudy officer you'd hear cursing and damning and swearing oaths.

Pegeen: Providence and Mercy, spare us all!

Christy: It's that you'd say surely if you seen him and he after drinking for weeks, rising up in the red dawn, or before it maybe, and going out into the yard as naked as an ash-tree in the moon of May, and shying clods against the visage of the stars till he'd put the fear of death into the banbhs and the screeching sows.

It is a language of simple syntax, the clauses accumulating in a loose structure uncluttered by subordinating connectives, held together by musical balance and carried forward by emotional impetus rather than logical process, making impact chiefly through its nouns and verbs. It is concrete and at the same time exuberant, capable of directness and at the same time of grandeur. With qualifications, one can say that it is the language of Yeats's own verse.

Yeats lacked the simplicity of nature which put Synge on easy terms with the country people, but he felt an equal need to identify himself with a whole people, to speak the language of an entire culture. His problem – it would have been Synge's also had he lived longer – was that Irish culture was originally Celtic and almost obliterated by centuries of English overlay. But this never entirely dismayed him. He believed that the creation of a vital society of peasantry and aristocracy, opposed in its whole spirit to the English hegemony, was possible, and he saw the sources for life for it in Irish myth. But since ancient myths are the basis of a much wider culture than merely national ones, and since they operate through dramatic and imaginative symbols rather than through rational concepts such as 'the greatest happiness of the greatest number', Yeats found himself drawn towards a far wider and more mysterious horizon of poetic thought than the politics of the 'Irish Renaissance' alone provided. He believed with increasing strength that all western civilisation was dying, not by any disease that politics could cure, but by an aridity which was destroying its spiritual roots.

Thus, by about 1920, Yeats was developing a theory of history with symbols of his own such as enabled him to dramatise poetically the rise and fall of civilisations. Such a symbol was the 'gyre', drawn from the spiral movement of a bobbin on a loom, according to which he envisaged a civilisation gradually unwinding into ever greater diversity away from the origins of its culture, until, as it lost all coherence, a new gyre would begin in the opposite direction. This is the subject of one of his most famous poems, 'The Second Coming', in the volume entitled *Michael Robartes and the Dancer* (1921):

> Turning and turning in the widening gyre
> The falcon cannot hear the falconer;
> Things fall apart; the centre cannot hold;
> Mere anarchy is loosed upon the world,
> The blood-dimmed tide is loosed, and everywhere
> The ceremony of innocence is drowned;
> The best lack all conviction, while the worst
> Are full of passionate intensity.
>
> Surely some revelation is at hand;
> Surely the Second Coming it at hand.
> The Second Coming! Hardly are those words out
> When a vast image out of *Spiritus Mundi*
> Troubles my sight: somewhere in sands of the desert
> A shape with lion body and the head of a man,
> A gaze blank and pitiless as the ʼun,
> Is moving its slow thighs, while all about it
> Reel shadows of the indignant desert birds.
> The darkness drops again; but now I know
> That twenty centuries of stony sleep
> Were vexed to nightmare by a rocking cradle,
> And what rough beast, its hour come round at last,
> Slouches towards Bethlehem to be born?

The ancient pagan world had been rocked to destruction by the birth of Christ, and now a new equally destructive birth was beginning its creative cycle: certainly a greater one than the rebirth of the Irish nation. Yet Yeats never forgot that he was an Irishman. The war had passed him by, but the Dublin Rebellion of 1916 deeply shocked and disturbed him, causing him to write another of his most famous poems – 'Easter 1916'. And although 'The Second Coming' may seem at first to have little in common with the language of Synge's peasants, examination shows it to have a comparable strength in the simplicity of its syntax, its achievement of impressive statement without ornament, its concreteness capable of arriving effortlessly at elemental grandeur.

T. S. Eliot (1888–1965)

. . . the poet has, not a 'personality' to express, but a particular medium, which is only a medium and not a personality, in which impressions and experiences combine in peculiar and unexpected ways. Impressions and experiences which are important for the man may take no place in the poetry, and those which become important in the poetry may play quite a negligible part in the man, the personality. T. S. Eliot: 'Tradition and the Individual Talent'

In this famous essay Eliot redefined the word 'tradition', so that its usual meaning of 'that which is continued because it has always been the same' is replaced by the meaning 'that which is different because it has to be continued'. Only a dead tradition, he explained, is merely reproduced; a living tradition is always a challenge to the poet for the development of it for new purposes. But a living tradition will not necessarily be manifest in the immediate past, and not necessarily in the channels of expression which recent writers have been accustomed to follow, for recent work may be merely imitative, accumulating in stagnant channels, whereas farther in the past and elsewhere among the literary currents there may exist much more vigorous sources. Sheer originality was in any case, for Eliot, a delusion, as it was for Yeats: it is no more possible to write without literary antecedents than it is to live without a genetic inheritance. But just as a man may use his genetic constitution in ways that were unforeseeable to his ancestors, so poets may use their inherited medium for work which is unprecedented.

Eliot settled in Britain in 1915, but he did not have to leave America to form these views. His essay 'Tradition and the Individual Talent' was published in 1917, in the same year as the publication of his first volume of poems, *Prufrock and Other Observations* (1917), and these were mainly written in America. It is not, however, easy to know this by internal evidence. One sequence, entitled 'Preludes', for instance, has an immediacy of place for the English reader whether it was written in Boston or London. The first of the sequence is as follows:

> The winter evening settles down
> With smell of steaks in passageways.
> Six o'clock.
> The burnt-out ends of smoky days.
> And now a gusty shower wraps
> The grimy scraps
> Of withered leaves about your feet

> And newspapers from vacant lots;
> The showers beat
> On broken blinds and chimney-pots,
> And at the corner of the street
> A lonely cab-horse steams and stamps.
>
> And then the lighting of the lamps.

The 'place' may of course be any big city, but it is the fact of being a city which gives the verse its immediacy of location. For over a century the majority of people – certainly of educated people – had lived in cities, and the novelists, notably Dickens, had long taken account of the fact. But English poets had continued to write as though life is normally passed in the country. This alone does something to explain why poetry had ceased to be a central preoccupation of the English reading public, who took holidays in poetry as they took them in the countryside, but read other literature when they wanted 'real life'. French poets had done otherwise, and Eliot, like James, regarding English literature from across the Atlantic in its English context, had learned more from Baudelaire and the French Symbolists than from Tennyson and the English Romantics. From the French, too, he had learned that rhyme could be used for its sting, whereas English poets, unless they were writing light verse or satire, had restricted it to its singing quality. The stinging, or biting, effect of the rhymes in *Prelude* counteracts the squalor and depression of the urban scene with an angry distaste, for the poet is not denying that the urban scene, unlike the rural one, is ugly and sinister. The rural setting can readily be made humane, but the urban one is the normal human setting, and to reach humanity through the environment requires a compassion which the environment itself inhibits;

> His soul stretched tight across the skies
> That fade behind a city block,
> Or trampled by insistent feet
> At four and five and six o'clock;
> And short square fingers stuffing pipes,
> And evening newspapers, and eyes
> Assured of certain certainties,
> The conscience of a blackened street
> Impatient to assume the world.
>
> I am moved by fancies that are curled
> Around these images, and cling:

82

> The notion of some infinitely gentle
> Infinitely suffering thing.
>
> Wipe your hand across your mouth, and laugh;
> The worlds revolve like ancient women
> Gathering fuel in vacant lots.

This is verse of a new dryness, apparently allowing itself a new licence, but in fact it is meticulously precise. The relaxed rhythm of the quatrain emits a glimpse of tenderness and pity promptly denied by the harsh, proselike rhythm of the last three lines: there is no space for compassion in this brutal world.

One can make a considerable list of the diverse influences acting upon Eliot early in his career. It would include the French Symbolists and Dante, the Metaphysical Poets and the later Jacobean dramatists, the idealist philosophy of F. H. Bradley and the theories of Ezra Pound about the nature of images. All these are important for understanding his work, but they do not by themselves bring one very close to appreciating the quality of his work unless one combines them with a study of how he understood the art of poetry, and in particular his own poetry. His attitude was paradoxical. On the one hand, his work is remarkable for its coherent development as well as for its scrupulous artistry. This points to a high degree of professionalism. Yet more than once in later life he declared to younger poets that he did not consider himself a poet so much as a man who from time to time was visited by the need to write poetry. This suggests a haphazard, inspirational view of poetic creation reminiscent of Housman, and, in fact, in *The Use of Poetry and the Use of Criticism* (1933) he acknowledges his kinship with Housman in this respect. How is one to reconcile this evident contradiction, between the professionalism of his work, its systematic development and coherence, and the hints he occasionally let fall about the private, inspirational way in which he actually wrote?

The enigma is explained if we consider the man and his work as they ask to be considered – as a whole. His career presents a number of paradoxes, each resolved on a further plane. We can see him as the American, leaving his native land with its democratic values, to go back to his ancestral Europe with its hierarchical cultures which he believed to be degenerate; as the thinker intensely aware of the materiality of the world, but educated in Bradley's idealism, according to which neither the subject nor the object is real, but only the spiritual entities which transcend them; as the sceptic who took his doubts so seriously that he was intolerant of indifference; as the literary critic for whom literature is never very important unless it is practised, in discipleship or antagonism, in the light of a religious system; as the poet who saw poetry as 'the emotional equivalent of thought', and held that it could not be practised without an intellectual discipline as stringent as that of philosophy. In each case there is a duality, and in each the duality is resolved: his pursuit of the emotional origins of culture took him beyond the immaturity of America and the degeneracy of Europe; his belief that the great dilemmas are spiritual overcame his internal distaste for the oppression of external matter; his faith in the viability of spiritual search carried him beyond his private scepticism and his despair at public indifference; his sense that poetry is below religion in a hierarchy of disciplines was for him a more logical justification for its existence than any pursuit of poetry as an absolute could be. Above all, although he did not believe that poetry could be a profession, he did believe that to create poetry a writer had constantly to study to make himself available for it, by cultivating his taste and that quality he attributed to Baudelaire – 'the sense of his age'.

The three qualities that characterise Eliot's work are, first, his own 'sense of his age'; second, his opinion that poetry is a medium which takes its start from the poet's emotions but is 'impersonalised' by the tradition in which the poet has to work, and third, his use of other writers in the tradition for irony, parody, and the deepening of poetic communication. The first gave him his unprecedented sensibility for the urban environment and for distinctively modern states of mind. The second gave him insights into the ways in which poetry could communicate as poetry, and not merely as a versified equivalent of the logically consecutive thinking natural to prose. His acute ear for rhythm made him aware that rhythm is never a mechanical choice of metre, but a means of achieving subtly varying tones of feeling, often dependent on the use of rhythm by other poets. In 'Reflections on Vers Libre', he wrote, in 1917:

... the most interesting verse which has yet been written in our language has been done either by taking a very simple form, like the iambic pentameter, and constantly withdrawing from it, or taking no form at all, and constantly approximating to a very simple one. It is this contrast between fixity and flux, this unperceived evasion of monotony. which is the very life of verse.

For the concept of 'free verse' itself he had no use: ' "Vers libre" does not exist'. He admired those poets – the Jacobean dramatists such as Shakespeare and Middleton, the Metaphysicals such as Donne and Herbert, the French Symbolists such as Baudelaire and Laforgue – whose rhythms were most subtle and flexible. In the same poets he found great freedom and flexibility of imagery. But imagery for Eliot was not essentially a literary concept; there was no class of images consecrated as 'poetic'. An image was the nucleus of an emotional complex, and every individual accumulates his stock. The difference for the poet is that a personal image may sooner or later find its place in the context of a poem, and achieve emotional illumination there, although this will not necessarily mean that its precise significance will be paraphrasable in prose.

This resistance to precise paraphrase by Eliot's poetry has caused more difficulties to readers than anything else. The reader accustomed to prose inevitably seeks in poetry what he has learnt to understand as a meaning: something portable, that he can carry away in his mind when he has closed the book. But for Eliot, meaning in this sense was not the point. Even poetry which can be paraphrased does not have 'meaning' in this sense as its main object:

The chief use of the 'meaning' of a poem, in the ordinary sense, may be ... to satisfy one habit of a reader, to keep his mind diverted and quiet. while the poem does its work upon him: much as the imaginary burglar is always provided with a bit of nice meat for the house-dog. (*The Use of Poetry*)

A poem has to be lived into, rather than what is normally meant by 'understood': it is an experience unified by rhythms and images the choice of which is dictated not only by the theme but by the echoes of that theme in other writers. This is the third of his three distinguishing qualities: his constant practice of adding a dimension to his own language by adapting the work of his predecessors.

Although the usual impression received by readers of Eliot is that he broke from the nineteenth-century English tradition, in one respect he continued it. Tennyson, Browning and other Victorian poets commonly wrote eclectically in established forms, but one they invented. In their different ways, Tennyson and Browning especially found it convenient to adopt the mask of some character in history or legend, or even that of an invention of their own, in order to dramatise a state of mind which was not exactly theirs, or, if it was theirs, one which they found convenient to disguise. This was the 'dramatic monologue', which Eliot continued in the three most important poems of his first two volumes. These poems are 'The Love Song of J. Alfred Prufrock' and 'Portrait of a Lady' in *Prufrock and Other Observations*, and 'Gerontion' in *Poems* (1919). But whereas the Victorians had always made their monologue characters speak consecutive speeches out of specific situations (Ulysses contemplates his last voyage, a Bishop explains how he reconciles his scepticism with his office), Eliot made the outline of his characters indistinct and their predicaments less specific so that both became humanly more generalisable, and at the same time their speech is unified through images and rhythms rather than by consecutive syntax, much as one's thoughts may take leaps which defy logic, but reflect a constant emotional pressure. Yet in summary, Eliot's characters do not differ markedly from Victorian prototypes in the form. Prufrock is a Bostonian, who finds that the conventions of his circle, its conformity by lip-service to a smart 'culture'—

> In the room the women come and go
> Talking of Michelangelo

have so conditioned his inner self that spontaneous expression of feeling is no longer possible for him. The young man in 'Portrait of a Lady' mocks a woman older than himself for her affectations of sensibility, only to find much later the doubt awakening in his mind whether it is not he who had looked the fool, by his complacent and vulgarly snobbish disregard of her craving for relationship. The difference between Eliot's poems and the Victorian ones is that he does not present us with characters in situations defined as not our own, so much as describe a consciousness such that it could be ours. This is particularly the quality of 'Gerontion', in which an old man addresses God at the end of a spiritually wasted life.

The name Gerontion is an ironic allusion to the mystical poem *Gerontius* by the great Victorian religious leader, Cardinal Newman. Gerontius is Greek for 'Old Man', and Newman's poem is about the soul reaching up to God at the moment of death. Gerontion, 'the little old man', is from the opposite end of the Victorian spectrum. The poem opens with a quotation from a sad letter written in old age by Edward Fitzgerald, author of a hedonistic version of the Persian poem, *Omar Khayyam*:

> Here I am, an old man in a dry month,
> Being read to by a boy, waiting for rain

But it is not Fitzgerald who is speaking, but a generalised figure, perhaps representative of civilisation itself. As the poem proceeds, the reader recognises (after re-readings, or with the help of commentators) a number of such allusions. First Thermopylae (meaning 'hot gates' –

> I was neither at the hot gates
> Nor fought in the warm rain)

– an ironical allusion to the wasting, fruitless war of 1914–18 by contrast with the classic victory of the Athenians over the Persians. Shortly there is a reference to the Pharisees in the Gospel: 'We would see a sign!' Then comes a sentence from the seventeenth-century theologian, Bishop Andrewes, alluding to the mystery of the Logos becoming incarnated in a speechless baby; again the allusion is ironical – the darkness of the mind is denser than speechless innocence. Into this world of decay and failure, a new image explodes:

> In the juvescence of the year
> Came Christ the tiger

The allusion is to Blake's poem 'The Tyger' ('Did he who made the Lamb make thee?'). But in what sense can Christ the Lamb of God be likened to the tiger? The poet does not explain directly; instead he immediately slides into a series of images of fictional characters:

> In depraved May, dogwood and chestnut, flowering judas,
> To be eaten, to be divided, to be drunk
> Among whispers; by Mr Silvero
> With caressing hands, at Limoges
> Who walked all night in the next room;
> By Hakagawa, bowing among the Titians;
> By Madame de Tornquist, in the dark room
> Shifting the candles; Fraulein von Kulp
> Who turned in the hall, one hand on the door. Vacant shuttles
> Weave the wind. I have no ghosts,
> An old man in a draughty house
> Under a windy knob.

After a tense passage to which I will refer later, the reader may recognise in the next passage but one an echo of a speech spoken by the dying heroine of Middleton's tragedy *The Changeling* (1623). If he does, it may help him to see how Eliot has been adapting for his own purpose the fluent rhythm of Jacobean blank verse. Here is Middleton:

> I am that of your blood was taken from you
> For your better health; look no more upon't
> But cast it to the ground regardlessly,
> Let the common sewer take it from distinction:

—and here is Gerontion:

> I that was near your heart was removed therefrom
> To lose beauty in terror, terror in inquisition.
> I have lost my passion: why should I need to keep it
> Since what is kept must be adulterated?

Very frequently this allusive technique frustrates appreciation by seducing the reader into a wrong approach. Suspecting literary references, but not identifying them, he resorts to a dictionary of quotations; suspecting historical references where none exist, he searches for Mr Silvero in a dictionary of biography. Such industry is not necessarily unrewarding, but it is mistaken insofar as it treats the poem as a crossword puzzle. The naiver and wiser reader will first hear the words and watch the images they evoke as they rise in his mind. Mr Silvero has a precious name and hands to go with it; Limoges is almost a trade name for precious enamels. But what keeps a man walking all night in the next room? This is the cosmopolitan, sophisticated, alienated and haunted world in which the Sacrament is consumed. But Gerontion, who does not consume it, has only his own vain, self-torturing speculations. The reader who does not spot the adaptations from Fitzgerald or Andrewes or Middleton misses less than the reader who is deaf to the nervous tautening of rhythm in the next passage, in which Gerontion turns from his contemplation of the world of cultivated Catholicism into the tense rationalising process of his own mind, as he seeks to explain how he has been trapped by his own scepticism first into indifference, and then into final recognition that unbelief is nullity of the self:

> After such knowledge, what forgiveness? Think now
> History has many cunning passages, contrived corridors
> And issues, deceives with whispering ambitions,
> Guides us by vanities. Think now

She gives when our attention is distracted
And what she gives, gives with such supple confusions
That the giving famishes the craving. Gives too late
What's not believed in, or if still believed,
In memory only, reconsidered passion. Gives too soon
Into weak hands, what's thought can be dispensed with
Till the refusal propagates a fear. Think
Neither fear nor courage saves us. Unnatural vices
Are fathered by our heroism. Virtues
Are forced upon us by our impudent crimes.
These tears are shaken from the wrath-bearing tree.

The tiger springs in the new year. Us he devours.

Because it is not wise to begin a study of an Eliot poem by refer-
ence-hunting, it does not of course follow that Eliot's allusiveness
is redundant. Most poems are to some extent allusive, and the
reader's response is always strengthened by his recognition of the
sources, though this recognition may be so instantaneous that he
may not be conscious of it as such. 'Gerontion' has many levels of
allusiveness: most readers will realise the association of Limoges
with previous works of art; few will be aware of Fitzgerald in the
opening lines, but if they are, they are enriched by their recognition of the contrast afforded by Newman's *Gerontius* and *Omar
Khayyam*. A poem is rarely an object to be acquired at first reading.
Nearly all the best require many readings, and the best of all, as
Eliot says of Dante, are such as 'one can only just hope to grow up
to at the end of life'. And for Eliot, to grow up to a great poem is
to grow up to a whole culture in which the poem is an element. Yet
even the first reading may be rich, if the reading can begin to cultivate what Eliot in *The Use of Poetry* calls the auditory imagination:

What I call the 'auditory imagination' is the feeling for syllable and
rhythm, penetrating far below the conscious levels of thought and
feeling, invigorating every word; sinking to the most primitive and forgotten, returning to the origin and bringing something back, seeking the
beginning and the end. It works through meanings, certainly, or not
without meanings in the ordinary sense, and fuses the old and obliterated
and the trite, the current, and the new and surprising, the most ancient
and the most civilised mentality.

Neither Eliot nor Yeats had achieved their best work by 1920,
but, different as they were, they had already changed for themselves
and for others the notions of the nature and scope of English poetry
that had been dominant only ten years before.

5

Diversification of the novel 1920-1930

Life is not a series of gig lamps symmetrically arranged; life is a luminous halo, a semi-transparent envelope surrounding us from the beginning of consciousness to the end. Is it not the task of the novelist to convey this varying, this unknown and uncircumscribed spirit, whatever aberration or complexity it may display, with as little mixture of the alien and the external as possible? We are not pleading merely for courage and sincerity; we are suggesting that the proper stuff of fiction is a little other than custom would have us believe it. Virginia Woolf: *Essay on Modern Fiction*

In any novel, the writer and the reader are implicitly 'placed' in relation to the characters in the story, and this implies that the writer knows his own relationship to the reader. The relationship of author and reader in mid-Victorian novels had been self-evident, relaxed and elementary. The reader was understood to surrender himself to a novel as to a world which was very much like the real world, but different inasmuch as he had the privilege of being guided through it by its omniscient creator. The reader moved among the characters and through the characters like an invisible spirit led by the hand, and from time to time the novelist–deity would turn and address him directly, amplifying and interpreting what the reader was perceiving. Such a technique worked as well or as badly as any other, and is indeed still the commonest in use, but it depends on a triple understanding between author and reader: that both have the same mental image of a working model of the real world, that both accept the same notions about how experience is received and should be transmitted, and that both agree about what experience is important or unimportant. If a novelist renounces any part of this compact, the novel changes its nature in more or less important ways: the reader is left to grope for himself, perhaps in a world that is altogether strange, perhaps in one which looks familiar, but which grows stranger as he proceeds. Most of the novelists who have best survived from the post-war period renounced one or another, or all three of the assumptions, and 1920–30 is consequently a decade of remarkable experiment and diversification.

It is perhaps helpful to group the innovators into three main categories, although this is inevitably a crude and provisional procedure, since it involves grouping together writers who were otherwise very different in their interests. Some novelists, impressed by the psychological fact that we are each of us isolated in our worlds of perception, chose the subjective technique of presenting the narrative through the minds and nerves of one or several of the characters. This first category includes James Joyce (*Ulysses*, 1922) and Virginia Woolf (*To the Lighthouse*, 1927). Others, disliking the perpetual dissolution of outline inescapable from subjectivism, sought an unprecedentedly clear objective presentation which left equally little room for the Victorian authorial mediator. This category includes the work of the painter–novelist Wyndham Lewis (*The Apes of God*, 1930) who brought to his writing the brilliant hardness of his pictorial delineation, and that of Ivy Compton-Burnett (*Pastors and Masters*, 1925) whose novels consist almost wholly of witty, sententious dialogue. These two categories are in extreme surface contrast, but they have in common that their works (whether huge in construction like *Ulysses* or slight and succinct like *Pastors and Masters*) make no concession to the reader's habits of thought about his ordinary, daily world. The personality of the author is at the same time nowhere directly evident in the novel, as though the act of creation was also an act of disengagement and retirement into anonymity, much as a work of ancient art may still impose its authority none the less for our total ignorance of its creator.

A third category of novelists differs from the other two in retaining a relationship with the reader, although it is not a homely one such as the Victorians had tolerated or even cultivated. Like the Victorian novelists, they still conceive it as their task to interpret the real world through their fictions rather than to present impersonally their constructions of a world: they are so far concerned with the reader's habits of thought that they evidently desire to change them. But, at least if he is alert, the reader will soon become aware that the novelist is insinuating a symbolic pattern into the tale which makes it by no means as apprehensible as its surface seems to promise. Works in this style include the masterpiece of

E. M. Forster's career, *A Passage to India* (1924), and much of Lawrence's later writing, for instance *St Mawr* (1925).

Such a categorisation by no means includes all the new kinds of fiction which found and retains admirers. It omits, for instance, Aldous Huxley's revival of the 'discussion novel' (*Point Counter Point*, 1928), the strange and witty fantasies of Ronald Firbank (*The Flower Beneath the Foot*, 1923), the satires by Evelyn Waugh (*Decline and Fall*, 1928), and the original, cinematic vision of Henry Green (*Living*, 1929). Moreover, novelists who were continuing the accepted tradition were still writing with full prestige, for instance John Galsworthy who completed his *Forsyte Saga* in 1921, Arnold Bennett (*Riceyman Steps*, 1923), and H. G. Wells (*The World of William Clissold*, 1926). One kind of justice, the justice of a balanced historical record, would require discussion of these and still others. But another kind of justice, according to which we need to debate those writers of the past who retain most power to challenge our judgements, requires rigorous selection. Among these in the 1920s James Joyce is conspicuous, and his work cannot be understood unless it is studied as a whole.

James Joyce (1882–1941)

The artist, like the God of creation, remains within or behind or beyond or above his handiwork, invisible, refined out of existence, indifferent, paring his fingernails. James Joyce: *A Portrait of the Artist as a Young Man*

It is at least as important a fact about Joyce as it is about Yeats that he was Irish, but whereas Yeats was Anglo-Irish, Joyce was mere Irish. Whereas Yeats came from the Protestant upper range of society, and therefore stemmed ultimately from the English immigration, Joyce was born of lower-middle class Catholic parents, and Catholicism, though he ceased to be a Catholic in name, never lost its hold on his imagination. The difference also shows in their choice of cultural influences. Yeats, as we have seen, felt the English tradition very strongly; indeed few poets have drawn more widely from English poets of the past in the shaping of their style. His urgent exploration of Irish mythology was perhaps less spontaneous: it seems that he felt the need of that cultural background to justify his vocation as an Irish writer, or at least as a writer who had to separate himself from the English cultural ambience. Joyce, on the other hand, as a Dubliner, felt no touch of this cult on his imagination; for him, it was dead matter appropriately forgotten, and he preferred to learn Norwegian in order to study Ibsen. The English influence upon him was in a way inescapable, since English was his native language as it was Yeats's. Yet Joyce was able to evade the English hold upon him as Yeats could not; he simply bypassed England by proceeding, physically and culturally, from Dublin to Paris, Central Europe and the Mediterranean.

It is of course a paradox that Joyce's choice of Ibsen for his early study instead of Celtic mythology is itself evidence of his essential Irishness. But there were political and cultural parallels between Norway and Ireland at the end of the nineteenth century, and suggestive parallels too in the careers of Ibsen and Joyce. Like Ireland, Norway was a small, poor country, which for centuries had endured the political and cultural dominance of its richer neighbours, just as Ireland had endured that of England. Both countries developed a new national self-consciousness in the nineteenth century, and both attempted to free themselves culturally through their folk mythology. But Ibsen, like Joyce, settled for modern society as his literary field, and both writers chose exile, yet never ceased to write about their native lands. Joyce, like Ibsen, faced the meagreness and poverty of his own native culture; he could never, as Yeats did, have brought himself to believe that a fine native culture might be generated from it. He knew Ireland as she was, and he pitied, loved and hated her as she was; the contemporary society of Norway was nearer to Ireland as he knew her than the mythical land of Cuchulain and Oisean.

But it might be objected that what Joyce knew was not Ireland, but its capital city, Dublin. For aside from his two slight volumes of verse, Dublin is the setting of all Joyce's fiction, and also of his single, not highly esteemed play in the manner of Ibsen, *Exiles* (1918). This is remarkable when one considers the scope of his fiction. It is true that it comprises only four volumes – *Dubliners* (1914), *A Portrait of the Artist as a Young Man* (1916), *Ulysses* (1922) and *Finnegans Wake* (1939) – but the last two show a scale of ambition comparable to that of such a novelist as Balzac. In contrast, the first two are almost slender: *Dubliners* is a portrait of the city projected through incidents in the lives of its inhabitants; *A Portrait* is a short autobiographical novel, which explains how Joyce came to abandon the city physically in order to abide in it imaginatively. So described, the themes of these two appear large enough for ampler books; yet Joyce's last two very ample ones seem to have very narrow themes: *Ulysses* is devoted to a single day in the life of one Dublin citizen, and *Finnegans Wake* to one night in the life of another, who, moreover, from first to last is fast asleep. The paradox is explained by the novelist's intentions: the first two books condense relatively wide themes into small space, like narrow, vertical shafts displaying the strata of massive mountains; the last two begin from trivia, but the trivia are used to display the largeness of implication in the experience of Everyman – and not merely Everyman of Dublin or even of Ireland, but of western civilisation in early twentieth-century Europe. To put it another way, Joyce began by exhibiting the narrow dimensions of the environment that had shaped him and imprisoned him; he went on to demonstrate that the dimensions of the individual psyche are vast in inverse proportion to the narrowness that confines the individual body. His imagination stayed with Dublin because Dublin had given him his physical existence, but he sought to show that the place of human origin is the point from which, in a psychic dimension, all human space can be evoked.

Joyce's purpose in writing *Dubliners* is best explained by his own words to a publisher:

My intention was to write a chapter of the moral history of my country and I chose Dublin for the scene because the city seemed to me the centre of the paralysis. I have tried to present it to the indifferent public under four of its aspects: childhood, adolescence, maturity and public life. The stories are arranged in this order. I have written it for the most part in a style of scrupulous meanness and with the conviction that he is a very bold man who dares to alter in the presentment, still more to deform, whatever he has seen and heard.

Though not published until 1914, the collection was completed in 1904; it is therefore a picture of Dublin society at the beginning of the century. We see a town in which poverty preponderates over prosperity, and prosperity is seldom better than modest; only one of the stories (and that, perhaps significantly, the least successful) deals with the really rich. It is an environment in which aspirations are limited by close horizons, idealism is undermined by slatternly scepticism, and passions are reduced to melancholy longings. Yet the accumulated image is not just a dreary one. Not only does Joyce shoot comedy and pathos through the drab texture so as to inspire sympathy with his characters even in their degradation, but he penetrates some of the stories with a dignity, tragedy and even majesty which transfigure the material.

An example is the first story, *The Sisters*. It concerns the death of a senile priest, seen through the eyes of a child who has known him well in life. The story is very brief, but Joyce uses it for extraordinary variety of effect. We are made to feel the unwholesome fascination which the decayed old man inspires in the intelligent boy, to whom he recounts the priestly mysteries; the pathos of the old man's sisters, whose devotion to him is blended with a kind of superstitious sanctimony; the obtuse vulgarity of the family friend, 'old Cotter', who unheathily relishes while he despises the priest's condition of mental 'paralysis' – a word which informs the story. So far we are shown an image of a great religion degraded into a ritual of superstition which is itself an added degradation to a dingy environment. But in the midst of this comes the unexpected impressiveness of the priest in death:

I went in on tiptoe. The room through the lace end of the blind was suffused with dusky golden light amid which the candles looked like pale thin flames. He had been coffined. Nannie gave the lead and we three knelt down at the foot of the bed. I pretended to pray but I could not gather my thoughts because the old woman's mutterings distracted me. I noticed how clumsily her skirt was hooked at the back and how the heels of her cloth boots were trodden down all at one side. The fancy came to me that the old priest was smiling as he lay in the coffin.

But no. When we rose and went up to the head of the bed I saw that he was not smiling. There he lay, solemn and copious, vested as for the altar, his large hands loosely retaining a chalice. His face was very truculent, grey and massive, with black cavernous nostrils and circled by a scanty white fur. There was a heavy odour in the room – the flowers.

Although this is the climax, it is not the end of the story. We return to the sitting-room, and one of the sisters explains how her brother's mental decline began with his accidentally breaking a holy chalice. The end is as follows:

She stopped suddenly as if to listen. I too listened; but there was no sound in the house: and I knew that the old priest was lying in his coffin as we had seen him, solemn and truculent in death, an idle chalice on his breast.

Eliza resumed:

'Wide-awake and laughing-like to himself . . . So then, of course, when they saw that, that made them think that there was something gone wrong with him . . .'

The half-demented priest with his senile laughter is like decadent Catholicism in impoverished, provincial Ireland; but in the silence of death, he becomes the symbol of the Church itself, the most ancient institution in the civilisation of Christendom. Characteristically, Joyce seems to stand with one foot in a Dublin back-street and the other implanted among the foundations of European culture.

Above all in *The Sisters* we have the theme of complex estrangement, of alienation severing and replacing the most intimate bond. It is a theme worth emphasising, because it is one of the most consistent features of Joyce's work. It is common to most of the Dubliner stories, most notably in the last and justly more praised of them, *The Dead*. In this, a middle-aged writer, Gabriel Conroy, a somewhat pompous and condescending leader of local culture, is shrivelled into insignificance, although enhanced into pathetic dignity, when he learns that his wife has never loved him as she loved a young man who has died for her long before, and whose memory is brought back to her at a party by a song he had been fond of singing:

One by one, they were all becoming shades. Better pass boldly into that other world, in the full glory of some passion, than fade and wither dismally with age.

In *A Portrait of the Artist*, Stephen Dedalus, Joyce's representative, abandons family, country and friends to pursue the vocation of art, which pursued in Ireland, would have stunted him at the level of a Gabriel Conroy, but he does not do so free of cost:

Cranly, now grave again, slowed his pace and said: Alone, quite alone. You have no fear of that. And you know what that means? Not only to be separate from all others but to have not even one friend.
 – I will take the risk, said Stephen.

In *Ulysses*, the central character is the type of the alienated man – Leopold Bloom, parody of the wandering Odysseus and exemplar of the wandering Jew. He wanders no farther than the confines of Dublin, on his business and haphazard pleasures, disturbed from time to time by pangs of self-pity when he recalls the faithlessness of his wife and the death of his little son. But Stephen Dedalus, the alienated, dedicated artist, becomes, momentarily, his adopted son: the alienated common man rescues the alienated artist, helplessly inebriated, from a brothel, and takes him home, where the solidity of facts and objects and the paralysis of their fatigue prevents them from achieving a personal communion. There can be no direct communion between the artist and the common man – such seems to be Joyce's thesis – and yet they exist in mutual need: the artist exists to raise the common man from ephemerality to permanence, and the common man exists as the artist's inexhaustible material. In *Finnegans Wake*, the sleeping protagonist, H. C. Earwicker, a Dublin pub-keeper, is another and vaster portrayal of the common man or Everyman, and in the release of his unconscious in sleep he is shown as more profoundly estranged – divided against himself; in rivalry with his two sons, Kevin and Jerry (Shaun and Shem) who are rivals of each other; divided between love for his wife Anna and incestuous love for his daughter Isobel. It is Anna who is given the last words of the book, as she slowly awakes to contemplation of her husband's faithlessness and her displacement by her own daughter.

However, the motif of estrangement, exile, loss and sacrifice in Joyce's fictions is countered – after *Dubliners* – by a recovery into strong affirmation. Dedalus leaves Ireland at the end of *A Portrait* in a spirit of exultation:

Welcome, O life! I go to encounter for the millionth time the reality of experience and to forge in the smithy of my soul the uncreated conscience of my race.

This is in spite of the grief he inflicts on his mother, whose sorrow is above all on account of his cold renunciation of his spiritual Mother Church. *Ulysses* ends with the passionate affirmation of Molly Bloom, the embodiment of sexual, procreative humanity, almost of Mother Earth:

. . . and then I asked him with my eyes to ask again yes and then he asked me would I say yes to say yes my mountain flower and drew him down to me so he could feel my breasts all perfume yes and his heart was going like mad and yes I said yes I will Yes.

Finally, the last mournful sentence of *Finnegans Wake* is left unfinished, to be completed by the first sentence, which begins midway. This was in keeping with a cyclic theory of history (not unlike Yeats's gyres) which Joyce took from the eighteenth-century Italian philosopher, Giambattista Vico, who believed that history passes through stages each of which ends in confusion, out of which a new age is born. It is in keeping with this affirmative movement in Joyce's writing that his last two works are often read as exuberant comedies, though their darker aspects are as indisputable.

But the affirmation, even when it is a human being that makes it, seems inhuman in the sense that it relates not to the individual so much as to the drive for continuance of art, of sex, of family or race. It is ruthless with a kind of self-sacrificing, impersonal ruthlessness characteristic of all Joyce's art after the stories. These indeed emanate from a tender, redemptive theory of imaginative perception according to which Joyce maintained that the artist perceives objects in the light of what he called their 'epiphanies'. The theory is explained in the lengthy but uncompleted first draft of *A Portrait of the Artist* entitled *Stephen Hero*. When an object is perceived aesthetically, it is seen transfigured, as the Three Kings saw God Himself in the form of the baby in the stable manger:

We recognise that it is *that* which it is. Its soul, its whatness, leaps to us from the vestment of its appearance. The soul of the commonest object, the structure of which is so adjusted, seems to us radiant. The object achieves its epiphany.

From his doctrine of epiphanies arises the compassion and the transparent beauty of the Dubliner stories. In *A Portrait*, the doctrine is blended with a kind of dialectical drama, and it is from here on that Joyce's writing takes on its special impersonality and ruthlessness. Stephen Dedalus is born into a family which, on the father's side, is laxly but unquestioningly patriotic, and, on the mother's, unquestioningly Catholic. The two are in agreement, or at least no uncomfortable issues divide them. But the unity is broken by the scandals surrounding the private life of the Irish leader Parnell who is condemned by the Church. In one of the best scenes Joyce ever wrote, at a stormy Christmas dinner, the boy watches his world being suddenly, unexpectedly, and irremediably fractured. For a time he becomes devoutly religious, but the tedious pettiness of the Church in its personal dealings wearies and disgusts him; on the other hand he is equally irresponsive to the bigotry and distortions of the nationalist politicians. On the seashore, he receives the experience of an epiphany as he watches a girl standing in the water and is enraptured by her beauty without experiencing any corrupting influence of lust. From this point he sees his vocation: dedication to the aesthetic vision will alone raise him above the entanglements that have entrapped his spirit, and

that alone has the spaciousness which will allow his spirit to soar:
'Daedalus' was an artist in a Greek myth who provided himself
with wings. But first he must leave Ireland:

When the soul of a man is born in this country there are nets flung at
it to hold it back from flight. You talk to me of nationality, language,
religion. I shall try to fly by those nets.

Joyce's total dedication to his art was a heroic choice, and it was
a disinterested one inasmuch as it went with the conviction that
only the artist (if he accepts isolation as his proper condition) can
achieve the necessary detachment to give back to the people a true
image of itself – 'to forge in the smithy of my soul the uncreated
conscience of my race'. He saw himself as a true artist, and perhaps
as the first to emanate from Ireland. On the other hand, the artist
must work in a medium, and Joyce's elevation of art as the crown-
ing activity of man raises the problem of whether he did not come
to make his medium all-important – more important, that is, than
the reality he strove to embody in it. What is the validity of the
almost hermetic but extremely elaborate aesthetic schemes he
worked into his last two narratives? Only the title 'Ulysses', to take
the most conspicuous example, is an overt clue to the intricate
parallels between that novel and Homer's *Odyssey*. More important, however, is the question of the validity of his experiments in
language.

These began in *A Portrait of the Artist* in which Joyce first made
use of the device known as 'the stream of consciousness'. According to this, the narrative proceeds along the current of the character's thoughts instead of by the author explicitly telling the story.
On inspection, it turns out to be as selective and artificial as the
more traditional method, but it has the enormous advantage, especially for the autobiographical novel, that it can denote the
scope of the character's consciousness at each stage of his existence. Thus *A Portrait* begins with infant language appropriate to
a very small child, develops into the speech of an intelligent and ob-
servant boy, and concludes in the range of a sophisticated university student. The stream of consciousness is again the pre-
dominating method of *Ulysses*, first for transmitting the consciousness of Dedalus in the opening three sections, then for Bloom,
and in the final section for Molly Bloom. *Ulysses*, however, includes almost every imaginable form of narrative. For instance

the dramatic form is used for the feverish, phantasmagoric episode in the brothel, and this is succeeded by a burlesque of traditional narrative in the sobered section that follows, when the still tipsy Dedalus and the weary Bloom take refuge in a cabman's shelter. This episode is followed by a narrative in questionnaire or catechism form, expressing the inertia of total fatigue in their final refuge of Bloom's home. These uses of language, though grotesque, are accountable, but there is a more questionable one in the fourteenth section in which the scene is the maternity department of a hospital, and the process of childbirth is symbolised by a long passage which parodies the development of English prose. Is Joyce doing more, here, than drawing attention to his own extraordinary versatility? Of course, the most notorious difficulties are those of *Finnegans Wake*, in which language is used as the vehicle of the unconscious and semi-conscious mind. Here Joyce fuses distinct words to form new ones, so subtly that a single sentence may and usually does have multiple meanings, rather as a cloud formation may simultaneously display several distinct resemblances, except that the images of the cloud are read into it by the observer, whereas Joyce's sentences are precisely calculated.

The defence of such linguistic strategies must be that in proportion as we submit ourselves to the demands that the language makes upon us, our perspective of what Joyce has to show us about the human condition will enlarge. Similarly, Joyce's use of episode from Homer's *Odyssey* as a loose framework of analogy for *Ulysses* may be to enlarge the novel and the human beings in it, as our detection of the analogies increases. The effect need not be merely ironical, contrasting the undignified Bloom to the mythologically heightened Ulysses; it may be enhancing. The small man, in his search for trivia among trivia, is still Man, lost and searching, although unaware of his potentiality and of the hidden significance of his search. Similarly, the dreams and nightmares of Earwicker are the dreams and nightmares of the human race. This is the defence, but against it, one may still put a doubt.

Joyce seems to have wished to carry the art of the novel to its extreme conclusion. The nineteenth-century realists and naturalists devoted a comparable intellectual energy to that of the nineteenth-century biologists to their study of living phenomena. In *Ulysses* Joyce brought as much artistic concentration as Flaubert and more than Zola's zeal for realism to his own presentation of urban life.

In *Finnegans Wake*, he broke through the restraints of naturalism on the principles of a later generation of scientists – the psychologists Freud and Jung. This alone gives him historic importance, but a writer lives, not by the extent to which he culminates the past but by the extent to which he fertilises the future. No one can doubt the originality of Joyce's genius. Yet a reader may still doubt whether his whole enterprise was not based on a false premise : that a work of art is absolute, superseding our reality by including it, instead of serving our reality by extending it. The great works of art, back to Homer, have all been fertile of later art; Joyce's last two works seem to stand aloof, monuments of language in a desert, or citadels of words defying the cities of life.

Virginia Woolf (1882–1941); Ivy Compton-Burnett (1892–1969)

The mind receives a myriad impressions – trivial, fantastic, evanescent, or engraved with the sharpness of steel . . . so that, if the writer were a free man and not a slave, if he could write what he chose and not what he must, if he could base his work upon his own feeling and not upon convention, there would be no plot, no comedy, no tragedy, no love interest or catastrophe in the accepted sense, and perhaps not a single button sewn on as the Bond Street tailors would have it.
Virginia Woolf: 'The Modern Novel' in *The Common Reader*

Real life seems to have no plots. And as I think a plot desirable and almost necessary, I have this extra grudge against life. But I think there are signs that strange things happen, though they do not emerge. I believe it would go ill with many of us, if we were faced with a strong temptation, and I suspect that with some of us it does go ill. Ivy Compton-Burnett: 'A Conversation' in *Orion I*

Virginia Woolf was, in a special sense, a feminist. The fact is worth mentioning in a study of her, not because of her specifically feminist polemic such as *A Room of One's Own* (1929), but because it explains the sense in which she was a self-consciously feminine writer. She had reasons for being one. Her father, Leslie Stephen (1832–1904), had been a distinguished critic and a philosopher in the Victorian agnostic school of thought, but in his family he had typified the self-centredness of the Victorian family man: indulgent towards his sons, self-pitying and demanding towards his wife and daughters. It was characteristic of Victorian radicals, of whom he was an example, that their boldness in challenging established beliefs was equalled by their conservatism in personal attitudes, especially towards women, as though the destructiveness of their doubt required the antidote of deference to their reason which produced it, so as to maintain them, at least in their families, in the position which the established beliefs would have conserved for them. Such a position began to look ill-founded, but so long as advanced education for women was still hard to come by, it was difficult to assail. Virginia Woolf did not so much seek to assail it as to counterbalance it. Masculine reason produced systems and destroyed them, replacing them by new systems which remained ascendant, but supposing masculine reason was mistaken in its basic premise, that truth is such that reason alone can command it? The truth that reason commands is the truth that can be verified by action, and action had always been the monopoly of the male. But women, who had been bred to understand the needs of the male, had thereby learned insights into his insufficiencies: his anxious striving for what is to be had leaving him helpless to respond to what is now, the life in the living moment.

All her best writing – her critical essays and her biographical studies as well as her fiction – has the quality of language which leaps out to catch the fleeting instant. It is a point of view which recalls Joyce's concept of the epiphanies, except that Joyce was concerned with the transfiguration of the object that is seen, whereas Virginia Woolf's concern is with the transfiguration of the mind that sees. What she calls reality is like a visitation—

What is meant by 'reality'? It would seem to be something very erratic, very undependable – now to be found in a dusty road, now in a scrap of newspaper in the street, now a daffodil in the sun . . . But whatever it touches, it fixes and makes permanent. That is what remains over when the skin of the day has been cast into the hedge; that is what is left of past time and of our loves and hates. Now the writer, as I think, has the chance to live more than other people in the presence of this reality.

(*A Room of One's Own*)

Joyce is not the only writer recalled by this; we also have Eliot on the compelling force of certain images:

Why, for all of us, out of all that we have heard, seen, felt, in a lifetime, do certain images recur, charged with emotion, rather than others? The song of one bird, the leap of one fish, at a particular place and time, the scent of one flower, an old woman on a German mountain path, six ruffians seen through an open window playing cards at night at a small French railway junction where there was a water-mill: such memories may have symbolic value, but of what we cannot tell, for they come to represent depths of feeling into which we cannot peer.

(*The Use of Poetry*)

102

By his stress on the subjectivity of such impressions, Eliot resembles Virginia Woolf rather than Joyce. Eliot's way was to allow such images to rise into fitting contexts of appropriate poems. But how is a novelist to make use of them? Virginia Woolf's solution in her best novels, *To the Lighthouse* and *The Waves*, was to use images as the organising principle of her narrative in place of story and plot.

She did not come to the solution easily. She only began publishing fiction after her marriage to Leonard Woolf, the publisher and socialist writer, in 1912. Her first two novels, *The Voyage Out* (1915) and *Night and Day* (1919) have nothing very new in their method. In 1921 she published short stories, *Monday or Tuesday*, which are experiments in the direction she was to follow, and these were succeeeded by the novels *Jacob's Room* (1922), which shows her particular originality but remains slight, and *Mrs Dalloway* (1925). This is the study of the sensibility of a woman who is brought very much alive, but she also is much slighter than Virginia Woolf seems to have realised: the sensibility contests with too little.

In *To the Lighthouse* (1927), on the other hand, Virginia Woolf seems herself to have been contesting with something very substantial – her own childhood background. Projecting the novel in her Diary (14 May 1925), she wrote:

This is going to be fairly short; to have father's character done completely in it; and mother's; and St Ives; and childhood; and all the usual things I try to put in – life, death, etc. But the centre is father's character, sitting in a boat, reciting We perished, each alone, while he crushes a dying mackerel.

St Ives, the scene of the Stephens' summer holidays, is substituted by the west of Scotland, and the Stephen family is given the name of Ramsay. They have a full house. Besides the Ramsay family, which includes the parents, four daughters and three sons, there are resident guests and some who come in and out of the house: Charles Tansley, the poor young philosopher with a chip on his shoulder; Lily Briscoe, who paints; Paul Rayley and Minta Doyle, who are in love; the genial, middle-aged William Bankes; the pathetic, enigmatic, silent Mr Carmichael who takes opium. The reader is not 'introduced' to the characters as he would be in a traditional style of novel; he comes upon them, one by one, as he would if he were himself a casual visitor, but he 'learns' them not in this way but more as he would the instruments and themes of an orchestral composition. Some – the Ramsay parents, the youngest son James, and Lily Briscoe – are dominant, although their pre-dominance varies: Mrs Ramsay prevails, slightly above her husband, in the first part, but in the third she is only an echo; her husband is the central figure in the third part though mainly a silent one; James is important at the beginning and the end; Lily Briscoe is consistently prominent, on a level with the Ramsay parents. Others play supporting themes, Charles Tansley, for instance, sup-porting the harsh notes of the father in Part I; the genial and shallow Mr Banks in Part I is replaced by the mysterious Mr Carmichael as a counter to Lily in Part III; or they make transient contributions as Paul Rayley and Minta Doyle do for Mrs Ramsay. The children play a harmonic bass to the dominant melodies.

A strong flow of life runs through the pages – to what effect? In Part I, 'The Window', nothing happens that the reader can distin-guish as the beginnings of the plot, for there is no plot. A projected visit to the lighthouse on the morrow is cancelled, to James's in-tense and resentful disappointment, by Mr Ramsay's declaration that 'it won't be fine'. Mr Ramsay is exorbitant to his wife, insensi-tive to his children, but a disinterested and strenuous thinker: he cares for the hardness of truth and the austerity of thought, and he pities and is indulgent to himself because no one knows the loneli-ness of the thinker, and the courage with which he has to face the conclusions of his thought. Mrs Ramsay understands his loneliness though she does not understand its cause; her main concern is to relate, not to distinguish; to bring and keep together the disparate components of her family and guests, and to resist the resolute independence of such as Lily Briscoe. Lily paints a picture of the house, with Mrs Ramsay reading to James on the steps of the French window, depicting the pair as a 'triangular purple shape' which puzzles Mr Bankes. James is taken to bed, and Mrs Ramsay is left with a moment of peace in which to think about herself:

Not as oneself did one find rest ever, in her experience (she accomplished here something dexterous with her needles), but as a wedge of darkness. Losing personality, one lost the fret, the hurry, the stir; and there rose to her lips always some exclamation of triumph over life when things came together in this peace, this rest, this eternity; and pausing there she looked out to meet that stroke of the Lighthouse, the long steady stroke, the last of the three, which was her stroke, for watching them in this mood always at this hour one could not help attaching oneself to one thing especially of the things one saw; and this thing, the long steady stroke, was her stroke.

In the second section, the house is left empty all through the war years, visited only rarely by Mrs McNab, the grotesque but industrious cleaner from the village. But the section is entitled 'Time Passes', and it is shown to pass even in an empty house. A shawl, placed over a mirror because the reflection in it scared a child at night, disturbs the silence as it gradually loosens; light and darkness pass across the glass; faint draughts from the sea play among 'the shrouded jugs and sheeted chairs'; Mrs McNab debates whether the family will ever return. In square brackets, events are recorded about the distant household: Mrs Ramsay dies suddenly; her daughter Prue dies in childbirth; her son Andrew is killed in France; Mr Carmichael brings out a book of poems.

'Then indeed peace had come.' In Part III, 'The Lighthouse', some of what is left of the household return: Mr Ramsay, James, the youngest daughter Cam, Nancy, Lily Briscoe, Mr Bankes much aged, Mr Carmichael. The expedition to the lighthouse is undertaken: Cam and James follow their father resentfully as the tyrant against whom they have always been disposed to rebel. But as the boat draws near, James compares the lighthouse of his memory with what rises before him:

'It will rain,' he remembered his father saying. 'You won't be able to go to the Lighthouse.'

The Lighthouse was then a silvery, misty-looking tower with a yellow eye that opened suddenly and softly in the evening. Now—

James looked at the Lighthouse. He could see the white-washed rocks; the tower, stark and straight; he could see that it was barred with black and white; he could see windows in it; he could even see washing spread on the rocks to dry. So that was the Lighthouse, was it?

No, the other was also the Lighthouse. For nothing was simply one thing. The other was the Lighthouse too. It was sometimes hardly to be seen across the bay. In the evening one looked up and saw the eye opening and shutting and the light seemed to reach them in that airy sunny garden where they sat.

James begins comparing his mother and his father and at last sympathy and understanding of his father awakens in him. Mr Ramsay lands:

'Bring those parcels,' he said, nodding his head at the things Nancy had done up for them to take to the Lighthouse. 'The parcels for the Lighthouse men,' he said. He rose and stood in the bow of the boat, very

105

straight and tall, for all the world, James thought, as if he were saying, 'There is no God,' and Cam thought, as if he were leaping into space, and they both rose to follow him as he sprang, lightly like a young man, holding his parcel, on to the rock.

At the same moment Lily Briscoe, hesitating on the focus that will complete her composition now that Mrs Ramsay is there no more, finds it, and the novel also is completed:

It would be hung in the attics, she thought; it would be destroyed. But what did that matter? she asked herself, taking up her brush again. She looked at the steps; they were empty; she looked at her canvas; it was blurred. With a sudden intensity, she drew a line there, in the centre. It was done; it was finished. Yes, she thought, laying down her brush with extreme fatigue, I have had my vision.

So the two visions of life, of the father and the mother, are complemented in the two aspects of the lighthouse, much as though shots of the moon surface were reconciled to the moon that has beamed on poets down the centuries; similarly, Lily Briscoe paints two pictures, one centred on Mrs Ramsay and one on her husband, but each is composed. The chorus of human phenomena is subordinated to this image-structure, because that is the truth which irradiates human phenomenalism.

With this book Virginia Woolf, too, had her vision; the three novels that followed need not be described as failures – the first of them is widely held to be an equal success – but none of them have the same assurance. *The Waves* (1931) was certainly a bold experiment. Six characters in monologue transmit their life experiences, not in any naturalistic use of the stream of consciousness, but as though the symbolic method is folded inwards instead of radiating outwards, so that at each stage the character discloses his or her secret life-pattern, the stages being divided by prose poems describing the waves meeting the shore at different hours of the day (corresponding to life phases) from early morning to nightfall. Interesting as it is, *The Waves* lacks the balanced unity of outer stimulus and inner event in a single composition shown by *To the Lighthouse*. After it, Virginia Woolf seems to have felt that she had carried narrative experiment as far as she could and in *The Years* (1937) she returned to conventional narrative. However her own description of this book in her Diary is 'a dank failure'. Her last novel, *Between the Acts* (1941), has moving episodes, but its ambitious symbolism is uncomfortably sustained on its normally realistic setting of a village festival.

To the Lighthouse has a comparable setting to that of all the novels of Ivy Compton-Burnett: family life, its antagonisms and rivalries, its surface cohesion, the psychic divisions it causes in its members, and its power of continuance. But indeed the methods and character of the two writers could hardly be more different. Virginia Woolf's settings are fairly contemporary, although her fictional biographies, *Orlando* (1928) and *Flush* (1933) are also historical novels; Ivy Compton-Burnett wrote entirely within the period of her youth, approximately 1890 to 1910. Virginia Woolf wrote sparingly and with painful effort; Ivy Compton-Burnett, once she discovered her peculiar manner in *Pastors and Masters* (1925), was prolific and confident. The former's novels vary greatly in style and character, whereas the latter's are often found bewilderingly similar in both; whereas the former is subjective, and always attempting to give form to the nebulous, the latter is objective and concrete; whereas the former uses description freely and dialogue rather sparingly, the latter relies almost wholly on dialogue, and hardly uses descriptions at all, at least of surroundings. The biggest contrast between them is perhaps this: Virginia Woolf rarely makes moral discriminations, although she discriminates severely about qualities of human perception, but Ivy Compton-Burnett's concern is above all with the propensities in human nature for the domination of others or immolation of the self, so that, so long as there is no suggestion that she preaches any ethic, she can fairly be called a moralist.

The limitation of her interest in morality might be said to be its pessimism. She presents the family unit in its last phase of strong cohesion, and reveals how within its framework the selfish and ruthless are unassailable; deadly crime is made possible within the system, and even made possible by it. Jane Austen, Ivy Compton-Burnett's literary progenitor, showed similarly that society is a game in which power comes most easily to the insensitive and un-scrupulous, but she also showed that those who are sensitive and vulnerable may also have their own cunning and can, with courage and some good fortune, liberate themselves without openly flout-ing the rules. Ivy Compton-Burnett, aridly but wittily, presents the system so as to afford them little hope – the virtues of the good are seldom proud enough and strong enough to win them independence.

107

One novel however – her seventh, entitled *A Family and a Fortune* (1939) – is nobly balanced, as well as illustrating the incisiveness of her art at its most accomplished.

The Gaveston family live in an old house on a still substantial but somewhat reduced estate. They are introduced to us – and unlike Virginia Wolf's characters they *are* introduced – as they come down to breakfast: Justine, the eldest; her mother, Blanche; the three sons, Mark, Clement and Aubrey; the father of the family, Edgar, and his brother, Dudley. Very little space is given to describing the characters, but the descriptions are graphically exact, and often most telling about small movements:

Mrs Gaveston dealt with the coffee with small, pale, stiff hands, looking with querulous affection at her children and signing in a somewhat strained manner to the servant to take the cups. She had rather uncertain movements and made one or two mistakes, which she rectified with a sort of distracted precision. She lifted her face for her children's greetings with an air of forgetting the observance as each one passed, and of being reminded of it by the next. She was a rather tall, very pale woman of about sixty, who somehow gave the impression of being small, and whose spareness of build was without the wiriness supposed to accompany it. She had wavy, grey hair, a long, narrow chin, long, narrow, dark eyes in a stiff, narrow, handsome face, and a permanent air of being held from her normal interest by some passing strain or distraction.

This is a good deal longer than customary; psychological and moral descriptions are terser still, and chiefly made when the characteristics have a central relationship to the system of relationships. Mrs Gaveston

really gave little thought to herself and could almost be said to live for others. Her children had for her a lively, if not the deepest affection, and she was more than satisfied with it. She would hardly have recognised the deepest feeling, as she had never experienced or inspired it.

We have in Mrs Gaveston, then, a good, weak woman, who lives by her feelings, and whose feelings are authentic but of low intensity. More attention is given her than is usual by the author, because Blanche's genuineness, innocence and weakness make a focal point of the book: what is there of her is real, but it is less than it is supposed to be. Her importance is the more because of the less simple, more dangerously negative qualities in her husband—

Edgar did not love his children, though he believed or rather assumed that he did, and meted out kindness and interest in fair measure. He had a concerned affection for his wife, a great love for his brother and less than the usual feeling for himself . . . Justine believed that she was her father's darling, and Edgar, viewing the belief with an outsider's eye, welcomed it, feeling that it ought to be a true one, and made intermittent effort to give it support.

The two elder sons, Mark and Clement, are in different ways the product of this emotionally under-nourished family. Mark, a placid young man, content to accept what is available for him, comes off best; Clement is introverted – not for that reason the more interesting, but certainly the less attractive and inwardly the more distorted. The daughter, Justine, supplies the difference between the extremely low temperature of family life and the temperature which, from lack of insight, the parents suppose it to possess; she does this the more for her personal, unacknowledged need to compensate for her own frustration as a woman never likely to be married. She is ingenuous and full of good will; girlish and incapable of artifice; her assiduous playing of her role saves her from the bitterness which – although she is totally unaware of the possibility – would overcome her in consequence of her dual deprivation. Real insight and deep feeling do however exist in the family on opposite poles of the periphery, in Dudley whose devotion to Edgar has caused him to give his brother support and to take second place all his life, and in the youngest son, Aubrey, who, academically the family disappointment and understood by no one except his uncle, is both painfully awake in his observation of the family and deeply sensitive in his feelings towards them.

It must be one of the acutest and sanest depictions of a very common kind of family ever made, and it is made chiefly through Ivy Compton-Burnett's stylised but richly revealing dialogue. Such a family can proceed equably until it undergoes stress, and the balance of this one is upset, and then restored, by its encounter with multiple stresses. Dudley receives an unexpected legacy, which the family coolly deprive him of, in innocent assumption that his known generosity has no limits. Mrs Gaveston's rapacious sister, Matty, comes to live in the lodge of the estate together with their aged but alert and egotistical father. Matty's friend, Maria Sloane, pays a visit, becomes engaged to Dudley, and is shortly taken off him by Edgar. Blanche, under the shock of discovering her family's greed and the strain of maintaining good relations with her impossible sister, has meanwhile died.

The legacy and the arrival of Maria are just the trials which the precarious emotional and moral economy of the family is not calculated to sustain. The legacy brings to life the latent egotism of its members, except Blanche, who has lived in total innocence that it is their strongest characteristic; by itself, however, it is disastrous only to her, since Dudley is sardonically willing to see his money go. Edgar's enticement of Maria, on the other hand, is more than Dudley can bear. His devotion to his brother has been entire, consistent, and the greater because it has been protective, since Dudley is the stronger as well as the superior nature:

It was a question in the neighbourhood which brother looked the more distinguished, and it was thought too subtle judgement to decide for Dudley. The truth was that Dudley looked the more distinguished when he was seen with his brother, and Edgar by himself, Dudley being dependent on Edgar's setting of the type, and Edgar offering the less reward to a real comparison.

Dudley's moral distinction is that while he is materially unselfish, although far from indifferent to material goods, he sees the human object of a man's devotion as inviolable, and he loves Maria as he has loved his brother.

Matty's impingement, however, has a different effect on the family. A monstrous and very clever egotist, she has known all her life how to use every occasion to gain ascendancy for herself over those about her. A youthful injury to her leg has turned her into a slight cripple, and she exploits this disability to gain further advantages, especially over her simple-minded, loyal, defenceless companion Miss Griffin, whom she turns out of doors on a winter's night and whom Dudley rescues. She is partly responsible for her sister Blanche's death, and all the more on that account the family, including Dudley, unite against her. In the end she recognises that she is quite alone, no longer able to impose on anyone, and she even begins to acquire pathos.

The novel is essentially about giving and receiving, getting and forgiving. The theme is a constant subject of conversation in it, especially in the mouth of Dudley, who treats it lightly and ironically until it threatens his very heart. To give in a significant sense is not possible unless the gift is from the nature of the giver and not merely from his lips; but receiving is equally unreal unless it is itself a giving by the receiver. A family which is as close in its feelings as it is contiguous in its daily life will give and receive as it breathes, but the weakness of feeling among the Gavestons (except the helpless Aubrey and his uncle) which is betrayed rather than concealed by Justine's euphoria, exposes the fiction of their family life, and the exposure is manifested in Blanche Gaveston's death. It is only in Miss Griffin that Dudley finds a kindred capacity for giving, and the corresponding capacity to receive. In one of the few tender scenes Ivy Compton-Burnett wrote (another is the death of Blanche) Dudley offers her restitution for her treatment by Matty:

'You would like a cottage of your own, and a little income to manage on, and perhaps a friend to live with you, who needed a home.'

'Oh, I know two or three people,' said Miss Griffin, in gladness greater than her surprise. 'I could have them in turn, to make a change for me and for them. Oh, I should like it. But I don't know why you should do as much for me as that.' Her voice fell more than her face. She depended on Dudley's powers, and would have liked so much to do this for someone, that she hardly conceived of his not feeling the same.

'I shall like to do it, and I can do it easily. I shall be the fortunate person. We will arrange for the money to come to you for your life. I shall not be living here, but that will make no difference.'

Miss Griffin hardly heard the last words. She stood with a face of simple joy. She believed that Dudley would not miss the money, would have been surprised by the idea of his doing so, and saw her life open out before her, enclosed, firelit, full of gossip and peace.

It is through finding Miss Griffin, who at last is able to receive as he is able to give, that Dudley finds it in himself at last to forgive Edgar.

The pair went out and walked on the path outside the house, and Justine, catching the sight from a window, rose with a cry and ran to fetch her brothers.

Ivy Compton-Burnett's prose has the clarity of fine lettering in stone; Virginia Woolf's has the flickering deftness of a brush scattering colours over a canvas. Both concern themselves with the nature of human responsiveness, but Virginia Woolf was more concerned with kinds of sensibility, whereas Ivy Compton-Burnett was concerned with moral resources. These are great differences, which can only be reconciled by a novelist with a philosophical level to his work. Such a novelist was E. M. Forster at his finest.

E. M. Forster (1879–1970)

Works of art, in my opinion, are the only objects in the material universe to possess internal order, and that is why, though I don't believe that only art matters, I do believe in Art for Art's Sake.

E. M. Forster: 'What I Believe' in *Two Cheers for Democracy*

In an earlier essay, entitled 'Notes on the English Character' (1920), Forster remarked: 'I had better let the cat out of the bag at once and record my opinion that the character of the English is essentially middle class.' Many writers in the year 1920 would have agreed with the remark, but perhaps not many of them would have made it. Some might have thought that, for good or ill, it was too obvious to be worth making; others that, obvious or not, it pointed to no further interest. But for Forster it was an important observation, because he was deeply conscious of himself as English middle class, and of the obstacles which his social stereotype imposed on the freedom of his mind and feelings. He went on:

Solidity, caution, integrity, efficiency. Lack of imagination, hypocrisy. These qualities characterize the middle classes in every country, but in England they are national characteristics also, because only in England have the middle classes been in power for one hundred and fifty years.

Both the virtues and the faults, as Forster saw them, constituted barriers, which operated within individuals against wholeness of feeling, within national society to frustrate communication, and internationally so as to keep the English insular, misunderstanding other national temperaments, and misunderstood by them. The institution which did most to mould this insularity was the English public school, whose products.

go forth into a world that is not entirely composed of public school men or even of Anglo-Saxons, but of men who are as various as the sands of the sea; into a world of whose richness and subtlety they have no conception. They go forth into it with well-developed bodies, fairly developed minds, and undeveloped hearts. And it is this undeveloped heart that is largely responsible for the Englishman abroad. An undeveloped heart – not a cold one . . . For it is not that the Englishman can't feel – it is that he is afraid to feel.

Fear, though not the same as incapacity, is apt to produce it, and Forster himself is apt to betray incapacity where he surrenders himself to the direct expression of strong emotion, when he is apt to become sentimentally rhetorical; where he seeks to express sexual passion, when he becomes commonplace, and where he presents a working-class character, when he shows his social inhibitions. In regard to these weaknesses, it is instructive to compare Forster with Rudyard Kipling (1865–1936). In modern cultural tradition, Forster is identified with humane liberal thought, sensitive and in some ways radical social criticism, and exploration of the conflict between the world of feeling and that of fact; Kipling (in spite of some recent changes in critical attitude) stands for reactionary chauvinism and social conservatism; for the public school ethic of a governing caste trained to stoicism of feeling. Yet it is Kipling, in his volumes of stories such as *Life's Handicap* (1891) and his volumes of verse such as *Barrack Room Ballads* (1892), who captures the mind and idiom of the common man; who in such a story as 'Without Benefit of Clergy' (*Life's Handicap*) conveys poignantly the love of a British officer for a socially humble Indian girl; who, in his novel *Kim* (1901) gives body to the simple folk of India as Forster, in his Indian novel, never attempts to do.

All the same, Forster was a very much more intelligent man and a far more discriminating writer than Kipling was. Whether or not Kipling's reputation as a reactionary is undeserved, Forster's status as a leader of Anglo-American liberal enlightenment is a reputation that he earned.

He earned it in a way comparable to that in which Matthew Arnold earned his reputation as the critic with most insight into nineteenth-century middle-class philistinism. Both writers were educated within the systems which they criticised, so that, in order to be critical of them, they first had to become exceptionally self-critical, and then to look elsewhere for foundations upon which to build their criticism constructively. Arnold looked back to the classics and outwards to France. Forster made extensive use of Greek mythology in his stories (*The Celestial Omnibus*, 1911), but above all he used the characteristics of foreign nations, emphasising in them (as Arnold emphasised in French culture) those qualities which he found most absent from the English character; only in his second novel, *The Longest Journey* (1907) does he use a different counterweight to his English middle class – that of the somewhat anachronistic peasant and rural England. In his first and third (*Where Angels Fear to Tread*, 1905, and *A Room with a View*, 1908) he sets the story partly in Italy, and contrasts the English tourist's view of the country considered as a museum with the native spontaneity of its inhabitants. In the fourth, *Howards End* (1910), the cultivated Schlegel household is opposed to the philistine Wilcoxes, and the Schlegel father is an emigrant German who stands for the strong and thorough reverence for culture of old German society.

It is possible to doubt whether Forster's reputation would now stand very high if he had stopped writing fiction after his fourth novel instead of after his fifth – leaving out of account the posthumous *Maurice*. It is true that his first four novels still read distinctively; he not only used in them irony and wit unmatched since Jane Austen for their delicacy, but – especially in the last of them – he developed a technique of symbolism which is less obtrusive than Virginia Woolf's and more at ease with the kind of narrative and social setting which the nineteenth-century novelist had made familiar. For it was one of his strengths that he combined an individual and qualified support for the doctrine of art for art's sake with an easy, communicative relationship with the reader. He was too fastidious to act the journalist like Wells, and too modest for the prophetic tone of Lawrence (whom he greatly admired), but he shared the desire of both of them that fiction should educate the reader's sympathies. He worked at this with a cunning which in some ways resembles Shaw's, but is more subtle – ambushing the reader's expectations with anticlimax, de-railing conventional opinion by revealing the unpredictability of human behaviour, sharpening perceptions by pointing banality into comedy. Yet, in spite of all their freshness, it is possible to wonder now whether the problems in these four novels are deep and convincing enough to move a modern reader. However, in his fifth novel, *A Passage to India* (1924), Forster found a theme of outstanding grandeur which he treated with exceptional depth; at the same time, by making India its whole setting, he exposed English middle-class culture to much more formidable attack.

This novel has often been read as a critique of Anglo-Indian postures just before and just after the war of 1914–18, when Forster was living in India. It is however more than that: it is also a study in cultural contrasts, and not merely the contrast between British and Indian cultures, but a triangular one of the British, the Moslem, and the Hindu. Most important of all, it is a study of the difference between a culture in which religion has lost its importance – the British; one in which religion has become chiefly a cultural support – the Moslem; and one in which religion is inherent in every context of life – the Hindu.

The setting is the undistinguished city of Chandrapore on the bank of the Ganges, an administrative station for the British Government. Mrs Moore comes here from England to visit her son, Ronny Heaslop, who is one of the officials; she brings with her Adela Quested, the girl to whom he is unofficially engaged. Their main intention is for Adela and Ronny to become better acquainted in the scene of his work; a secondary one is to get to know 'the *real* India' – a much more difficult enterprise than the first, or than either of the women anticipate. They find that the British officials do not want close relations with either Moslems or Hindus, but that the Education Officer, Fielding, is more liberal and willing to serve as an intermediary. In Chapter 7, a tea-party takes place at Fielding's house; he has invited the two women, Ronny Heaslop, Dr Aziz – a Moslem medical officer at the station, and Professor Godbole, a Hindu who works in the education department under Fielding.

Mrs Moore and Aziz have already met, when she has visited his mosque alone and at night, and he has rebuked her for intruding (Chapter 2), but he was impressed when he learns that she has removed her shoes, and apologises—

'Yes, I was right, was I not? If I remove my shoes, I am allowed?'
'Of course, but so few ladies take the trouble, especially if thinking no one is there to see.'
'That makes no difference. God is here.'

This statement has pleased him enormously; but it is a question whether she really understands her own statement, and what he understands by it. His meditations before he has seen her have been aesthetic and emotional, but it is difficult to say that they should be called religious—

Here was Islam, his own country, more than a Faith, more than a battle-cry, more, much more . . . Islam, an attitude towards life both exquisite and durable, where his body and his thoughts found their home.

Mrs Moore's Christian faith is overtly explicit, but inwardly perplexed. Unlike the religion of Aziz, it is strongly ethical; she preaches it to her son as the only proper basis for government, but only succeeds in making him anxious about her – 'He knew this religious strain in her, and that it was a symptom of bad

115

health.' He himself, like most of the other British, 'approved of religion as long as it endorsed the National Anthem, but he objected when it attempted to influence his life.' Mrs Moore, on the other hand,

felt that she had made a mistake in mentioning God, but she found him increasingly difficult to avoid as she grew older, and he had been constantly in her thoughts since she entered India, though oddly enough he satisfied her less. She must needs pronounce his name frequently, as the greatest she knew, yet she had never found it less efficacious. Outside the arch there seemed always an arch, beyond the remotest echo a silence.

Personally, Mrs Moore is a brave and generous woman with strong and generous intentions to all about her; her son is a capable and completely honest magistrate. But he, like his fellow officials, has the 'undeveloped heart' which can now be re-expressed (more satisfactorily?) as a lack of capacity for spiritual growth, whereas his mother's perplexities show that such capacity is still alive in her, or perhaps has been re-awakened. We are left, among the British, with Fielding and Adela, both indifferent agnostics of the intelligentsia. Asked (in Chapter 9) by his Indian friends whether it is true that the educated British are mostly atheists, Fielding replies, carelessly and to their scandal, that he believes it to be so. But do his honesty and openness of mind really make him superior to his prejudiced and conventional compatriots? His virtues are genuine, but Fielding, who prides himself on 'travelling light', also suffers from the undeveloped heart. Thinking of Aziz—

'I shall never really be intimate with this fellow,' Fielding thought, and then 'nor with anyone.' That was the corollary. And he had to confess that he really didn't mind, that he was content to help people, and like them as long as they didn't object and if they objected to pass on serenely. Experience can do much, and all that he had learnt in England and Europe was an assistance to him, and helped him towards clarity, but clarity prevented him from experiencing something else.

Only the Brahmin, Godbole, is religious in the full sense of the word, but only late in the novel is his religion defined at all, and it remains mysterious to the very end. At Fielding's tea-party he is asked to describe the Marabar Caves, the only interesting tourist sight within reach of Chandrapore. But they are not holy, nor are they ornamented. In what, then, lies their importance? He is unable, or unwilling, to say anything. However, at the end of the party, just as the guests are departing, Godbole elects to sing a Hindu song, which, though not about the caves, provides what is to prove a clue to them.

Only the servants understood it. They began to whisper to one another. The man who was gathering water chestnut came out of the tank, his lips parted with delight, disclosing his scarlet tongue. The sounds continued and ceased after a few moments as casually as they had begun – apparently half through a bar, and upon the subdominant.

'Thanks so much: what was that?' asked Fielding.

'I will explain in detail. It was a religious song. I placed myself in the position of a milkmaiden. I say to Shri Krishna, "Come! come to me only." The god refuses to come. I grow humble and say: "Do not come to me only. Multiply yourself into a hundred Krishnas, and let one go to each of my hundred companions, but one, O Lord of the Universe, come to me." He refuses to come. This is repeated several times. The song is composed in a raga appropriate to the present hour, which is the evening.'

'But he comes in some other song, I hope?' said Mrs Moore gently.

'Oh, no, he refuses to come,' repeated Godbole, perhaps not understanding her question. 'I say to him, Come, come, come, come, come, come. He neglects to come.'

Ronny's steps had died away, and there was a moment of absolute silence. No ripple disturbed the water, no leaf stirred.

The Marabar Caves, as it turns out, are important for one thing only: they have an echo. The echo sickens Mrs Moore, who fights her way out to relax in a deckchair, but it will not leave her:

The crush and the smells she could forget, but the echo began in some way to undermine her hold on life. Coming at a moment when she chanced to be fatigued, it had managed to murmur, 'Pathos, piety, courage – they exist, but are identical and so is filth. Everything exists, nothing has value.' If one had spoken vileness in that place, or quoted lofty poetry, the comment would have been the same – 'ou-boum'. (Ch. 14)

The visit to the caves changes her personally, and it is decisive too in many other lives. Adela Quested has the delusion that in the darkness of one of the caves Aziz tried to rape her. He is imprisoned, to await trial; Fielding, who stands by him, is ostracised by the other British who draw together in courageous solidarity; the latent hatred of the Indians ferments. In the midst of this crisis, Godbole visits Fielding to ask his advice about the name of a new school. Fielding is astounded; for him, at the moment, there is only one question:

'Is Aziz innocent or guilty?'

'That is for the Court to decide. The verdict will be in strict accordance with the evidence, I make no doubt.'

'Yes, yes, but your personal opinion. Here's a man we both like, generally esteemed; he lives here quietly doing his work. Well, what's one to make of it? Would he or would he not do such a thing?'

'Ah, that is rather a different question from your previous one, and also more difficult: I mean difficult in our philosophy. Dr Aziz is a most worthy young man, I have a great regard for him; but I think you are asking me whether the individual can commit good actions, and that is rather difficult for us.' He spoke without emotion and in short tripping syllables.

'I ask you: did he do it or not? Is that plain? I know he didn't, and from that I start. I mean to get at the true explanation in a couple of days. My last notion is that it's the guide who went round with them. Malice on Miss Quested's part – it couldn't be that, though Hamidullah thinks so. She has certainly had some appalling experience. But you tell me. Oh, no – because good and evil are the same.'

'No, not exactly, please, according to our philosophy. Because nothing can be performed in isolation. All perform a good action, when one is performed, and when an evil action is performed, all perform it. To illustrate my meaning, let me take the case in point as an example.

'I am informed that an evil action was performed in the Marabar Hills, and that a highly esteemed English lady is now seriously ill in consequence. My answer to that is this: that action was performed by Dr Aziz.' He stopped and sucked in his thin cheeks. 'It was performed by the guide.' He stopped again. 'It was performed by you.' Now he had an air of daring and of coyness. 'It was performed by me.' He looked shyly down the sleeve of his own coat. 'And by my students. It was even performed by the lady herself. When evil occurs, it expresses the whole of the universe. Similarly when good occurs.'

The singular fact about Godbole's account is that, in the light of the whole novel, it turns out to be the only satisfactory one. But *was* an evil action performed? We never learn, but it seems that Adela's belief that Aziz assaulted her was due to hysteria. Before entering the cave – absent, bored, and oppressed by the heat – two thoughts had passed across her mind for the first time: that she did not love her fiancé, and that Aziz was sexually attractive to her. This reversal of feeling in a young woman who has never given much attention to her feelings, plus her physical exhaustion and the sudden darkness, are the nearest we get to diagnosing the cause of the evil situation which she has unintentionally projected. But Aziz is also responsible for it, because he has organised the expedition, not out of authentic good will but out of vanity, to prove that he could be as good a host to English ladies as any European: the mood and spirit of the party has been false and insincere from the start. The guide's responsibility is characteristic inefficiency; Fielding's responsibility is that he has indirectly fostered hostility to his colleagues by the careless indifference with which he has encouraged his Indian friends' suspicion of the British officials; Godbole has also been responsible by his characteristic indifference to practical matters, which had incidentally caused both himself and Fielding to miss the expedition – with Fielding present to give his personal attention to the two women, the disaster would certainly not have occurred. The students are responsible because they are ready to use any pretext, good or bad, against their rulers, and Adela – most responsible of all – had been the victim of her physical and psychological condition. Godbole alone, with his embracing religious philosophy, is able to see the human situation whole; but just because it is a philosophy in which the individual can never be finally responsible, he is indifferent to and incapable of practical action.

Yet it is not a philosophy of indifference to good and evil. He goes on to explain to Fielding—

'in my own humble opinion, they are both of them aspects of my Lord. He is present in the one, absent in the other, and the difference between presence and absence is great, as great as my feeble mind can grasp. Yet absence implies presence, absence is not non-existence, and we are therefore entitled to repeat, "Come, come, come, come".'

The echo in the cave is important to Hindus because it resembles BYOM, the word for emptiness in Sanskrit, and because it is the supreme sound in religious chants and meditation, evoking ultimate and ineffable consciousness. Hearing the echo, Mrs Moore is made to realise the appalling disparity between her individual will for good action and the weakness of her spiritual grasp. She feels the absence of Krishna, whereas for Godbole the same syllable expresses his reality. It is as though she and Godbole touch fingers in the dark. She collapses into a hard and total egoism – a condition which, because of the passion of her despair, she nonetheless expresses with a poetic intensity achieved nowhere else:

'My body, my miserable body,' she sighed. 'Why isn't it strong? Oh, why can't I walk away and be gone? Why can't I finish my duties and be gone? Why do I get headaches and puff when I walk? And all the time this to do and that to do and this to do in your way and that to do in her

119

way, and everything sympathy and confusion and bearing one another's burdens. Why can't this be done and that be done in my way and they be done and I at peace? Why has anything to be done, I cannot see. Why all this marriage, marriage? . . . The human race would have become a single person centuries ago if marriage was any use. And all this rubbish about love, love in a church, love in a cave, as if there was the least difference, and I held up from my business over such trifles. (Ch. 22)

The impressiveness issues from the authenticity and depth of the feeling: Mrs Moore's truthful egoism does more than her good intentions could ever have done – it shakes Adela, for a moment, out of her hysteria, so that she realises that she has deceived herself about Aziz. The moment of truth is soon overlaid, but in the tense, cool objectivity of the court-room (Chapter 24) the moment of truth returns; she again, and this time finally, recognises the deception of her senses. It is a prodigious defeat for the British officials and an illusory triumph for their Indian opponents; the real triumph is for the western intellectuals, Adela herself and Fielding. Despite their scepticism, they have after all their own creed, and this is acceptance of the absolute obligation to be honest before the fact. Fielding has never much liked Adela personally, but they come to recognise in each this fundamental kinship:

A friendliness as of dwarfs shaking hands, was in the air. Both man and woman were at the height of their powers – sensible, honest, even subtle. They spoke the same language, and held the same opinions, and the variety of age and sex did not divide them. Yet they were dissatisfied. When they agreed, 'I want to go on living a bit', or, 'I don't believe in God', the words were followed by a curious backwash as though the universe had displaced itself to fill up a tiny void, or as though they had seen their own gestures from an immense height – dwarfs talking, shaking hands and assuring each other that they stood on the same footing of insight. They did not think they were wrong, because as soon as honest people think they are wrong instability sets up. Not for them was an infinite goal behind the stars, and they never sought it. But wistfulness descended on them now, as on other occasions; the shadow of the shadow of a dream fell over their clear-cut interests, and objects never seen again seemed messages from another world.

A Passage to India is not a philosophical statement about religion and culture, but a novel which presents individual experience in an actual setting. Thus it would not be relevant to protest that deeper exponents of Christianity could be found than Mrs Moore, or that Aziz and Godbole are not necessarily representative of their creeds. The physical context of India, and in particular of Chandrapore, the political relationships of the British and the Indians in a particular decade, the individual motives current in certain social classes, are all elements which define the scope of the religious theme; so also is the point of view of the novelist himself, who stands close to the character of Fielding. The very great distinction of *A Passage to India* is the coherence through delicately reiterated symbolism with which Forster builds up in the reader's mind an image of a double contrast: the endless confusion of India in the dimension in which the British mind, immersed though it is in the confusion, retains a cool and practical order; and another dimension in which the Indian mind perceives an infinite order and the western psyche knows only the darkness of confusion. If these are truths, they are truths only in personal experience, and as such Forster conveys them. The truthfulness of the experience is in the convincingness of the characters themselves, but it is also testified by Forster's refusal to build wishful bridges. Differences may be apprehended, and thus deepen self-understanding, but they cannot be annihilated any more than can geography. At the centre of the book is the yearning for friendship of Fielding and Aziz, representing west and east, but by the end, the crisis of the caves has only defined and clarified what holds them apart:

'Why can't we be friends now?' said the other, holding him affectionately. 'It's what I want. It's what you want.'

But the horses didn't want it – they swerved apart; the earth didn't want it, sending up rocks through which the riders must pass single file; the temples, the tank, the jail, the palace, the birds, the carrion, the Guest House, that came into view as they issued from the gap and saw Mau beneath: they didn't want it, they said in their hundred voices, 'No, not yet,' and the sky said, 'No, not there.'

6

The critical decade 1930-1940

What a decade! A riot of appalling folly that suddenly becomes a nightmare, a scenic railway ending in a torture-chamber.

George Orwell, reviewing *The Thirties* by Malcolm Muggeridge, 25 April 1940

The decade of the thirties opened with a world crisis in trade and ended in the Second World War. It was a period of economic bankruptcy and unemployment; of moral bankruptcy among the democracies facing terror and mass hysteria in the dictatorships; a decade of slither from the rather heady excitement of the twenties into apathy and evasiveness. It was not, then, conducive to vigorous imaginative activity, and besides, the figures who had most distinguished the previous decade were many of them in one sense or another removed: Lawrence died in 1930, and Forster had ceased writing fiction; Virginia Woolf was in decline and James Joyce had become arcane; Eliot and Yeats were still achieving great work, but they now dominated the skyline rather than the immediate scene; Ivy Compton-Burnett's special voice seemed content to address itself to what had become her special public. In the place of these, the younger generation of new talent did not match either the originality or the distinction of their elders. However it is cultural fallacy to assume that the interest of a period depends on its production of masterpieces or at least works of imaginative originality. The very fact that the thirties were a decade of crisis and disillusionment in public conduct and private expectations stirred up critical life; not only did literary criticism begin to take new directions, but imaginative writing became critical and didactic in reaction against the pessimistic inertia which writers felt in their society.

The best writers of the twenties, poets and novelists, had tried to see beyond or to one side of current events: either the immediate scene was used only as a medium through which the writer could reach a permanent essence of the human condition, or it was ignored in favour of a scene a little removed in time, and therefore more easily seen in perspective. But by the early thirties current events had become so pressing that they demanded attention for their own sake; sides had to be taken and judgements made when it seemed that society might break down internally by its own inadequacies, or be destroyed from without by unprecedented barbarism. Feeling chilly from the exposure of their lack of principles, the official parties were huddling into coalition; the intellectuals consequently felt it their duty to take a political stand, usually outside the narrow range of British parliamentary politics. Traditionally, the British intelligentsia in time of crisis had been radical; so now many of them were drawn towards Communism. Right-wing politics, for the young, were not intellectually respectable, or at least did not include a body of opinion acceptable to humane thinking, so that the principal counter-attraction to Communism was Catholicism – not necessarily of the political right. Thus we find that a group of new poets – Wystan Auden, Stephen Spender, Cecil Day Lewis, Louis MacNeice – all have Marxist or near-Marxist sympathies, and that two of the ablest young novelists, Graham Greene and Evelyn Waugh, are Catholic converts. If we ask why it is the poets who have the political sympathies and the novelists the religious ones, a ready if superficial and provisional answer is that the poets, being elliptical and didactic, found that Marxism helped to epitomise their comment, whereas the novelists found Marxism too tight a constraint on their discursive form; the long and more supple traditions of Catholicism allowed them the amplitude of movement that they needed while sustaining their requirement for a framework of judgement.

But while the younger generation sought anchorage in the extreme left or in a new and radical Catholicism, their seniors – Eliot, Yeats, Pound and Wyndham Lewis – were on the right, and Lawrence in his later years had often divulged anti-democratic and authoritarian opinions. They did not often adhere to specific parties, however – only Pound, now in Italy, became closely involved with Fascism. Their aversion from the left was dictated on the whole by their need for independence. This implied a refusal to let themselves go with currents of opinion, which usually, among intellectuals, meant 'left' opinion; a mistrust of the public who were so easily swayed by propaganda; a deep assumption that since thought is necessary to life and the ability to think is rare, the function should remain the responsibility of an elite. Above all, this generation were inclined by their development to discount immediate crises as mere symptoms, however agonising, of a much deeper human sickness. It must be remembered too that these men had in their youth already outlived the facile left-wing optimism of the early years of the century – the optimism of Shaw and of the young Wells.

However, the younger generation shared with the older one a disdain and hostility for the conservative establishment in both politics and letters – the establishment that revered Kipling for the wrong reasons, still considered Galsworthy to be the outstanding novelist of the century, and the new Poet Laureate, John Masefield, its outstanding poet. But there was an establishment within this establishment (and opposed to it) which was also exposed to their criticism and, sometimes, outright attack. This was the 'Bloomsbury Group', so-called because it had centred on the house of Leonard and Virginia Woolf in Gordon Square, although it owed its origins as much to a circle in Cambridge centring on the philosopher G. E. Moore. At its heart, among the most famous, were the Woolfs, the economist Maynard Keynes, the art critics Roger Fry and Clive Bell, the painters Duncan Grant and Vanessa Bell; E. M. Forster was on its fringe. As individuals, each had his or her distinctive achievement which was sometimes great, but as a group Bloomsbury had a different collective presence which in a curious way had come to seem formidable. The phenomenon is curious because the group had no organisation, no clear-cut doctrine, no direction; it was little more than a chance collection of friends, all of whom happened to be intellectuals, some of them eminent. It was formidable because it constituted a cultural climate, and had even, for many, come to seem the climate of culture itself. Yet it was so far from being that, that its critics were asking whether true culture could even survive in such a climate.

Perhaps the criticisms of Bloomsbury could be epitomised by a sentence of Virginia Woolf's on Clive Bell's book, *Civilisation*: 'He has great fun in the opening chapters but in the end it turns out that civilisation is a lunch party at No. 50 Gordon Square.' Individually, the members of the group could often see through each other, and some of them had great social concern. Collectively, they cultivated the aesthetic rather than the moral sensibility;

valued the pleasures of conversation as much as the obligation for thought; accepted the superiority of reason over the passions; practised the virtues of scepticism and doubted those of faith. It was evident to many in the 1930s that if this was the climate of culture, then it was the climate of a greenhouse, irrelevant to such as could not afford it or pursued other goals, and defenceless against any who had the power and the will to smash it and sweep it away as an inconvenient obstruction. If culture and civilisation mean anything, they must be the spirit and the body of the values of a whole society; no individual is irrelevant to it and no department of activity can monopolise its production. Bloomsbury had grown up in the first two decades of the century and flourished in the third, but on the whole the best minds of that decade had either held aloof from it, like Eliot, or had actively hated it, like Lawrence. Those who had frequented it (Forster and Virginia Woolf) betray some of its weaknesses (as well as its virtues) even in their best work.

The younger writers felt the need of stronger allegiances than Bloomsbury believed safe, and a wider reference to human exprience than it had thought necessary or possible. On the other hand the younger intellectuals were in some respects not so different from Bloomsbury as they supposed. They accused Bloomsbury of being a sheltered enclave which had been able to cultivate its refinements and its scepticism because the society of the twenties happened to afford it protection; yet they themselves were in their own way sheltering themselves in faiths and hopes which many of them were later to abandon when they became inconvenient. Looking back, one can see what writers observed at the time – that there was often a facile quality in the commitments of the 1930s.

Some of the writers who saw this were also those who understood most clearly the difficulty of commitment, and themselves worked hardest to achieve and sustain it. They were individuals and impossible to place in categories, but it is they on the whole who have provided the most valuable influences from the late 1930s: the critic F. R. Leavis; the journalist George Orwell, and, more doubtfully and obscurely, the novelist L. H. Myers. In the rest of this chapter we shall discuss them in their appropriate contexts, with other writers who invite comparison or contrast with them.

W. H. Auden (1907–73); George Orwell (1903–50)

To do the useful thing, to say the courageous thing, to contemplate the beautiful thing: that is enough for one man's life.

T. S. Eliot on Charles Eliot Norton: *The Use of Poetry and the Use of Criticism* (1932)

The stars are dead; the animals will not look:
We are left alone with our day, and the time is short and History to the defeated
May say Alas but cannot help or pardon.

W. H. Auden: 'Spain 1937'

Eliot's lectures on *The Use of Poetry and the Use of Criticism* contain insights to which one returns, but at publication they seemed disappointing. Their perspective is so long, their reserve is so fastidious, their disengagement from harassing anxieties reminded one too much of a doctor whose diagnosis is deep but who refuses to prescribe for immediate relief. In earlier essays Eliot had taught the public to recognise that most poems were unnecessary actions: only indispensable communication of a kind that could take no other form fully justified a poem. But he did not, at least in these lectures, satisfy the craving for a supplement to the news – for a response to our immediate anxiety and an antidote to our impulse to escape from it.

When we took up Auden's first volume, *Poems* (1930), we felt that this new poet was doing just that. He gave us, in 'The Watershed' (XI) for example, the present scene of industrial inertia:

> Who stands, the crux left of the watershed,
> On the wet road between the chafing grass
> Below him sees dismantled washing-floors,
> Snatches of tramline running to the wood,
> An industry already comatose,
> Yet sparsely living.

Like Eliot's, the language is modern idiom, though differently heightened by Auden's characteristic use of ellipsis; like Eliot's, the detail is of a contemporary environment. But unlike Eliot's (usually urban) environments, the scene is not a mask for the state of the soul, but a stage for a state of mind. The poem, that is to say, is not about a timeless spiritual predicament expressed in current terminology, but about anxiety, depression, fear, in the contemporary scene of the slumped industrial north. It ends:

> Beams from your car may cross a bedroom wall,
> They wake no sleeper; you may hear the wind
> Arriving driven from the ignorant sea
> To hurt itself on pane, on bark of elm
> Where sap unbaffled rises, being spring;
> But seldom this. Near you, taller than grass
> Ears poise before decision, scenting danger.

This is difficult to paraphrase. The 'stranger' addressed in the poem is in a car the headlights of which reflect on the walls of empty houses. He may sometimes listen to the wind as to a suffering thing as it beats against the windows and trees, but he will seldom be aware of the reviving life within the trees themselves. He is watched (is he aware of it?) by some lurking animal, suspicious and alert to make its quick escape. But why need the sea be described as 'ignorant'? How can the ears 'scent' danger? And who is the stranger? In the middle of the poem, the poet admonishes him:

> Go home, now, stranger, proud of your young stock,
> Stranger, turn back again, frustrate and vexed;
> This land, cut off, will not communicate,
> Be no accessory content to one
> Aimless for faces rather there than here.

The 'stranger' to such a land comes from another social climate: he has children whom he can afford to nourish and educate; he is a tourist who likes scope for his idle curiosity – 'aimless for faces rather there than here'. Such a man will receive no response from a land with its own heroisms, which he will not be asked to admire, and desperations which he will not be able to relieve. The land is thus not only its earth and elements but its human inhabitants. Both will repudiate him, but perhaps he may sense its suffering in the wind from the sea, which is 'ignorant' perhaps as the economic forces are ignorant of the dereliction they cause. He may even be sensitive enough to feel that forces of resurgent life are at work here as elsewhere, but more evident than this will be the suspicion, represented through metonymy – a characteristic device of Auden's – by the just visible ears of a concealed and watchful animal, directed at him because, as a stranger, he cannot be a friend to this land enclosed in its own misery. It is the poet himself, perhaps, who is this stranger; it is also the reader; the land is a region of his own country, and the reader is made to feel estranged to himself in being made to experience this estrangement.

127

The imagery, the diction, the scene of these first poems made us feel that this was a poetry of our country expressing a state of mind that was also ours; their compression and obscurity gave the less discomfort because they seemed an assurance against facile answers to our large and haunting problems. They were thus gnomic rather than cryptic; not just codes to be deciphered, but wise utterances only intelligible by an effort comparable to the energy that had produced them. The voice was evidently post-Eliot, inasmuch as the poems could not have been written without Eliot's work, but they also showed other influences which were less familiar – Old English, for example, in the frequent elision of the definite article and the occasional use of emphatic alliteration.

But Auden was soon to exhibit many influences and to practise many manners. He was a prolific poet: between 1930 and the end of the decade, just after he had left England for the United States, he produced ten more volumes, some of them plays, including four works which were collaborations with Christopher Isherwood and one with Louis MacNeice. He was widely receptive to ideas: at first to Marx tentatively and Freud and other psychologists more distinctly; he became after the war a professing Christian. Although these influences lay at times too much on the surface of his verse, so that the techniques and the thought seemed ostensible rather than assimilated, his receptivity increased his readership, but what extended his popularity most – though it disillusioned some of his first admirers – was his formal and rhythmical versatility. He could use, or parody, the singing ballad ('As I walked out one evening'); he renewed unfashionable forms such as the sonnet and the ballade ('Paysage moralisé'), so successfully that they seemed never to have dated; he wrote light verse and doggerel as amusingly as Byron. Above all, and in this he also resembled Byron, he could combine conversational ease and grace with stanzaic and rhythmical tunefulness:

> Easily, my dear, you move, easily your head,
> And easily as though the leaves of a photograph album I'm led
> Through the night's delights and the day's impressions,
> Past the tall tenements and the trees in the wood,
> Though sombre the sixteen skies of Europe
>   And the Danube flood.

('A Bride in the 30's)

This is from *Look Stranger!* (1936). We have a tourist again, as in 'The Watershed', still travelling lands oppressed by fear, but now with a bride to divert him from the issues, as well as his own relative security to cushion him from them. Although the manner is so much more relaxed, the verse sustains from the first volume certain constants which Auden retained to the end: the focussing on current crisis; the admonitory tone; the theme of division and divisiveness, social, psychological, ethical. 'A Bride in the 30's' shows tenderness rather than depth of feeling, and it does not have much depth of thought. Yet it epitomises the predicament of the man who, at a time when so many others are facing present or imminent anguish, sees that his own happiness may be a kind of treachery, and is thus his own spiritual antagonist. The graceful movement of the stanzas carries with it sadness and nostalgia, but also a painful urgency. Here is the close of the poem:

> Be deaf, too, standing uncertain now,
> A pine-tree shadow across your brow,
> To what I hear and wish I did not,
> The voice of love saying lightly, brightly –
> 'Be Lubbe, be Hitler, but be my good
>   Daily, nightly.'
>
> The power that corrupts, that power to excess
> The beautiful quite naturally possess;
> To them the fathers and the children turn,
> And all who long for their destruction,
> The arrogant and self-insulted, wait
>   The looked instruction.
>
> Shall idleness ring then your eyes like the pest,
> O will you, unnoticed and mildly like the rest,
> Will you join the lost in their sneering circles,
> Forfeit the beautiful interest and fall
> Where the engaging face is the face of the betrayer
>   And the pang is all?
>
> Wind shakes the tree; the mountains darken;
> But the heart repeats though we would not harken:
> 'Yours is the choice to whom the gods awarded
> The language of learning and the language of love,
> Crooked to move as a moneybug or a cancer
>   Or straight as a dove.'

On the other hand, the very ease and charm of this may themselves be a source of uneasiness to the reader. Is the poem itself a little too like the ambivalent beauty of the girl who is being admonished? Perhaps Auden's work suffers in the end from a facile compatibility between two stances: that of the fearless self-analyst and didact with a warning finger, the seer into dark secrets, and that of the eternal spectator, stranger and tourist, who is never far away from the dangerous frontier and never far from the safe side of it.

Other poets of the decade, such as Robert Graves and Dylan Thomas – both of whom achieved their biggest reputation after the war – were personal, sometimes light-hearted, sometimes indulgent or self-indulgent, without raising the sort of doubts that Auden raises because they offered no precepts. Another poet, whose work is almost entirely contained within the decade, is personal in yet another sense. This is William Empson, whose two volumes, *Poems* and *The Gathering Storm*, appeared in 1935 and 1940. An objection that has been made to some of his poems is that they are private exercises for the wits, like superior crossword puzzles, but the best have that kind of authority which seems impersonal because it is personal feeling made universal. He is different from Auden, as well as from Thomas and Graves, especially in his ability to make his poem absorb his self-consciousness; this is evident in his use of images. Like Auden, he used images very deliberately, but whereas Auden implied or symbolised emotion through them, Empson followed the seventeenth-century Metaphysical Poets, such as John Donne, in using images to advance the thought of the poem, so that the emotion becomes subsumed in the idea until the poem is a whole articulation of feeling. His two thin volumes contain a number of such fully substantiated poems; one looks in vain for any in Auden's much larger output.

And yet Auden achieved in the thirties something like that peculiar distinction of being the voice of his time, rather as we may think of Dryden as being the voice of the Restoration. This is testified by the respect accorded him by the group of talented writers of like sympathies who cohered about him – Christopher Isherwood, Louis MacNeice, Stephen Spender, Cecil Day Lewis – and whose reputations were to some extent enhanced by reflecting his, although MacNeice at least had a strong poetic personality of his own. Together they gave the generation of the thirties – or at least that part of it that sought a projection of its moods and preoccupations – a self-diagnosis and a kind of public confessional. However, to say that a writer is the voice of his time is not to give him the highest praise: the phrase suggests that he is representative rather than original – although to be representative is already a great distinction, far greater than to be merely 'typical'. But whereas we value the representative writer by the extent to which he enables us to recognise his time, we value the original writer because he enables us to judge it by the extent to which, although he is rooted in his time, he also excels it. And there is room for a third category, which we may call that of the 'independent' writer, who is a critic of his own time without going beyond its own values. We esteem him not because he is representative, although he is that, nor because he is original, which he is probably not, but because he is truthful in the sense of testing the assumptions on which his contemporaries base their values. Cobbett was such a man in the early nineteenth century, and he was a journalist. In the 1930s Eric Blair, who wrote under the name of George Orwell, was such another, and he also is best described as a journalist.

The difference between his mental outlook and Auden's is succinctly shown by a comment he made in his essay 'Inside the Whale' (1940) on a stanza in Auden's poem 'Spain 1937' – which Orwell describes as 'one of the few decent things that have been written about the Spanish War':

> Today the deliberate increase in the chances of death,
> The conscious acceptance of guilt in the necessary murder;
>   Today the expending of powers
>   On the flat ephemeral pamphlet and the boring meeting.

The second stanza is intended as a sort of thumbnail sketch of a day in the life of a 'good party man'. In the morning a couple of political murders, a ten-minutes' interlude to stifle 'bourgeois' remorse, and then a hurried luncheon and a busy afternoon and evening chalking walls and distributing pamphlets. All very edifying. But notice the phrase 'necessary murder'. It could only be written by a person to whom murder is at most a *word*. Personally I would not speak so lightly of murder. It so happens that I have seen the bodies of numbers of murdered men – I don't mean killed in battle, I mean murdered. Therefore I have some conception of what murder means – the terror, the hatred, the howling relatives, the post mortems, the blood, the smells. To me, murder is something to be avoided. So it is to any ordinary person. The Hitlers and Stalins find murder necessary, but they don't advertise their callousness, and they don't speak of it as murder; it is 'liquidation', 'elimination' or some other soothing phrase. Mr Auden's brand of amoralism is only possible if you are the kind of person who is always somewhere else when the trigger is pulled. So much of left-wing thought is a kind of playing with fire by people who don't even know fire is hot.

131

In later editions of the poem, Auden substituted 'the fact of murder', but he complained to a friend (in a letter quoted by Munroe K. Spears in his book on Auden) that 'To kill another human being is always murder and should never be called anything else' and that '*If* there is such a thing as a just war, then murder can be necessary for the sake of justice.' However, Orwell would surely not have accepted the argument, which merely clarifies their disagreement. To say that 'killing is always murder' is to make a philosophical statement, not a statement of experience. Both men came from a middle-class professional background, and found as they grew up that they could not live in that traditional security. Auden looked across the frontier, and saw nebulous menaces and exigencies which he epitomised in phrases, but it was an inward frontier rather than an outward one – a confrontation with ideas rather than actualities.

Orwell, on the other hand, identified his inner psychic frontier with the outer social one; as Tom Hopkinson, one of his commentators, has said, it was his way at any moment to *do* what seemed important. Thus he did not merely observe extreme poverty; he lived, for a time, the life of extreme poverty, and reported it in his first book *Down and Out in Paris and London* (1933). Later, when he was commissioned by a left-wing publisher, Victor Gollancz, to make a personal survey of the depressed areas of the north, he did not merely live with unemployed workers but with the most depressed among them, publishing his report in *The Road to Wigan Pier* (1937). By the time this book was out, Orwell was fighting on the Government side in the Spanish Civil War, having enlisted, not with the International Brigade, but with P.O.U.M., a dissident communist movement with anarchist affiliations. He reported on these experiences, after he had been wounded by a bullet through the neck and had escaped from Spain with the secret police behind him, in *Homage to Catalonia* (1938), a book which includes an analysis of the events leading to the suppression of the movement in whose forces he had served.

These are his best-known books from the thirties decade, although he is probably still better remembered from that period by a handful of descriptive and critical essays: 'A Hanging' (1931); 'Shooting an Elephant' (1936); 'Marrakech' (1939); 'Charles Dickens', 'Boys' Weeklies' and 'Inside the Whale' – all in 1940. Most of it amounts to reporting, but reporting of the kind to which a man is driven when he has no other desire to write beyond the communication of what he is certain should be known. In fact, however, Orwell was not such another as H. G. Wells, who preferred the description of journalist to that of artist. In his essay 'Why I Write' (1946), he declares that from early childhood he had had an ambition to be an imaginative writer, and that only the nature of the times had turned him into 'a sort of pamphleteer'. It was literary ambition as well as dislike of imperialism which made him resign his post in the Burmese branch of the Indian Imperial Police in 1927. He set about writing his first novel, *Burmese Days* (1934), and by 1940 he had written three more: *A Clergyman's Daughter* (1935); *Keep the Aspidistra Flying* (1936), and *Coming Up for Air* (1939). Yet as novels, these books are not memorable; it is still as reporting that they retain some vivid life. *Burmese Days*, for instance, compels comparison with Forster's *A Passage to India*, published ten years before: it contains so many parallels with and parodies of Forster's characters, and the structure of the story is also analogous, with its setting of an administrative centre run in an atmosphere of racial hatred, its catalyst of an English girl fresh from England, and its theme of an Englishman standing alone against his colleagues in defence of his Indian friend. But the comparison shows up the comparative lack of distinction of Orwell's book. The characters are, except for the hero, presented as stereotypes rather than as living people, and so are the racial and religious phenomena. The conflicts and the types are more bitterly delineated but also more thinly: no one, except Flory and his Indian friend Veraswami, has any generosity of feeling to counteract the sourness of their prejudice or the remorselessness of their egotism, and even these two are shown as temperaments rather than as products of whole cultures. In 'Why I Write', Orwell was to acknowledge that his literary allegiance had been to Zolaesque Naturalism which emphasised the inescapability of environmental and hereditary conditioning. This may have supported Orwell's propensity for reporting, but it suggests little scope for Forster's kind of imaginative moral exploration.

There are, however, two features of *Burmese Days* which help to explain some of the nature of Orwell's imaginative writing, though they are perhaps evidence of its weakness rather than its strength. One of these is the birthmark which disfigures his hero, Flory:

Seen from the left side his face had a battered, woebegone look, as though the birthmark had been a bruise – for it was a dark blue in colour. He was quite aware of its hideousness. And at all times, when he was not alone, there was a sidelongness about his movements, as he manoeuvred constantly to keep the birthmark out of sight.

It is a strange disadvantage for a novelist to inflict on his central character, for it seems quite arbitrary: Flory's predicament – roughly the same as that of Fielding in Forster's novel – is quite awkward enough without any added disadvantage. Orwell may only be attempting to exemplify one of the tenets of the Naturalist school of fiction, which emphasised that chance inheritances, taints in the blood, may influence our destinies in ways that we have no freedom to remedy. But in fact the birthmark has no decisive influence on the story; in some episodes – those of lovemaking for instance – where one might expect it to have importance, Flory – or Orwell – seems to forget about it. Orwell's intention appears rather to have been to give an external sign to a personal disadvantage which he himself possessed, for Flory is plainly as close to himself as Fielding is to Forster. 'Until I was thirty', he writes in his autobiographical fragment, 'I always planned my life on the assumption not only that any major undertaking was bound to fail, but that I could only expect to live a few years longer.' His sense of a personal doom and alienation is worth mentioning because Orwell is not so solitary in it as perhaps he thought. Many intellectuals in western nations have felt it in this century, and it may have been more than usually acute among intellectuals of the English middle classes in the second quarter of it. The tight and prestigious system of middle-class private and public school education, with its narrow but strongly instilled expectations, intensified it after the First World War, when sensitive individuals with other values were least likely to respond to those in which they had been educated. In Orwell's case, it seems to account for his strenuous and even extravagant attempts to get outside his middle-class milieu – to know by direct experience how classes inferior to his own lived, and it helps to explain the painful theme of failed relationships which runs right through his novels to his most notorious success, *Nineteen Eighty-Four* (1949).

The other feature of diagnostic interest in *Burmese Days* is a character who has no analogy in Forster's novel. This is the aristocratic young military officer, Lieutenant Verrall, who is sent to help suppress a rumoured rebellion. He is Flory's anti-type, immune to pity and impervious to hatred, because his self-sufficiency is shown to be in itself a kind of perfection. He himself hates no one, because it is not worth his while: he merely dominates by the perfect coordination of his mind and body, by his complete mastery over all that he desires to master. His power arises from the British class system; and the physical culture it has perfected – he is an extreme example of Matthew Arnold's aristocratic Barbarians – has engrained in him that his egotism is unassailable, just because it happens to be his. Verrall is a slight figure from a passing era, but he portends another kind of Orwellian monster: the 'norms' at the heart of the new totalitarianism which Orwell identified most of all with Stalinism, such as the pig Napoleon in *Animal Farm* (1945), and O'Brian in *Nineteen Eighty-Four*. His belief that societies can produce such characters, and perhaps must produce them, partly explains the pessimism of his last novel, for when the unassailable individual commands the irresistible technology, it seems that there is no issue from social despair.

These two qualities in Orwell's mind, his inward sense of personal alienation and his outward sense of the invulnerability of the human products of strong social systems, are weakening inasmuch as they permeate his work with excessive pessimism. Yet they are reverse indications of his strength. His very facing of them so remorselessly is a sign of his insistence that the individual can only release himself from the terror of ugly truth by recognising it, and he can only recognise the truth consistently by cultivating in himself a habit of indefeasible truthfulness. One of the constant themes of his writing is what he considered to be the principal danger within the society of his time: the expedients we constantly use to evade recognition of the truth, especially by misuse of language. This is the subject of some of his best essays, for instance 'Inside the Whale' (1940) and 'Politics and the English Language' (1946); it is also a strong element in *Animal Farm* (1945), in which he shows how the principles at the foundation of the republic of animals are increasingly eroded of meaning by plausible modifications of their phrasing. It is strongest in the best feature of *Nineteen Eighty-Four* – the invention of Newspeak. Orwell explains the objective of this new language in an appendix to the novel:

It was intended that when Newspeak had been adopted once and for all and Oldspeak forgotten, a heretical thought – that is a thought diverging from the principles of Ingsoc – should be literally unthinkable, at least so far as thought is dependent on words. Its vocabulary was so constructed as to give exact and often very subtle expression to every meaning that a Party member could properly wish to express, while excluding all other meanings and also the possibility of arriving at them by indirect methods. This was done partly by the invention of new words, but chiefly by eliminating undesirable words and by stripping such words as remained of unorthodox meanings, and so far as possible of all secondary meaning whatever. To give a single example. The word free still existed in Newspeak, but it could only be used in such statements as . . . 'This field is free from weeds' . . . since political and intellectual freedom no longer existed even as concepts, and were therefore of necessity nameless. Quite apart from the suppression of definitely heretical words, reduction of vocabulary was regarded as an end in itself, and no word that could be dispensed with was allowed to survive. Newspeak was designed not to extend but to *diminish* the range of thought, and this purpose was indirectly assisted by cutting the choice of words down to a minimum.

The right use of language – the use of it to convey truth freely and nakedly – was the more indispensable to Orwell since he believed that language might not only be falsifying and narrowing to the mind, but was essential, in its healthy state, to the very existence of psychic life, for how can an individual feel a positive and enriching idea if he has no language with which to give it embodiment?

Orwell's practice of always acknowledging publicly the painful experiences of his very active life is the source of much of his most memorable writing, because he was able to convey the relevance of what is personal to what is general without neutralising its personal vividness. Perhaps his very best contribution is that he abjured self-pity, to which his temperament might have tempted him, and substituted for it the insistent reminder that we can allow no generalisations to escape from their only vital testing ground – that of individual experience in the lives of humans and also of animals, since both enjoy and suffer. It was thus that he projected socially his personal suffering. Only in *Animal Farm* did he escape from his own personality in the scene. This unusual freedom perhaps allowed the special incisiveness and wit which has made the book so famous, but, as Raymond Williams has noted in his study of Orwell, the freedom was a loss as well as a gain. It is Orwell himself who is his most important contribution to literature. He left a request that no biography would be written of him: the request has a point which he probably did not intend, for his entire work is a kind of autobiography, a record of the man of letters exposed to the temptations and stresses of his public function. He is that rare phenomenon described by Carlyle as 'the hero as man of letters'; as such, he has achieved almost mythic stature in twentieth-century English literature.

Graham Greene (b. 1904); L. H. Myers (1881–1944)

She said, 'Of course you could – renounce.'

'I don't understand.'

'Renounce your faith,' she explained, using the words of her European History.

He said, 'It's impossible. There's no way. I'm a priest. It's out of my power.'

The child listened intently. She said, 'Like a birthmark.'

Graham Greene: The Power and the Glory

For the last six days Jali had been travelling over the desert and disappointment had befallen him – disappointment but not disillusion. He clung to the truth of appearances as something equal to the truth that underlay them. There were two deserts: one that was a glory for the eye, another that was weariness to trudge. Deep in his heart he cherished the belief that some day the near and the far would meet.

L. H. Myers: The Near and the Far

No English novelist alive and working today has a larger public of admirers than Graham Greene. His prestige is due not merely to the vividness with which he conveys distinctively twentieth-century scenes, but to the difference of tone with which he pervades them by what has become for many people an unusual hypothesis – that God is not dead. The priest explains the difference to his fellow-prisoners in *The Power and the Glory*:

The voice said with contempt, 'You believers are all the same. Christianity makes you cowards.'

'Yes. Perhaps you are right. You see I am a bad priest and a bad man. To die in a state of mortal sin' – he gave an uneasy chuckle – 'it makes you think.'

'There. It's as I say. Believing in God makes cowards.' The voice was triumphant, as if it had proved something.

'So then?' the priest said.

'Better not to believe—and be a brave man.'

'I see—yes. And, of course, if one believed the Governor did not exist or the jefe, if we could pretend that this prison was not a prison at all but a garden, how brave we could be then.'

137

'That's just foolishness.'

"But when we found that the prison was a prison, and the Governor up there in the square undoubtedly existed, well, it wouldn't much matter if we'd been brave for an hour or two.'

'Nobody could say that this prison was not a prison.'

'No? You don't think so? I can see that you don't listen to the politicians.'

So, although fear may sometimes be an unnecessary emotion, it is as foolish not to feel fear of God if he really exists as it would be not to feel fear of the Governor. The priest's comparison of the prison to a garden is not as naive as it looks, because just as the prisoner is a citizen whom the politicians like to believe is living in a happy society, so God allows the soul to delude itself into forgetting that it is a prisoner of the flesh: the arrogantly pious make the same mistake as the complacent materialists. This is an ancient Christian commonplace, but Greene revives it for the modern consciousness by making it a pretext for emphasising the oppressiveness and delusiveness of the modern material world. Thus he is far from transfiguring this world by his religious themes, nor does he transfigure the people who live in it, who are as meagre and deprived as their surroundings. He does, on the other hand imply that fear and squalor are never merely that, because they are the obverse of glory, although it is an unseen, unfelt glory; and one which the ordinary sinner may never enjoy. The 'God hypothesis' is thus no release, in Greene's novels, to the oppressiveness of matter; it is rather an added oppression.

This doubling of material oppressiveness with spiritual significance in Greene's novel is underlined by the fact that his attempt to distinguish two classes in his fiction leads to a division which is not objectively clear. *The Power and the Glory* (1940) was his tenth novel, excluding short stories, and he defines three of its predecessors as 'entertainments'. These belong to the 'thriller' category of fiction, involving crime, detection and pursuit. But *Brighton Rock* (1938) was published in England as a novel and in America as an entertainment; its matter is the criminal underword, but it is also Greene's first distinctively Catholic novel. The blending is more evident than the difference: 'thrillers' rely for their suspense on violence in society, and Greene, especially in the thirties, has concerned himself in both novels and 'entertainments' with violent society, the intensity of the violence being increased rather than mitigated by the addition of the pursuit of the soul by God to the pursuit of the body by the police. Thus there is great density of psychic pressure in Greene's fiction, and this sense that his characters are constantly under test recalls Conrad, a comparison to which we must return.

A superficial resemblance between the two writers is that both drew their material from widely separated areas of the world. *The Power and the Glory* resulted from a journey to Mexico in 1938 to investigate religious persecution there, the first fruit of the visit being a report entitled *The Lawless Roads*. The federal constitution of Mexico meant that repression of religion was exerted very un-evenly in the different provinces: in some, the priests were syste-matically driven away or killed off, while in others they survived comfortably and even exercised their functions within fairly generous restrictions. Thus the priest in the novel, based on an actual prototype in *The Lawless Roads*, is one of two survivors in a state from which the rest of the clergy have fled; the other one, Father José, has bought safety by taking a wife – a step which is more satisfactory to the atheistic government than his death would be, since it exposes him and his office to contempt. But if Father José is a laughing-stock, his colleague regards himself as no better: he is a 'whiskey priest' – a confirmed drinker, the father of a child, conscious of every susceptibility to human weakness. Yet he never doubts his duty to carry out his priestly function among the miserably poor but unquestioningly devout peasants, always at the risk of his own life and often imperilling theirs. His sense of his own moral abjectness is no barrier to the execution of his function, because he never questions the Church's doctrine that in its most crucial form the priestly office is separate from the character of the man who exercises it: the Sacrament is as holy when a bad priest administers it as when it is received by a saint. His self-contempt does, however, prevent him taking any credit for his remarkable courage in remaining under constant threat instead of seeking refuge in the safety of the adjacent province. And yet it is not his present lust and greed that he despises most, but his complacency which he recalls from the days when he presided over well-to-do, self-satisfied parishioners, ignoring the material misery of the masses who still crave for the Sacrament which is their only release.

The narrative line of the novel is the priest's adventures as he moves from parish to parish with the police never far behind him, until he eventually escapes, only to be brought back by his conscience, entrapped, and eventually shot. This is the 'entertainment' line of the story, heightened beyond entertainment by the priest's sense of a parallel pursuit by Divine Judgement, whose Mercy he cannot conceive to compensate for his own unworthiness. The theme that deepens this plot is the religious one of spiritual consequences: we have the priest's ignorance of how and among whom his actions are indeed profitable, and his acute insight into those whom they do not profit – into the blindness of the faithful and of the Church itself, insofar as it is an earthly institution whose officers misconceive the efficacy and inefficacy of their ministrations. In his knowledge, he is aware that what passes for piety among believers is often the inhumanity of the Pharisees, and that the 'goodness' of the individual is not synonymous with his loyalty to the Church and to the letter of doctrine. In his ignorance, he is unaware that, although his own child is a moral outcast who despises him, he has acquired a kind of spiritual paternity over the Protestant American child who takes upon herself to give him shelter and refreshment, and that by his martyrdom he converts (temporarily at least) the boy who is wearied by the pious tale which his mother reads aloud night after night, but equally wearied by the drabness of the political secularity of the society in which he is growing up.

The book is structured so as to underline the irony of the difference between the real and the supposed good and evil. The unceasing pursuit of the priest runs coincidentally with the pursuit of a gangster at large in the province; it is to his deathbed that the priest is summoned, and to which he goes, still in fulfilment of his function, yet fully knowing that he is walking into a police trap. The gangster knows this too, and is more concerned that the priest shall save himself than that his own soul shall be saved by a deathbed absolution. The Lieutenant, who heads the pursuit of both, is a murderous and fanatical atheist, but his atheism is derived from a genuine compassion for the misery of the people and a conviction that the Church has exploited this by a system of lies. It is he, the priest, and the gangster who are the 'good' men, because, in error or not, they sacrifice themselves to faithfulness to their beliefs. On the other hand, the little outcast who is the immediate instrument of the priest's betrayal, who has hung round the police like a jackal

GRAHAM GREENE; L. H. MYERS

in his hope of reward, is shown to be too wretched in his understanding, too naive in his greed, to be an evil man: he too is a sinful
child of God, not intrinsically worse than the unctuous women who
confess what they suppose to be their sins in blank ignorance of
their real spiritual shortcomings.

The Power and the Glory is thus a richly worked novel, and its
resemblance to the work of Conrad is borne out by the high tension
of its action, its constant moral insistence, especially its insistence
on fidelity. And yet the comparison with Conrad immediately brings
a doubt to the mind: the doubt is whether such a comparison shows
Greene to be truly a moralist at all. When we look closely at the
characterisation, are we sure that the moral qualities arise from
within the characters, as they do in Conrad, or are we being offered
social stereotypes whose morality is an attribute of their typicality?
It is not of course possible to dissociate social types from moral
assumptions common among such types, but a moral typology of
society is not the same as a moral exploration of how an individual
comes to face or to evade the demands of his moral experience. A
distinguished moralist, such as Conrad is, causes his reader to
recognise moral predicaments as though he had discovered them
in himself; in Greene, the reader is brought to recognise moral
predicaments as they may exist socially on this or that social hypothesis; for God (and the question whether He exists or not) becomes
a social hypothesis in *The Power and the Glory*. The priest of course
is a special case, because we are shown into his mind much more
than into the minds of the other characters, but his self-contempt
raises another awkward question about Greene's moral vision:
whether belief in the Divine Sacrifice and in Divine Judgement
does not entail subjective disbelief in the validity of the believer's
personal identity. In their valuations of the lives of others, the
atheist Lieutenant does not differ markedly from the priest: despite
their contrasting beliefs, both men have positive, 'felt' moralities
which bring them together in contrast to the other characters,
atheists and Christians, for the most part with none. But whereas
the Lieutenant has a self-respecting dignity, the priest broods so
long and painfully on the contrast between his own relatively trivial
sinfulness and the infinite goodness of his Creator, that one begins
to wonder whether self-mortification – hard, sometimes, to distinguish from self-pity – is not for Greene one of the highest
spiritual virtues. For the reader, what is blocked, once again, is the

141

process of exploration: the difference between the infinite and the finite, after all is always the same, however much the finite may itself vary. *The Power and Glory*, in short, portrays sympathetically and vividly the difference made to a wretched society when it also happens to be a believing one: it explores the social condition, but not the moral experience, of human beings, and bears a closer resemblance to Wells's *The Island of Dr Moreau* than it does to Conrad's *Heart of Darkness*.

L. H. Myers, on the other hand, a much less famous novelist than Greene, owes his continuing reputation to the consistency with which he made moral exploration his whole endeavour. He is indeed differentiated by his emphasis on moral search as a natural and specific concern of human consciousness. In the work of others – James, Conrad, Lawrence – moral implications are an inescapable outcome of their characters' experience in society: such implications are the fruit of judgements which they and the reader are impelled to make on the very nature of that experience. In Myers, the search is the very action of his characters, who are therefore in an unusual relationship to their physical setting: they are in it rather than of it, motivated by a desire for a participation which will be liberated from the mere force of their circumstances. He was averse from the usual propensity of novelists to actualise the foreground of the social environment, especially insofar as this led to a stress on the aesthetic rather than the moral sensibilities, and stated his objection to this in the preface to his major work, *The Near and the Far*:

When a novelist displays an attitude of aesthetical detachment from the ordinary ethical and philosophical preoccupations of humanity, something in us protests . . . Proust, for instance, by treating all sorts of sensibility as equal in importance, and all manifestations of character as standing on the same plane of significance, adds nothing to his achievement, but only draws attention to himself as aiming at the exaltation of a rather petty form of aestheticism.

This helps to explain why, in his novels with a twentieth-century setting – *The Orissers* (1922), *The 'Clio'* (1925), and *Strange Glory* (1936) – the material environment is indistinct, as though it was an embarassment to the novelist instead of the very medium in which the characters have to shape their lives; its pressures limit and frustrate their perceptions of the range and depth of potential choice. In his major, more satisfactory work he escaped the embarrassment by choosing – almost inventing – a society beyond the bounds of his time and of European civilisation, with the intention of illuminating the perplexities which underlay his own society.

The Near and the Far (1929) was followed by sequels – *Prince Jali* (1931) and *Rajah Amar*; the three were published together in 1935 under the title of *The Root and the Flower*. In 1940 he added *The Pool of Vishnu*, and the tetralogy was republished in 1943 under the title of its first volume, *The Near and the Far*. The setting is India in the sixteenth century, under the rule of the Emperor Akbar. By this choice, it might seem that Myers had faced himself with an even worse difficulty – that of actualising an equally material world in an age and society remote from his own, but he denied that he was writing a historical novel; only four of the characters – Akbar, his two sons, and the statesman Mobarek – have historical existence. He was really attempting something unique: the construction (rather than the reconstruction) of a society whose human components are near enough to the men and women of his own time to be recognisable, while far enough from them for him to be able to exclude from their attention the distracting issues of his time so as to bring into the foreground of his narrative the spiritual problems which those issues disguise. The India of Akbar's reign exhibits a vast confusion of competing religions and ways of life which Akbar tried to synthesise in a state religion called the Din Ilahi, with the Emperor himself figuring as the representative of God. This great theatre enabled Myers to imagine a society peopled by characters who were in communication, even close friends, while driven by profoundly different motivations and professing the most various faiths.

The novel opens with a great court assembly of the princes of the Empire summoned by Akbar to his capital city of Agra; a small boy, Prince Jali, is standing on the terrace outside his room in one of the palaces, looking out over the desert. Jali is the son of a sophisticated Buddhist, Raja Amar, and a Caucasian Christian, Ranee Sita. His favourite relative, apart from his parents, is his uncle by marriage, Hari, a sceptical renegade Moslem who is still on close terms with Amar and Sita although he lives in separation from Amar's sister, Ambissa, a woman whose whole interest is social and political intrigue. The most intimate family friend is the Hindu Brahmin scholar, Gokal, deeply immersed in the conflict of a life of learning and carnal desire, in the anxieties of his own precarious political status, and in the personal crises of his friends. The most evident of these crises is political and centres on Amar, who is inevitably involved in the intrigues surrounding the rivalry of the Emperor's sons – the drunken, foolish Prince Salim and the sophisticated but trivial and evil-minded Prince Daniyal. Amar is in the dilemma that, on the one hand, his sole desire is to abdicate and abandon the world for life as a holy man, and, on the other, that he cannot do this until he has secured his principality against whichever of the competing forces seems most likely to win power on the old Emperor's death. Beyond this is the further dilemma that his allegiance to one or other of the worthless princes may involve violating his conscience. The world of politics (for Amar, though not for the others, it is Maya – illusion) makes demands on the individual quite disproportionate to its intrinsic significance: it can neither be respected nor ignored. How is this world to be encountered and yet duly subordinated to the other realms of the mind? How is action to express the spirit without subjecting the spirit to the ephemerality of the stuff of action? This is the theme which is explored through the diverse temperaments of the main protagonists.

On the whole Myers seems to have escaped the charge that he should have written a historical novel but evaded the challenge; at least in the first three volumes the network of intrigue and the physical environment are substantial enough to sustain the narrative convincingly, even grandly. A commoner accusation is that *The Near and the Far* is not so much a novel as a philosophical fable, peopled by personifications of attitudes rather than by substantial characters. Yet the characters are not simplified; they are complex, representatives but not emblems of their styles of motivation. The choices they face are real and arise out of concrete situations. An example is the division between Amar and Sita which Gokal tries to heal:

'I, for my part, shall always affirm what Amar denies. Between us there is a great gulf.'
Gokal leant forward earnestly. 'The gulf lies not between those who affirm and those who deny, but between those who affirm and those who ignore. Listen!' he went on. 'Fundamentally your mind and Amar's are similar in type; you both raise the same problems and the answers you give are the same in essence, if their substance is not the same. You advocate life's intensification, Amar its extinguishment; but you both recognise imperfection and you both aim at perfection!'

144

Myers was right in his belief that deliberate moral search is a leading constituent of fully developed human experience. If we do not receive this without protest, it is a symptom of our deprivation, not of his eccentricity: Renaissance readers would not have felt the difficulty.

The real obstacle to the attainment of classical status by Myers's novels is a subtler one. The novel form itself has grown up from the realisation that human experience moves from denser atmospheres to rarer ones, and that the denser experience must be assimilated before the finer. In the first three volumes of his tetralogy, Myers provided some of this denser basis in the politics of Akbar's reign, but even these intrigues are presented so much from a philosophical plane of vision that we hardly know whether the stuff of his characters is too like our own for the remoteness of their culture, or too far removed. The symptom of this failing is in the dialogue – even in the brief extract just quoted – for speech betrays all levels of the personality, when it is fully alive, even in the most highly developed minds. The language of Myers's characters is our language, but too often it reads bodilessly. In *The Pool of Vishnu*, the theatre of political intrigue is abandoned, and though a different social context replaces it, the problem in that novel becomes more acute. Thus Myers reaches ranges of interest which Greene has never attempted and which only the greatest novelists command, but what Greene has attempted, he makes us feel as what by comparison is an almost brutal factuality. This explains why Greene's novels of the thirties are still widely read despite their limitations, while Myers, with perceptions which are far more spacious but have much less density, continues to be neglected.

Literary criticism in the critical decade

A critic must be able to *feel* the impact of a work of art in all its complexity and its force. To do so, he must be a man of force and complexity himself, which few critics are.
D. H. Lawrence: 'John Galsworthy' in Phoenix I

. . . I don't believe in any 'literary values', and you won't find me talking about them; the judgements of the literary critic are judgements about life.
F. R. Leavis: 'Luddites? Or there is only one culture' in Lectures in America

For the common reader, criticism is often a different category of writing from other kinds usually classified under 'literature'. He may neglect poetry because he feels that it is 'not for him', but he will recognise at least that it is addressed to him; he is more likely to feel that literary criticism is addressed to the student, that it is 'books about books' and not about life, as imaginative literature is. And we must admit that much literary criticism is susceptible to that kind of description: 'books about books' is what it is, and not necessarily negligible for that reason, yet negligible by the busy man or woman who works in another industry.

Two kinds of literary critic, however, from time to time break down this barrier which isolates them in the public mind from the 'creative' writer. The first is the imaginative writer who, as Wordsworth put it, 'creates the taste by which he is enjoyed', whose criticism may, at the lowest level, gain the interest of the public by the curiosity which he has already aroused through his other work. T. S. Eliot, D. H. Lawrence and W. B. Yeats were all critics of this sort. The second is the critic who, whether or not he is also a creative writer, extends the range of what is usually recognised as literary criticism, tumbling down the wall of 'books about books' by exposing the non-existence of its assumed foundation. This false assumption is that the books about which the critic writes are *about* life; on the contrary they *are* life in the sense that reading them is, or should be, vital experience. It follows that there should be, in what is called literature, no books about books: the critic's books should be as directly living experience as the writing which are their subject, because he should be communicating their vitality or (in some instances) the vitality which they are without. Two outstanding critics of this sort arose between 1920 and 1940: I. A. Richards and F. R. Leavis.

'The arts', wrote Richards in *Principles of Literary Criticism* (1924)

are our storehouse of recorded values. They spring from and perpetuate hours in the lives of exceptional people, when their control and command of experience is at the highest, hours when the varying possibilities of existence are most clearly seen and the different activities which may arise are most exquisitely reconciled, hours when habitual narrowness of interests or confused bewilderment are replaced by an intricately wrought composure . . . They record the most important judgements we possess as to the values of experience.

Imaginative literature, the most central of the arts for Richards's attention, is also made central to the activities of society, since no science or technology can by its own means project a currency of values, and conventions merely harden into habits. This conception of literature as the means by which we educate ourselves in values recalls Matthew Arnold's famous essay 'The Study of Poetry' (1888), in the opening paragraph of which Arnold predicted that, since 'our religion has materialised itself in the fact', it was the destiny of poetry to become the 'criticism of life' and the touchstone of value for our civilisation. And indeed Richards chose this paragraph as epigraph to his own essay, *Science and Poetry* (1926 and 1935) which was republished as *Poetries* and *Sciences* in 1970.

However, the title of Richards's essay indicates the difference of his approach: where Arnold saw poetry as communication of the human spirit permeating fact, Richards was concerned with poems *as* facts: he sought to investigate what they are, how they are and ought to be read, and what effects they have on the reader, bearing in mind that every reader involuntarily carries with him a private poetry compounded from his personal fears, desires, regrets and remorse. This is the subject of his three most influential books of criticism: the *Principles* and *Science and Poetry* already mentioned, and *Practical Criticism* (1929). The books were immensely liberating, especially in the practice of criticism and the teaching of literature, because they demonstrated that literary study could be an enhancement of the whole consciousness of the reader, expanding Coleridge's dictum in *Biographia Literaria* (1817) that 'the poet, described in ideal perfection, brings the whole soul of man into activity'. Richards's challenge to the culture of his time was positive, moreover, because he revealed a new cultural landscape in which totally different activities – the practical and the theoretic, the scientific and the artistic – need not be pursued in separate compartments but were shown to be not only consonant with one another, but complementary. Yet his importance appears now to have been above all on the theoretical level of communications; significantly, from the later 1930s, he gave his main attention to the devising and expounding of Basic English as a possible international language. This judgement does not of course lessen his achievement, but problems of communication arise in a material context: what moves freely on the level of ideas may remain suffocated within actual social forms and practices. A culture which so baffles itself is in crisis, and it has been the lifework of F. R. Leavis, especially in the great review, *Scrutiny*, which he edited from 1932 till 1953, to show that such a crisis existed, and to assess those writers and forces which offered promise of survival.

Leavis is a critic who has aroused perplexity amounting sometimes to bewilderment, as well as hostility. The hostility has been due to his intransigence, although this is also one cause of the perplexity. Another perhaps is the total absence of theory in his writings – the absence, that is, of an abstract scheme of ideas such as other critics may find conveniently portable, classifiable, and disposable at convenience. Instead he has insistently repeated a simple challenge which no writer can evade once he has been faced with it: that a writer's work must either sustain and enhance the reader, or it will corrode and waste the life of the reader's mind and heart. He has owed much to the critical work of two imaginative writers – T. S. Eliot and D. H. Lawrence. Eliot's contribution was his discernment of the importance of a living tradition in national literature, surviving only through the active sensibility of every generation of readers. Lawrence, who shared with Leavis the seriousness of the tradition of religious nonconformity in their backgrounds, contributed the central relevance to literature of the sense of morality, considered not as a conventional code, but as the force from which the coherent meaning of our experience derives.

The basis of Leavis's own work can be expressed in two principles: first, that literature matters, not to any special group who choose to make it their recreation, but to all of us; the second, that since it matters, its best values must be kept vital by the strenuous, collaborative attention of dedicated minds. Neither principle, certainly not the first, seems to invite antagonism; both, for many readers, amount to commonplaces. But Leavis's insistence is that just because both are commonplaces, the first is taken for granted without being a felt truth, so that the need for the second is not in fact recognised. One of the consequences of the first principle, for instance, is that not all writers and works of acknowledged importance in the past can matter equally for every generation, so that the study of literature demands repeated attempts at reassessment and fresh discernment, and unless this effort is sustained, there will be no firm basis for the truly great writers of the present. Leavis borrowed from Eliot the phrase 'the common pursuit of true judgement'; Eliot had used it in his essay 'The Function of Criticism', in which he pointed out that few critics in fact contribute to such a function. In the thirties, Leavis attributed the failure to three kinds of inertia: that of the Marxist doctrinaires, who believed that culture could look after itself so long as society was set right according to the correct principles of economic justice; that of the established writers and teachers, especially such as derived from Bloomsbury, who fattened themselves on literature as parasites on their host, and that of the commercial forces, which, by now lacking the positive energy of Victorian industrialism, obliviated the mind by the mechanical operation of their technologies.

Because he has not been a theorist, either in the sense in which Richards was one, of exploring and enlarging ideas, or in the sense of teaching a specific doctrine like the Marxists, Leavis's creative achievement has been above all in his critical assessments of specific writers – of poets in *New Bearings in English Poetry* (1932) and *Revaluation* (1936), and of novelists in *The Great Tradition* (1948), *D. H. Lawrence, Novelist* (1955), and (with his wife, Q. D. Leavis) *Dickens the Novelist* (1971). The influence of this work has been very great in education where his criticism opened new possibilities in the training of response and judgement – aspects which are emphasised in his books *Education and the University* (1943) and *English Literature in Our Time and the University* (1969). But in the thirties, his influence can perhaps be best expressed as that of a moralist. He inspired, that is, the realisation that life, whatever our political or religious allegiances, is valuable as it is valued, and that it is valued to the extent that we can enlarge our awareness of the scope and intensity available to the human consciousness. He rightly perceived that literature was a means to this end, not an end in itself, but that without this means we may lose sight of the end itself.

7

Yeats and Eliot: the climax

> O body, swayed to music, O brightening glance,
> How can we know the dancer from the dance?
> >   W. B. Yeats: 'Among School Children'

> From wrong to wrong the exasperated spirit
> Proceeds, unless restored by that refining fire
> Where you must move in measure, like a dancer.
> >   T. S. Eliot: 'Little Gidding'

Some periods of crisis stimulate the young writer, others mislead or constrain him; the second decade of this century was an example of the former kind, the fourth was of the latter. Only if a writer has already achieved strong maturity without hardening into repetitive mannerism can he sustain self-direction in such a period, and if he does, this ability to offset his younger contemporaries may enhance his impressiveness for later generations. This is true of both Yeats and Eliot, the greatest poets writing in English in this century, although the reputations of both have suffered some loss by the denigrations of mid-century critics, themselves victims of the spiritual collapse of our mid-century society.

Yeats was in his sixties in 1930: he had just produced one of his two most important volumes of verse – *The Tower* (1928) – and in 1933 he published his second – *The Winding Stair*. Eliot was in his forties, and he was already showing that consistency of development which gives his work its unusual coherence, in contrast to Yeats's unpredictability. And yet both poets have in common a resurgence of greater genius after what looks at first like a point of exhaustion. When Yeats published *The Wild Swans at Coole* in 1919, the fine critic Middleton Murry (as Leavis points out in *Lectures in America*) described the book as the poet's swan-song: he was continuing to be an artist only 'by determination', for 'his sojourn in the world of the imagination, far from enriching his vision, has made it infinitely tenuous'. In 1922 Eliot published the most notorious of his works, *The Waste Land*, commonly interpreted as a desperate vision of the state of European civilisation, and he followed it in 1925 with 'The Hollow Men', which later he once refused to read in public because he had come to doubt the right of an artist to give voice to such despair. Yet it was in 1930 that he published *Ash-Wednesday*, a poetic document of rebirth, and by the end of the decade he was bringing out his greatest work, *Four Quartets*.

After the Irish won their independence in 1922, Yeats lost the public theme which had inspired much of his earlier work without finding cultural inspiration in the provincialism of the Free State. He had in any case never been a politician at heart: 'I am no Nationalist,' he was to write in 1937, 'except in Ireland for passing reasons; State and Nation are the work of intellect, and when you consider what comes before and after them they are, as Victor Hugo said of something or other, not worth the blade of grass God gives for the nest of a linnet.' His true inspiration had always been those forces of the imagination which, for him, vitalised the human soul, and these attracted him to mythology, esoteric studies and magic, exemplified in his prose work *A Vision* (1925). Yet in spite of his occasional solemnity about it, his attitude to the occult became increasingly ironic. His central theme was the destructive and creative passions, and this became a concern with the tension between passion and the ageing body, burdened less by physical decay than by memory and knowledge of transience:

> Bodily decrepitude is wisdom; young
> We loved each other and were ignorant.
>
> ('After Long Silence')

The theme is of course in one word, mortality, an ancient commonplace. What gives it importance in Yeats's rendering of it is his refusal to betray his youth. This betrayal – a merciful one – occurs in many ageing people in two forms: the memories may fade, and with them their pain, or they may survive only in their joy; in the former case the facts are obliterated, and in the latter, their significance. For Yeats the dilemma could only be resolved in art, especially tragic art, which perpetuates the fact in the form and gives it dignity in the thought.

His finest rendering of the theme is 'Among School Children' in *The Tower*. The poem consists of eight seven-line stanzas, and describes a visit he paid as a senator to a school taught by nuns. The visit does not interest him much, but as he watches the children, and watches them watching him, his mind leaps back to a girl he had loved in his own youth, and he places that image beside his present image of her as an old woman. This leads him to generalise: what mother, given a vision of her baby as an ageing man, would feel the pain of his birth to be compensated? What philosophers have reconciled nature, ideality, and the cost of suffering? It is the image that focusses desire, but the image mocks it too:

> Both nuns and mothers worship images,
> But those the candles light are not as those
> That animate a mother's reveries
> But keep a marble or a bronze repose.
> And yet they too break hearts – O Presences
> That passion, piety or affection knows,
> And that all heavenly glory symbolise—
> O self-born mockers of man's enterprise;
>
> Labour is blossoming or dancing where
> The body is not bruised to pleasure soul,
> Nor beauty born out of its own despair,
> Nor blear-eyed wisdom out of midnight oil.
> O chestnut-tree, great-rooted blossomer,
> Are you the leaf, the blossom or the bole?
> O body, swayed to music, O brightening glance,
> How can we know the dancer from the dance?

The spontaneity of desire (to put this very much in other words) is life, and its object is the image of whole and harmonious beauty, but between the desire and its object come change and suffering – the forces that destroy and disillusion even while they shape. But the tree is not identifiable with any of its parts, and no part of it, seen separately, seems consonant with any other part, yet it blossoms spontaneously through the free coordination of all its parts. The dancer is not the dance, but the magic and mystery of the dance is that it transfigures the body which is at the same time indispensable to it. In both nature and art beauty is self-fulfilling; soul is not divided from body. But in human life there is a chasm between them.

If the dancer cannot be distinguished from the dance, nor of course can the words from the poem, although just as the dancer, when not dancing, pursues the normal activities of life, so the words have common usage. Very few poets have enabled common speech to carry such weight of majesty as Yeats did at his best, nor to convey so gracefully such variety of tone. There is a great difference between the eloquence of the last two stanzas and the matter-of-factness and mild irony of the first:

> I walk through the long schoolroom questioning;
> A kind old nun in a white hood replies;
> The children learn to cipher and to sing,
> To study reading-books and histories,
> To cut and sew, be neat in everything
> In the best modern way – the children's eyes
> In momentary wonder stare upon
> A sixty-year-old smiling public man

and yet there is no incongruity. The variety is achieved by a sure and subtle command of rhythm and music, combined with an unusual confidence in the emotions to be communicated. Yeats himself only achieved this fully in a few poems.

Yeats's problem was that the theme of human mortality was no longer sustained in the public imagination by great religious, philosophical and mythological systems, so that he had to sustain it by his own. In his earlier work, we hear a great deal about 'gyres', those phases of history which constitute the rise and fall of civilisations; about the phases of the moon, each of which evokes a style of human experience; of masks which the poet uses to dramatise styles of experience not his own yet of an aspect of himself. He wrote in *The Trembling of the Veil* (1922):

I was unlike others of my generation in one thing only. I am very religious, and deprived by Huxley and Tyndall of the simple minded religion of my childhood, I had made a new religion, almost an infallible church of poetic tradition, of a fardel of stories, and of personages, and of emotions, inseparable from their first expression, passed on from generation to generation by poets and painters with some help from philosophers and theologians.

But such an enterprise, the purpose of which was to establish an impersonal basis for a fully human art, was itself an immensely personal one, so that the very endeavour to release his ego into the impersonality of art too often makes itself felt in the rhetoric of an over-dramatised ego, so distasteful to some modern critics who confuse self-depreciation with humility. Yeats's dilemma is expressed in one way most succinctly in the series entitled 'Vacillation' (*The Winding Stair*), the seventh of which is a dialogue between the Soul and the Heart:

153

The Soul. Seek out reality, leave things that seem.
The Heart. What, be a singer and lack a theme?
The Soul. Isaiah's coal, what more can man desire?
The Heart. Struck dumb in the simplicity of fire!
The Soul. Look on that fire, salvation walks within.
The Heart. What theme had Homer but original sin?

The temptation that the Heart is resisting is clearly religion, symbolised by the coal of fire set upon the prophet's lips, purging him of sin. Isaiah was not struck dumb, for he went forth to preach to his nation, but for the Heart he was dumb to speak henceforth on the complexities of the human heart. As the poet writes in the next in the series, addressed to a Catholic theologian:

> I – though heart might find relief
> Did I become a Christian man and choose for my belief
> What seems most welcome in the tomb – play a predestined part.
> Homer is my example and his unchristened heart.

He rejected religion then because, in its contemporary form, religion rejected human complexities, and yet the complexities, as he aged, were a personal torment that cried out for resolution, and in two of his greatest poems, 'Sailing to Byzantium' in *The Tower* and 'Byzantium' in *The Winding Stair*, he presented his tragic nostalgia for a fictitious one. In a passage in *A Vision* he expresses this nostalgia in prose:

> I think that in early Byzantium, and maybe never before or since in recorded history, religious, aesthetic and practical life were one, and that architect and artificers – though not, it may be, poets, for language had been the instrument for controversy and must have grown abstract – spoke to the multitude and the few alike.

The earlier of the two poems announces his retreat from Ireland ('That is no country for old men'), and, in the second stanza, his fidelity to his art, for whose sake he seeks in Byzantium 'monuments of its own magnificence'. The third stanza evokes the contrast between the man and the artist, calling upon the sages of Byzantium to

> Consume my heart away; sick with desire
> And fastened to a dying animal
> It knows not what it is; and gather me
> Into the artifice of eternity.

'Artifice of eternity' implies the transcendence of nature by art, and in the last stanza Yeats envisages himself – as a man – transcended by taking the form of a work of art whose function it is to transmit art

> to sing
> To lords and ladies of Byzantium
> Of what is past, or passing, or to come.

The man is taken up into the artist, into a world wholly taken up into art, within a universe conceived as a single great artifice. The poem is a fantasy, but a fantasy that conveys mockery at its own wishfulness. *Byzantium* deepens the fantasy:

> I hail the superhuman;
> I call it death-in-life, and life-in-death

for the death that is in life breaks life's 'bitter furies of complexity', and the life in death leaves the 'complexities of fury'—

> Dying into a dance,
> An agony of trance
> An agony of flame that cannot singe a sleeve.

But the sea of living images that storm against the cold fixities of marble, mosaic and metal – 'Those images that yet Fresh images beget' – is endless, as though the poet were himself storming against his own insatiable yearning for an absolute which is itself the creation of his passionate adoration.

What defied him was not the logical fallacy of a straining for transfiguration into what was itself his creation, for in a sense Byzantium both existed and exists. The poems have tragic power partly because the goal is a mockery in the world of now, and partly because the poet knows that he has in any case rejected it : 'the fury of complexities' he so desires to release himself from is also his predestined element, without the context that offered it dignity. In 'Coole and Ballylee, 1931', he commemorates Lady Gregory, his former associate :

> We were the last romantics – chose for theme
> Traditional sanctity and loveliness;
> Whatever's written in what poets name
> The book of the people; whatever most can bless
> The mind of man or elevate a rhyme;
> But all is changed, that high horse riderless,
> Though mounted in that saddle Homer rode
> Where the swan drifts upon a darkening flood.

Part of his suspension between human passion and the fastidious-ness of the artist was his suspension between the aristocrat and the simple man, the elevated style and elemental starkness. In his last four books, he cultivated the second, no doubt because his consistent determination to be himself enabled him to see – in the light perhaps of twentieth-century depth psychology – that his dramatisations had been so often in essence self-dramatisations motivated with less dignity than he had supposed. This last phase is movingly expressed in 'The Circus Animals' Desertion' (*Last Poems, 1936–39*):

> Players and painted stage took all my love,
> And not those things that they were emblems of.
>
> Those masterful images because complete
> Grew in pure mind, but out of what began?
> A mound of refuse or the sweepings of a street,
> Old kettles, old bottles, and a broken can,
> Old iron, old bones, old rags, that raving slut
> Who keeps the till. Now that my ladder's gone,
> I must lie down where all the ladders start,
> In the foul rag-and-bone shop of the heart.

It is tempting to say that this is where Eliot started, but the two poets were in so many ways different that there is a danger of making the contrast too symmetrical. Still, it can be said that Eliot felt keenly the 'foul rag-and-bone shop of the heart' early in his career, and had by the end of it found his ladder.

The Waste Land, remarkable poem as it is, does not show full mastery, and might have shown less of it had it not been for the assistance, amounting almost to collaboration, of Ezra Pound. It is not truly what it is often said to be, a poem about twentieth-century civilisation, but a poem about the sterility of body and spirit, drawing on past treatment of the theme in English and European literature from the very first lines:

> April is the cruellest month, breeding
> Lilacs out of the dead land, mixing
> Memory and desire, stirring
> Dull roots with spring rain.

This echoes the opening of Chaucer's *Prologue to the Canterbury Tales*:

> Whan that Aprille with his shoures swote
> The droghte of Marche hath perced to the rote,

– which also implies ('perced' – 'pierced') the pain of fertilisation, but which in a single sentence passes from the impulses to genera- tion in nature to the cosmopolitan impulses to religious pilgrimage in human beings. Eliot, on the other hand, passes from nature to the smart cosmopolitan woman, for whom the change of season is merely excuse for another form of expensive holiday.

The poem is a succession of images presented through changing rhythms which vary the emotional tone. In human life the prevail- ing image for fertility is woman; in nature it is water. These two dominate the poem, which is in five unequal parts, entitled 'The Burial of the Dead', 'A Game of Chess', 'The Fire Sermon', 'Death by Water' and 'What the Thunder Said'. The image of woman is principal in the first three, with water not absent but subsidiary. Allusions to women are numerous in the first part, but fleeting – all of them of reduced, frustrated, or self-frustrated female energy. The second has only two women, but they are extended portraits. The first of them begins with a line –

> The Chair she sat in, like a burnished throne

– which echoes the opening of Enobarbus' description of Cleopatra in Shakespeare's play. The second ends with the line spoken by Ophelia as she makes her first exit in the 'mad scene' in *Hamlet*:

> Good night, ladies, good night, sweet ladies, good night, good night.

Cleopatra, earthly Venus, Queen of a lavishly sensual country, dominated men by her sexuality, but she overplayed her powers and ended by making love to death; Eliot's Cleopatra lives a death- in-life amid claustrophobic and richly erotic surroundings. Ophelia was the helpless and innocent victim of men; Eliot's Ophelia is the sexual drudge of a returned soldier who is likely to betray her. In the third section water (the River Thames) occupies equal space with woman, the two being brought together in the speeches of the three Thames daughters, analogous to the Rhine-daughters in Wagner's *Rheingold* and *Götterdämmerung*, but the section centres on the typist and her part-time activity of loveless, sterile, amateur prostitution. She is to the city what the Thames daughters, grieving for the material and spiritual pollution of their river, are to the Thames: victims of sterility. The short fourth section is entirely given over to water – the element that destroys and then

157

restores in a new form, and in the final one, water predominates by its absence:

> Here is no water but only rock
> Rock and no water and the sandy road
> The road winding above among the mountains
> Which are mountains of rock without water . . .

It is this last section which points the real elusiveness of *The Waste Land*. This is not the unconventionality of the poem's structure, the abandonment of logical connecting links between the sections; that is a language influenced perhaps by the contemporary artistic school of Futurism, according to which the act of disconnection enables the poet to imply new and unexpected connections, and as a language it can be learnt. The elusiveness is really a loosening of grasp, not of the logical sort, but spiritual. The Thunder speaks the Sanskrit words of redemption: Da, Dayadhvam, Damyata – Give, Sympathise, Control – but does it bring rain? We are left in doubt:

> Then a damp gust
> Bringing rain
>
> Ganga was sunken, and the limp leaves
> Waited for rain . . .

It is a doubt, one feels, in the poet: to know the means of release is not the same as to receive the means.

Yet *The Waste Land* is not so utterly pessimistic as it is often reputed, nor perhaps is the poem that succeeds it, 'The Hollow Men'. They are the Yeatsian emblem of the scarecrow, the empty man without heart, in Yeats, but for Eliot (who never centred himself on the Heart as Yeats did) they are the men whose ideals have not grown from a centre of regeneration, so that – like Conrad's Kurz, in *Heart of Darkness*, who is mentioned in the poem's epigraph – they cannot move upwards, but can only fall. We live in dreams, the poem tells us, and these may be the death of the spirit or life-giving visions, but it is the cost to be paid for the attainment of life that men fear. Prayer can only be stammered:

> Between the desire
> And the spasm
> Between the potency
> And the existence
> Between the essence
> And the descent

Falls the Shadow
  For Thine is the Kingdom
For Thine is
Life is
For Thine is the

This is the way the world ends
This is the way the world ends
This is the way the world ends
Not with a bang but a whimper.

Yet 'The Hollow Men' is a fine poem, and fine poems cannot proceed from total desolation of spirit.

It is in Eliot's *Ash-Wednesday* and his Ariel Poems (so-called not by his intention but from the name of the edition in which they were published) that regeneration begins. *Ash-Wednesday* is a fine series, but it is an expression of painful process rather than of realisation. But in 'Marina', one of the Ariel poems, the clouds all at once lift: the experience is, for once, joy. The poem is based on a scene in Shakespeare's late and controversial play, *Pericles*, a scene which enacts the mutual recognition of a father and a daughter. They have been lost to each other, and Pericles in consequence has sunk into silent despair from which no one can arouse him. Marina is brought to him on the deck of his ship, because in the course of her own wanderings she has become renowned for her marvellous singing, which baffles assaults on her virtue and heals the broken spirit. Separated from her father in infancy, she has no more knowledge of the identity of the sick king than he has of hers, but as she sings his spirit awakens and he knows her for his daughter. Eliot's poem is an expression of this resurrection from death into life; life is restored to him as if in a dream, yet at the same time with the poignancy of a reality which has been known but never before received:

What seas what shores what grey rocks and what islands
What water lapping the bow
And scent of pine and the woodthrush singing through the fog
What images return
O my daughter.

Those who sharpen the tooth of the dog, meaning
Death
Those who glitter with the glory of the hummingbird, meaning
Death

159

Those who sit in the stye of contentment, meaning
Death
Those who suffer the ecstasy of the animals, meaning
Death

Are become unsubstantial, reduced by a wind,
A breath of pine, and the woodsong fog
By this grace dissolved in place

What is this face, less clear and clearer
The pulse in the arm, less strong and stronger—
Given or lent? more distant than stars and nearer than the eye

Whispers and small laughter between leaves and hurrying feet
Under sleep, where all the waters meet.

So far we have the awakening of the spirit; the body is now likened
to a ship, sea-worn, in disrepair, whose life has been all life to
Pericles until this moment. The poem ends with the ship moving
towards a new shore, with new menaces but also new promise:

What seas what shores what granite islands towards my timbers
And woodthrush calling through the fog
My daughter.

The antinomies of soul and body, of spirit and matter, have been
devalued in our time, partly for sound philosophic and scientific
reasons which have given a different geography to the human organism, partly for unsound ones which have flattened the human
dimensions. Eliot's peculiar importance is that he is one of the few
who have kept alive the distinctions by communicating their reality
as experience – the only truth they can have, since they can no
longer be defined scientifically or philosophically. His most important achievements in this way as the *Four Quartets*: 'Burnt Norton'
(1935), 'East Coker' (1940), 'The Dry Salvages' (1941) and 'Little
Gidding' (1942). The first is named after a ruined house in Glouces-
tershire; the second, a village in Somerset whence his ancestors
derived; the third, from a group of rocks off the coast of Massa-
chusetts, and the fourth from a hamlet in Huntingdonshire, where
an Anglican community existed in the reign of Charles I, of which
only the chapel now survives. Each title indicates one of the four
traditional elements – air, earth, water and fire – both in their
material and their symbolic forms. Through them all runs the
theme of time: past, present, future; the revolutions of day and
night, life and death; time as destroyer and as preserver; time as

160

occasion; time ending and beginning. Time is linked with space through movement: the movement forward of a journey, the circular movement of a dance, the movement out of space and time of the timeless vision. Time, space and movement are all both related and cancelled by the 'still point' – the centre of the dance, the centre around which a form is shaped, the eternal 'now' which is both at the centre of time and supersedes it.

The mark of a great poem, at least of this metaphysical kind, is that it is a liberation of meaning; that is, it says more than one had thought it possible for language to say before one has read the poem, and at the same time it conveys that still more remains to be said, so that the reader's mind is carried beyond the poem itself and is enlarged by the renewal of the sense of mystery – which is very different of course from a sense of perplexity. But a poet cannot do this by conveying meaning as we all do, with more or less success, on the single dimension of speech or prose. In addition he offers the harmonic dimensions or kinds of meaning evoked by verbal music and image, and also a sort of counterpoint, by which one use of language is counteracted by another use, so that the reader is offered a variety of approaches to the central significance. In exemplification of this last point, each of the Quartets is divided into five parts, and these correspond in character throughout the four. Thus every first movement sets a scene, evoked by the place of the title, and induces the reader to participate in the mood which the setting arouses. The second movement is always divided into two parts, the first of which is a tightly organised lyric the meaning of which is enclosed in its images, and the second is a meditation in a relaxed, conversational rhythm and idiom. The third movements are argumentative, sometimes polemical, and the fourth is again a lyric using symbolic language, but this time more expository than gnomic. The fifth and last movements are again meditations but more condensed, less discursive, summative of what has come before in the poem.

The first paragraph of the fifth movement of 'Burnt Norton' is as follows:

> Words move, music moves
> Only in time; but that which is only living
> Can only die. Words, after speech, reach
> Into the silence. Only by the form, the pattern,
> Can words or music reach

> The stillness, as a Chinese jar still
> Moves perpetually in its stillness.
> Not the stillness of the violin, while the note lasts.
> Not that only, but the co-existence,
> Or say that the end precedes the beginning,
> And the end and the beginning were always there
> Before the beginning and after the end.
> And all is always now. Words strain,
> Crack and sometimes break, under the burden,
> Under the tension, slip, slide, perish,
> Decay with imprecision, will not stay in place,
> Will not stay still. Shrieking voices
> Scolding, mocking, or merely chattering,
> Always assail them. The Word in the desert
> Is most attacked by voices of temptation,
> The crying shadow in the funeral dance,
> The loud lament of the disconsolate chimera.

We can use this passage as an indication of what Eliot is seeking to achieve in *Four Quartets*. This is not to express a philosophy or doctrine, still less a mood, but to communicate a spiritual poise within an emotional and intellectual ambience to the attainment of which doctrine, thought, moods, and all the accidents of experience contribute as means, though they have all been mistaken as ends until they have been surpassed, when they are recognised as beginnings. To express this spiritual poise requires delicate disciplines of language, by which words are made to lose their inert meanings by being played against each other in a kind of dance, so that the meaning lives in the mind instead of lying in it. But language by its nature – or by the nature of our use of it – resists this disciplined animation. The poet can only use current language, and the currency for his purposes has become devalued, intensifying the difficulty of his task: words which should be precise have become vague; their denotations and connotations unreliable. Moreover when we seek the centre of meaning, the Word, the point of balance for all experience, our minds are distracted and our hearts dismayed by the formless, ever-changing menaces which bar our progress. Hence the poet offers a kind of dialectic: the disorder of our consciousness is set against the harmony which we can also conceive, and by including both in the harmony of the whole poem (regarding the series as one) he presents a symbol for the ultimate attainment of pure movement which is also pure rest.

Such is an account, not a paraphrase, of the passage, suggested as a clue to the whole of the *Four Quartets*. The sequence is in one sense a very personal document since it is the summation of Eliot's own spiritual progress. But in another sense it is unusually impersonal, because it points to the elimination of the pronoun 'I', because this is brought into accord with otherness. The use or absence of this pronoun is an indication of the difference between Yeats and Eliot. In Yeats's poems it occurs frequently; it fixes our attention on the poet, and though we cannot always be sure that the poet is to be identified with the man, we know that its use is an insistent reminder that the poet would regard the abandonment of the man as a betrayal of the humanity of the poetry. Eliot uses it more seldom: at first, in the early dramatic monologues such as *Gerontion*, to identify a fictional but generally representative persona, and later, in *Ash-Wednesday*, with a curious effect of impersonality, so that we do not identify the first person with the poet so much as with the poem itself. In *Four Quartets* the first person is used rarely, and in the most conspicuous place in one of the argumentative sections, with a tone of weary irony:.

> You say I am repeating
> Something I have said before. I shall say it again.
> Shall I say it again? . . . ('East Coker' III).

One might sum up the difference by saying that Yeats was determined to 'stand by' himself at whatever cost of self-exposure, and that Eliot sought to escape the sense of self – had he not said in 'Tradition and the Individual Talent' that poetry is 'an escape from personality'? – in order to discover, or establish, a true selfhood which has no need of egoism.

The point is of some importance for the literature of the thirties, for this decade showed a sense of the oppressiveness of selfhood in so many of its writers. Writers were middle class, and in the conditions of the time felt themselves constrained by their class. Should they abandon it, and lose themselves in the working class? But how could this be done, and what sort of solution would it provide? At the same time, the totalitarian regimes of Germany, Italy, Russia made individualism into a social virtue despite itself. It was a twentieth-century dilemma, which earlier phases of our civilisation had not encountered. Yeats's attempt to resolve it by creating his own mythology of history merely enlarged it; Eliot's spiritual conservatism and poetic radicalism was a unique resolution.

8

Drama 1900-1940

M'Comas: There is only one place in all England where your opinions
   would still pass as advanced.
Mrs Clandon (*scornfully unconvinced*): The Church, perhaps?
M'Comas: No: the theatre.
                                     Bernard Shaw: *You Never Can Tell* (1897)

B: Blasphemy is a sign of Faith. Imagine Mr. Shaw blaspheming! He
   could not.
                          T. S. Eliot: *A Dialogue on Dramatic Poetry* (1928)

Shaw notoriously cultivated provocative statement: he sought
to bring out that part of any truth which public opinion ignored
and exaggerated it. But M'Comas's scornful dismissal of the English
stage at the end of the nineteenth century does not now, when we
look back on the period, seem much beyond the truth. It is also true
that a revival had already begun: Oscar Wilde and Shaw himself
are evidence of it. But as yet the evidence was tenuous, and it is
fair to say that as literature – though not as theatre, since drama is
a composite art, requiring producers and actors as well as writers –
English drama scarcely breathed in 1900. The causes of the mori-
bundity were two. The first was that the theatre, for reasons which
are too complex for short exposition, had come to be a place where
nothing substantial could be said, unless the plays, like
Shakespeare's, happened to be sanctified by history. The second
was that those who attempted to say something in dramatic form –
the poets and the novelists – no longer knew how to write a play.
Summarily, one could put it that English dramatists lacked either
technique or matter, but this is superficial, for any art requires a
mastery of both. Deficiency in either always implies some deficiency
in the other, and though some advance can be made in one without
the other, no drama can thrive when the stage is mere entertainment, nor when it is merely a platform of opinion. Elsewhere in
Europe, the great geniuses of Ibsen, Strindberg and Chekhov had

164

already learned this lesson and profited from it. The English dramatists were slow to learn it. The towering influence of the nineteenth-century novel impelled gifted writers such as Granville Barker (*The Voysey Inheritance*, 1905) and John Galsworthy (*Strife*, 1909) to emulate the novel in the social substance of their plays, and they seem to have thought that this was the only lesson that Ibsen transmitted. They did not understand, what Ibsen knew very well, that a play is a shape of experience which is different from that of the novel, and that what merely emulated prose fiction was better done by it. The Irish, who had never produced a great novelist, learned the true meaning of dramatic art much quicker, and part of the subject of this chapter will be the uprising of a distinctively Irish theatre. However, the comparative backwardness of the English theatre was also due in part to the very success of the Irishman, George Bernard Shaw.

It is clearly paradoxical to say of a writer that by his genius he exerts a retarding influence, although Shaw is not a unique case of it. In his case, the paradox can be explained in two ways: Shaw, beyond a certain point, was a bad critical influence on the drama, and his own achievement, so startling despite its inferior critical basis, was too idiosyncratic to be a creative influence. Shaw's lack of critical depth shows in his well-known remark in 1895, already quoted, that Ibsen's *Doll's House*

will be as flat as ditchwater when *A Midsummer Night's Dream* will still be as fresh as paint; but it will have done more work in the world; and that is enough for the highest genius.

If a play does 'work in the world' this of course is nothing against it, but it says nothing for it as a work of art. Ibsen, who knew very well what a work of art was and intended *A Doll's House* to be one, did not approve of its being regarded as a feminist tract. Shaw, in fact, made the mistake common in England to this day of supposing that Ibsen was a superior journalist, and the mistake came the more naturally to him, because, like Wells, he did not despise this description of himself. It is not that Shaw was a bad critic of the *craft* of the theatre: his own dramatic reviews, which still read excellently even when the plays he is discussing have been totally and justifiably forgotten, show him to have been admirable within the limits that make destructive criticism profitable. But as a creative critic he was without what he also lacked as a creative artist: he could not see how drama could create a new vision of human nature, as Shakespeare had done, and as Ibsen, Strindberg and Chekhov also did.

However, if Shaw was like Wells in his pride in the title of journalist, he was unlike Wells in his very strong regard for art, in his definite ideas about the nature of art, and in his consciousness of his own artistic practice. He had been a music critic (1888–94), and an exceptionally fine one before he became a dramatic critic (1895–8); in the 1880s he had also learnt to become a public speaker, and had taught himself the art of public speaking with the care, as he said, that a singer takes in practising scales. Speech and music were thus associated in his mind, so that it is not surprising that he also associated dramatic speech with the art of opera. He learnt to write plays, according to his own testimony, by studying the operas of Mozart. Some of his best scenes seem on the surface to be untheatrical, portraying debates which hold up the action, and might, by their matter, seem calculated to send an audience to sleep. And yet it is often such scenes that hold the attention most: even when the matter has grown familiar to us, or stale, Shaw's sense of antithetic styles, mannerisms and rhetoric give them a force which is greater than their content, much as an audience at an opera may be held by the arias although they are sung in a foreign language. What is said ceases to matter, because how it is said is all our pleasure. The effect is not only gained by contrast of styles, but by countering predictability and surprise: some characters are stable elements, while others elude expectation, overturning our initial sympathies or antipathies, and gaining victories when they would seem to be incontestably in the wrong.

A good example is *The Doctor's Dilemma* (1906, published 1911). The opening lines are a miniature of the technique of heightening what could have been a flat dialogue into a lively debate with an unexpected victory. The scene is a doctor's consulting-room; we have a medical student, Redpenny, and the doctor's Cockney servant, Emmy:

Emmy (*entering and immediately beginning to dust the couch*): There's a lady bothering me to see the doctor.
Redpenny (*distracted by the interruption*): Well, she can't see the doctor. Look here: what's the use of telling you that the doctor can't take any new patients, when the moment a knock comes to the door, in you bounce to ask whether he can see somebody?

166

Emmy: Who asked you whether he could see somebody?
Redpenny: You did.
Emmy: I said there's a lady bothering me to see the doctor. That isn't asking. It's telling.

As the scene develops, doctor after doctor enters to congratulate Dr Colenso Ridgeon on his knighthood, announced in the morning papers. Ridgeon himself is in early middle age, serious and humane, and believed to have discovered a cure for tuberculosis by inoculation, but his serum exists only in small supply. He is however kept in low relief to offset the characters of his visitors, each of whom has a pronounced individual style. We have Schutzmacher, who has acquired wealth by his formula 'Cure guaranteed', and yet is not the fraud he seems, nor nearly so dangerous as some of his more celebrated colleagues. Next comes Sir Patrick Cullen, retired, gruff, cynical, direct, who believes that all important scientific discoveries have been made before. Cutler Walpole, an energetic surgeon, is obsessed with the idea that all sickness is a form of blood-poisoning, and that blood-poisoning is caused by an organ he calls the nuciform sac. Sir Bloomfield Bonington, on the other hand, believes the one thing necessary to be 'the stimulation of the phagocytes'; he is bombastic, foolish and sentimental, and yet the most successful of them all. Last to enter is Blenkinsop, a failed doctor, who has forgotten his science, and can barely find the means to live. Each character contributes his own style to the discourse, which becomes, in effect, a debate about the medical profession. The tone rises from the quietness of Schutzmacher, through the astringency of Sir Patrick and the energy of Cutler Walpole to heady comedy with Bloomfield Bonington, and then abruptly sinks to pathos with Blenkinsop. And all the time we are reminded at intervals, without intrusive artifice and yet so as to stimulate our interest, that there is a lady waiting downstairs desperate to capture Sir Colenso and his serum to save her dying husband. She succeeds by the end of the act, but the drama, the doctor's real dilemma, has not yet begun.

One can use *The Doctor's Dilemma* to distinguish the art of Shaw's dramatic writing from the craft, and from his dramatic intention. The first and the third acts admirably illustrate the art. In the latter, Louis Dubedat, Sir Colenso's patient, a brilliant artist but also, even in the moment of his death, an amoral egotist, turns the tables in his debate on morality with the doctors, although it

167

would seem that he has no shadow of defence for his viewpoint. Shaw's art comes out in his sensibility to the games we unconsciously play with language. The third act is a serious game, since it challenges, as Shaw so often does, our assumptions about the relationship of our behaviour with our ideas about our behaviour. But if it is by his art that Shaw's plays survive best, it was as much by his craft that he gained his audiences at the beginning of the century. The nineteenth-century theatre had exploited the audiences' capacity for sentimentality and their taste for melodrama. Shaw repeatedly takes stock sentimental and melodramatic situations and then deliberately travesties them, thus first arousing the audience's expectations and then frustrating them – a dangerous ploy for a less gifted playwright, but successful as he contrives it, since the shock of reality supersedes conventional entertainment. Thus the doctor's dilemma is superficially whether the rest of the serum – enough in its present supply for one or more patient – should be used to save the gifted but noxious Louis Dubedat or the useless but harmless and conscientious Blenkinsop. The dilemma is made easier by Sir Colenso's certainty that Louis will, if he survives, end by breaking his wife's heart, but it is made much more difficult by the fact that Ridgeon has fallen in love with the wife, intending to marry her if she becomes a widow, so that the death of the artist is the doctor's personal gain. The situation would be a promising one for the sentimental dramatist, who might have brought about an equally gratifying happy or sad ending in various ways, but Shaw deliberately abjures such possibilities. Sir Colenso Ridgeon contrives that Louis Dubedat is handed over to the prestigious Sir Bloomfield Bonington, whose incompetence can be relied on to kill the patient, and it does. But Ridgeon is not given the chance to console Mrs Dubedat in marriage, nor (another possibility) does he nobly abstain from asking for her hand in order that his act of allowing Louis to die in order to save her happiness shall be truly disinterested. All he gets is her cool contempt, based on the belief that he has allowed a great man to die from envy at his greatness, and mild astonishment that anyone as old as Sir Colenso should have any expectations from a woman as young as herself. If one is comparing the play to sentimental melodrama, this ending clearly seems much closer to life, but now that the traditions of sentimental melodrama, at least of the Victorian kind, are gone, it appears no more than an anticlimax, the more so because Mrs

Dubedat's adoration of her truly detestable husband is itself in-comprehensible – a romantic and silly convention in itself.

Ibsen, Shaw's master, would have been too concerned with the realities of human beings to have depicted so fatuously infatuated a character as Mrs Dubedat without making more constructive use of her passion. That Shaw did, and that he frequently created characters who, though central, lack inherent interest, raises the question of his dramatic seriousness. What were his intentions in *The Doctor's Dilemma*? The first act seems to promise satire on the medical profession : 'all professions are conspiracies against the layman' is one of the famous remarks in the play, and to Shaw medicine was one of the most overrated. The doctors' prestige, it turns out, has less to do with their scientific ability than with their capacity for self-advertisement and with good luck. Bloomfield Bonington is not a better doctor than Blenkinsop, but he is sure he is, and has the gift of broadcasting his self-confidence in a way that is much naiver but no less self-advertising than Schutzmacher's 'Cure guaranteed'. Sir Colenso's knighthood might have been due to his genuine merit, but in fact he owes it to a happy accident. However as the play develops, it becomes clear that Shaw's real concern is social morality. The doctors, as doctors, are morally enclosed in their science; their interest in their patients is the scientific interest which the latter provide as cases. It is only when Sir Colenso is forced into his dilemma that he has to consider a principle of basic morality in the use of science, and only at the end of the play does he realise that he can strictly be accused of having 'murdered' Louis Dubedat. On the other hand, as men, faced with the amoralism of Dubedat, they are highly moral, but they take their moral code, like most of us, at second-hand, so that his unconventional but thought-out logic defeats them polemically at every point. To this extent the play is brilliant – and yet, morality carries no conviction unless it is bound up with vividly realised emotional living, and this is where Shaw's intentions fall so far short of great art : Louis Dubedat is a caricature; his wife is a doll.

It is often said that Shaw is a dramatist of ideas, and it is true that his plays are essentially ideological debates. The great dramatist creates living characters – Hamlet or Hedda Gabler – who, through the action, bombard the mind of the audience with ideas; Shaw reverses the process: it is the ideas which are the centre of his plays, and the characters are just their vehicles. Even this may be to estimate his genius too highly, for was it really *ideas* that interested him? He was indeed an ideological playwright, influenced by certain thinkers: by Marx, who inspired his socialism; by Lamarck, Schopenhauer and Bergson, who gave him his vitalism – the belief that life on the planet is imbued with a drive towards mastery and advancement; by Nietzsche, with his doctrine of the superman. But, perhaps with the exception of his socialism, Shaw uses his ideologies more as pieces in a game than as ideas that nourish his imagination; when he writes about them directly, as in *Back to Methuselah* or the dream scene in *Man and Superman*, he produces his dullest work. On the other hand, he was immensely astute at diagnosing public opinion, and his genuine humanitarian passion gives his own opinions considerable emotional force. It is thus perhaps truer to say that Shaw was a polemical dramatist of opinion rather than of ideas. He was a supremely witty artist in the Comedy of Manners tradition of Congreve, Sheridan and Wilde, widening its scope by centring his plays on opinions in preference to modes.

It would be too neat to say that Shaw was a genius of the theatre rather than of drama, but at least the difference is suggestive, because clearly it ought not to exist, and clearly it often does. There is a great difference, that is to say, between the writing of plays for a place of entertainment or propaganda, however popular or fashionable, and writing plays to dramatise the conflicts in a society. The second sort of theatre is not necessarily more congenial to the society; it may even arouse enraged protest in the audiences, but at least it will not easily be disregarded, and the very protests that are intended to silence it may well be evidence that it has touched the social quick. But for such a drama to exist, it seems likely that there must be an impulse within the society to dramatise itself, otherwise it is likely that a different literary form will concentrate the social consciousness; Shaw, the Irishman writing in and for England, knew that he had to compete with the English novel, and he attempted to do so partly by designing his plays to be read as much as to be performed. Ireland, on the other hand, in the first quarter of this century, was experiencing an intensifying consciousness of itself in its struggle for national independence. This is an aspiration which lends itself to drama, not necessarily of the political conflict, but of the search of a people for its own identity, of what it means to be Irish. It was Yeats's sense of this, and the fact that a native dramatic instrument already existed in W. G. Fay's Irish National Dramatic Company, that impelled him in 1904 to initiate the Dublin Abbey Theatre, home of the Irish National Theatre Society, and for three decades the most original and vigorous theatre to have existed in the British Isles since the Elizabethans.

In his book *In Search of Theater*, the American critic Eric Bentley has written of Yeats's own dramas:

Yeats's whole theory and practice were devised in revulsion from the whole Ibsenite-Shavian movement. He proposed two alternatives. The first was to cut below it. Beneath the surface of middle-class civilization there still lurked, in Ireland at least, a peasant culture possessing a living speech and not yet wholly robbed of simple human responses. Not feeling competent to tap this vein himself, Yeats pushed Lady Gregory and J. M. Synge into doing so. For him, the second alternative: to rise above 'the play about modern educated people', a drama confined to 'the life of the drawing-room', in a drama of symbol and myth.

The result was a series of twenty-six plays by Yeats, most of them in verse, many of them drawn from Irish myth and legend, some of the later ones influenced by the Japanese Noh plays which used ritual movement and stylised character, and nearly all directed at private audiences of fastidious taste rather than the mixed audiences of a public theatre But Yeats showed more intelligent understanding of the problems of dramatic structure than any poet in the English language since Milton had written *Samson Agonistes* – and many had tried their hands. He did not succeed in reviving the poetic drama, but his experiments, as Eliot discovered, are indispensable to a study of the problem.

What the problem was, insofar as Yeats did not master it, can be illustrated by the one short play in which he clearly did, although it is too short to be an important exception. This play is *Purgatory* (1939), written at the very end of his life, and for once the incident is drawn from modern times. The characters are two: a boy and an old man, both standing before a bare tree and a ruined house:

Boy: Half-door, hall door
           Hither and thither day and night,
           Hill or hollow, shouldering this pack,
           Hearing you talk.
Old Man: Study that house.
           I think about its jokes and stories;
           I try to remember what the butler

Said to a drunken gamekeeper
In mid-October, but I cannot.
If I cannot, none living can.
Where are the jokes and stories of a house,
Its threshold gone to patch a pig-sty.

The house is the birthplace of the old man, who is now a tramp, and it has left on him a legacy of hate. He killed his father, who had set the house on fire in a fit of drunkenness, and before the end of the play he kills the boy – his son. Yet the legacy of hate was initiated by love for his mother who had stooped to marry his father, a drunken groom, whence the old man has derived his own sense of degeneracy, and his crazed belief that his son has inherited it and will pass it on. Both crimes are to expiate his mother's guilt, but as he leaves the scene he hears the hoofbeats of his father's horse again: the squalor of his own begetting is to be eternally re-enacted.

Twice a murderer and all for nothing,
And she must animate that dead night
Not once but many times!
    O God,
Release my mother's soul from its dream!
Mankind can do no more. Appease
The misery of the living and the remorse of the dead.

Short and spare as the play is, it dramatises much more than one might suppose that it could contain – even the sense that a nation may continue in remorse for the loss of a grandeur that it never truly possessed, a permanent dream of dereliction. The pungency and pathos of the language in this play contrast with Yeats's usual dramatic style. This has the austerity of his later non-dramatic poetry, but in the context of a play, it shows also as a rather mannered grandeur:

I thought to find a message from the King.
You are musicians by these instruments,
And if as seems – for you are comely women—
You can praise love, you'll have the best of luck,
For there'll be two, before the night is in,
That bargained for their love, and paid for it
All that men value. You have but the time
To weigh a happy music with a sad,
To find what is most pleasing to a lover,
Before the son of Usna and his queen
Have passed this threshold.   (*Deirdre*, 1907)

172

What Yeats did not achieve – the creation of a style of dramatic speech which would match in dignity and distinctive life the speech of the rich poetic dramas of the past – John Millington Synge did achieve in prose, in at least two plays, by the use of Irish popular idiom. His life was a short one – born in 1871, he died in 1909 – and his career as a dramatist was even shorter. His first play, *In the Shadow of the Glen*, was produced in 1904, and he was still engaged on his sixth and last, *Deirdre of the Sorrows*, when he died. It was Yeats who rescued him from the life of a minor cosmopolitan belle-lettrist in Paris by pointing out to him the rich unexplored field of Irish peasant life still available to writers, but it was the humility and responsiveness of his own nature which enabled him to acquire command of the peasant idiom, not as the alienated Protestant Anglo-Irishman that his education had made him, but as the friend and equal of the peasants among whom he lived for a time in the Aran Islands. Directly out of this experience he wrote his short tragedy *Riders to the Sea* (1905), usually regarded as one of his two masterpieces, although Yeats criticised it acutely as 'too passive in suffering'. The other masterpiece, *The Playboy of the Western World* (1907), is ostensibly a comedy, but in truth one of those rare works which defy classification, as do the plays of Chekhov, by challenging the critic to think again about his use of the terms 'comedy' and 'tragedy'. It is also a challenge to our conventional acceptance of the term 'dramatic poetry'; it forces us to ask whether true dialogue ever is prose, or at least whether it need be, any more than verse dialogue is inevitably poetic.

The action is set in a public house in a village in Mayo on the western coast. Its hero is Christy Mahon, a young man, little more than a boy, who is in flight, and its heroine is Pegeen Mike who keeps the pub for her father, Michael James. When Christy enters, he is distraught with terror and fatigue, and almost at once he admits that he is trying to escape the police. This is not so naive as it might be in another country, for the peasants, accustomed for centuries to an alien rule, take for granted that the representatives of authority, at least of political or police authority, are any man's natural enemy:

Michael (*going after him*): Is it yourself is fearing the polis? You're wanting, maybe?
Christy: There's many wanting.
Michael: Many, surely, with the broken harvest and the ended wars.

Interrogated in a friendly but close way by Michael, Pegeen and their friends about the likely and (humanly speaking) 'normal' crimes that he might have committed, Christy eventually lets out that he has killed his father by striking him down with a heavy spade. Instead of this confession being received with horror, Christy finds himself the object of awed admiration, especially by Pegeen. The word 'father', after all, expressed the essence of authority to the peasants, and to kill one's tyrannical father (symbolically) was to achieve the emancipation from authority which every peasant craved. At the same time, with its fear of authority and of desperate men alike, the community chiefly respects those who have the native force to take care of themselves and of those attached to them.

Christy's reception gives him confidence, and his confidence grows with Pegeen's admiration when he expatiates on his father's terrible power and tyranny. It culminates when he finds that she is the envy of the girls of the village for her prior possession of him – there was in any case a shortage of men in Ireland – and he wins all the village sports. Yet in the end the village turns against him. Too hard-headed to be destroyed by a blow from a spade, Old Mahon turns up (instead of the police, who would have done Christy's reputation no harm) in pursuit of him. The respect accorded to him is transferred to his father, whose bandaged head is enough to convince Pegeen and the villagers that Christy's action has not been an act of symbolic heroism but of crude (and bungled) brutality. As she says:

I'll say, a strange man is a marvel, with his mighty talk; but what's a squabble in your backyard, and the blow of a loy, have taught me that there's a great gap between a gallous story and a dirty deed.

But Christy has undergone one transformation, from the timid, frightened boy who struck his father only under desperate provocation into a village hero; he is not to be reduced again. Instead he becomes a third kind of man: he fights himself free of the villagers and assumes the bullyhood that is his father's style:

Go with you, it is? I will, then, like a gallant captain with his heathen slave. Go on now and I'll see you from this day stewing my oatmeal and washing my spuds, for I'm master of all fights from now. (*Pushing Mahon.*) Go on, I'm saying.

He leaves, with his father behind him, for the open road, and Pegeen laments

Oh, my grief, I've lost him surely. I've lost the only Playboy of the Western World.

The play caused an uproar of indignation at the Abbey Theatre; it was alleged to be indecent, because there was mention in it of a woman's 'shift' or undergarment, but clearly the real cause was that it dramatised not the dignity and heroic suffering of the common Irishman (as did *Riders to the Sea*) but his superstition, credulity and ignorance. The ordinary Irish public could not see that Synge had given Irish speech a glory that excelled all other uses of dramatic speech at the period: he made it eloquent from the meanest level of social life, to the extent that the characters who walked other stages looked like ghosts compared to his. Still less could they see that the thought latent in the play not only epitomised the Irish condition but also an issue common to the culture of western Europe. This was the relationship of art to the actualities of life.

The human imagination is always greater than the meanness of common human circumstances, and never has the disparity been greater than in this century. 'I call people rich', says Ralph Touchett in James's *The Portrait of a Lady*, 'when they're able to meet the requirements of their imagination.' The class that had always been able to do this had been the aristocracy, a fact that explains Yeats's constant allegiance to it, and his bitter nostalgia for its passing. Neither the middle class which had superseded the aristocracy nor the lower classes could, for different reasons, afford to meet these requirements; their use of imagination is for escape from their consequent sense of deprivation. It is this that has isolated the artistic function from the other social functions in our time, unless the artist has been prepared to prostitute his art to the prevailing wishfulness. The mental environment becomes fact, generalisation from fact, and theory deduced from generalisation, in mounting bafflement of the emotions: the more we know, the less we are able to grasp. The peasant, however, living in ignorance and isolation, uses his imagination differently from the other classes: fact is for him only what he witnesses; the rest of reality is what his emotions dictate, but at least he is not faced with the awkward dilemma of the other classes of having to acknowledge that what they dictate is a lie, since he has no system of generalisation and theory to belie it. Thus Christy Mahon innocently and unconsciously dramatises for the village their secret desire, and embodies

175

in himself a new folk hero; when he regresses to the common Irish bully and departs, he takes with him the drama that has momentarily released them – he was 'the only Playboy of the Western World'. But Synge has shown that at least in Ireland, where the only pure peasantry in the British Isles survived, an artist could arise and receive recognition by accident; in the middle-class and urbanised civilisation elsewhere, he did not even stand this chance.

Some time after Synge's death in 1909, the reputation of the Abbey Theatre and of the Irish drama was sustained by Sean O'Casey, whose most famous plays – *The Shadow of a Gunman* (1923), *Juno and the Paycock* (1924) and *The Plough and the Stars* (1926) were all produced there. Like Synge, O'Casey was of Protestant parentage, but unlike Synge he had a poverty-stricken background in the Dublin slums, and he was intimately and passionately concerned with the Irish Nationalist movement. The three plays are set in Dublin slum tenements, and dramatise the desperation of poverty and the confused and violent dissensions of the Irish movements – nationalist and socialist, loyalist and rebellious, Protestant and Catholic – which gave this desperation its peculiar terror. He knew his characters as one of themselves and presented them with humour and compassion, mingling their degradation, absurdity and pathos with their dignity and intermittent grandeur. As documents, the plays are moving records of Irish suffering, and something more, for they anticipate the squalid and terrifying urban wars that have become the nightmares of great cities in the second half of the century. As dramas of the human spirit, they are much more local in their interest. O'Casey's urban language has much less imaginative reach than Synge's cool and majestic command of the peasant idiom; the ugliness of the slum-dwellers' life gives it brutal vitality in scenes of violence, and grotesque vitality in scenes of comedy, but in the tragic scenes it can only convey the intensity of emotion without articulating it. For instance, Mrs Boyle laments her dead son at the end of *Juno and the Paycock* :

Maybe I didn't feel sorry enough for Mrs. Tancred when her poor son was found as Johnny's been found now – because he was a Diehard! Ah, why didn't I remember that then he wasn't a Diehard or a Stater, but only a poor dead son! It's well I remember that then he wasn't a Diehard or a Stater, but only a poor dead son! It's well I remember all that she said – an' it's my turn to say it now: What was the pain I suffered, Johnny, bringin' you into the world to carry you to your cradle, to the pain I'll suffer carryin' you out o'the world to bring you to your grave! Mother o'God, Mother o'God, have pity on us all! Blessed Virgin, where were you when me darlin' son was riddled with bullets? Sacred Heart o'Jesus, take away our hearts o'stone, and give us hearts o'flesh! Take away this murdherin' hate, a' give us Thine own eternal love!

This is a dirge, and it has intensity, but its power relies greatly on traditional phrases and invocations. If we compare it with Maurya's speech when her drowned son, the last of her family, is carried in, we see how Synge, in *Riders to the Sea*, makes his language enact the tragedy:

They've all gone now, and there isn't anything more the sea can do to me . . . I'll have no call now to be up crying and praying when the wind breaks from the south, and you can hear the surf is in the east, and the surf is in the west, making a great stir with the two noises, and they hitting one on the other. I'll have no call now to be going down and getting Holy Water in the dark nights after Samhain, and I won't care what way the sea is when the other women will be keening . . . It isn't that I haven't prayed for you, Bartley, to the Almighty God. It isn't that I haven't said prayers in the dark night till you wouldn't know what I'd be saying; but it's a great rest I'll have now, and it's time, surely. It's a great rest I'll have now, and great sleeping in the long nights after Samhain, if it's only a bit of wet flour we have to eat, and maybe a fish that would be stinking.

The difference is between emotion half baffled by language and emotion elucidated by language.

Synge's achievement was unique for evident reasons. It resulted from the encounter of an illiterate culture and a highly educated mind with extraordinary powers of sympathy. The culture was not long to survive; the mind was too rare to recur; the encounter could have no parallel elsewhere in these islands. The Irish dramatic renaissance was local in its origins, and ephemeral as a phase of even Irish history. It offered no prospects for English drama. Shaw, as we have seen, was equally unique, and the vein from which he extracted such brilliant ore was a thin one, its brilliance more striking than its substance. In the second half of our period, the most interesting advances were therefore in a different direction, and, in spite of the slenderness of his actual dramatic achievement, it was Yeats who offered the best prospects outside the Irish setting.

No culture which has once experienced supreme mastery in any medium can lose its fascination with that medium. The English had produced the greatest poetic drama of Europe in the reigns of Elizabeth I and James I, and poet after poet in succeeding generations sought to emulate the Elizabethans in that art. None succeeded, for reasons which Yeats was to make clear by his practice: the poets had failed either because they had tried to repeat Elizabethan successes, which meant imitating the Elizabethan voice instead of finding their own, or because they had sought an alternative in the style of classical, or French neo-classical drama, suitable for France with its Latin basis of culture, but unsuitable for England whose culture was ultimately northern. Yeats showed that the only way to recover a living poetic drama was to evolve a new language, by putting the Elizabethan tradition beside other traditions and evoking thereby a fresh idiom. In his advocacy of a small, private theatre, he probably made a wrong diagnosis of his times and the kind of poetic drama that could thrive in them, but we have seen that he achieved at least one success, and this was the success that influenced Eliot.

T. S. Eliot, over fifteen years before he published his first complete play, wrote critical reappraisals of the Elizabethan and Jacobean dramatists, particularly distinguished for what they showed about the evolution of dramatic blank verse and its suppleness in registering variety of tone and emotion in dramatic character. In his own poetry, he continued the Victorian tradition of the dramatic monologue, partly derived from the Elizabethan soliloquy, as a means of transmitting emotion through the voice of an imaginary character – Prufrock, Gerontion, and the young man in 'Portrait of a Lady'. *The Waste Land* is based on the effect of tones and voices, correcting, conflicting and contrasting one another, sometimes in direct speech; it is a poem which stands somewhere between the monologue and the true dramatic form. In 1932, he published *Sweeney Agonistes*, subtitled *Fragments of an Aristophanic Melodrama*. 'Fragments' are all it is, but the poem has an entirely new kind of dialogue – a pungent parody of common speech influenced by the syncopated rhythm of jazz:

Sweeney: Nothing at all but three things
Doris: What things?
Sweeney: Birth, and copulation and death.
      That's all, that's all, that's all, that's all,
      Birth, and copulation, and death.
Doris: I'd be bored.

Sweeney: You'd be bored.
Birth, and copulation, and death.
That's all the facts when you come to brass tacks:
Birth, and copulation, and death.
I've been born, and once is enough.
You don't remember, but I remember,
Once is enough.

Sweeney Agonistes is not so much the fragment of a play as a ritual, symbolising the brutality of the twentieth-century city at its starkest; it reminds us that in Eliot's *Dialogue on Dramatic Poetry*, speaker *E* declares 'that the consummation of the drama, the perfect and ideal drama, is to be found in the ceremony of the Mass'. In 1934, Eliot was commissioned to write the speeches for a religious pageant-play, *The Rock*.

So much of his work seems to have been impelling him in the direction of the drama, that it seems surprising that he only became a playwright late in his career, and by this time he had become so deeply Christian that it was natural enough that he should write Christian plays. However this faced him with a problem peculiar to his time: the temperament of the age, whether or not it can in any sense be called religious, is largely indifferent to Christianity, its nominal faith, so that specifically Christian plays would be regarded as directed at a special audience. It was a problem different from but analogous to his intention to revive dramatic poetry, for the audiences that would not go to a Christian play would also avoid a play in verse. His first play, *Murder in the Cathedral*, did not, as he himself says in his essay *Poetry and Drama* (1951), solve either problem, for it was designed for performance in Canterbury Cathedral to celebrate the martyrdom of St Thomas à Becket, and its explicitly religious subject and verse medium – original and contemporary though this was – both, in his opinion, received special tolerance from the circumstances. In his later plays (*The Family Reunion*, 1939; *The Cocktail Party*, 1950; *The Confidential Clerk*, 1954; *The Elder Statesman*, 1959) he tried to solve the dilemma and to capture the theatre audiences of London and New York.

Religiously, his method was to use the concept of the 'problem play' which Shaw had stamped on serious modern drama, but to change the problem from a social one into a psychological one, and then to show that the psychological problem was really spiritual.

179

Poetically, he devised a rhythm (learned from the later Jacobean dramatists such as Middleton, Massinger, and late Shakespeare) which would be imperceptible to the audience as a verse rhythm, and at the same time would be able to lift the language from the banality of common talk so as to convey the tensions of the mind when it is deeply moved. Tension, after all, until it reaches breaking point, is essentially rhythmical; rhythm arises from a tension between the static monosyllable and the tendency of language to become a shapeless fluid. Thus, in *The Family Reunion*, Eliot conveys the banal exchanges of the dull uncles and aunts in this form:

Gerald: Well, as for me,
I'd just as soon be a subaltern again
To be back in the East. An incomparable climate
For a man who can exercise a little common prudence;
And your servants look after you very much better.
Amy: My servants are perfectly competent, Gerald.
I can still see to that.
Violet: Well, as for me,
I could never go South, no, definitely never,
Even could I do it as well as Amy:
England's bad enough, I would never go South,
Simply to see the vulgarest people—
You can keep out of their way at home;
People with money from heaven knows where—
Gerald: Dividends from aeroplane shares.

An audience used to drawing-room comedies by Noël Coward would not notice that each line has four lightly accented stresses, nor the patterning repetitions ('Well, as for me . . .', 'I would never go south . . .') which give the inanities a style. On the other hand the same rhythms and patterning intensify scene 3, where Amy (the hero's mother) challenges her sister for having deprived her of her son:

Amy: I was a fool, to ask you again to Wishwood;
But I thought, thirty-five years is long, and death is an end,
And I thought that time might have made a change in Agatha—
It has made enough in *me*. Thirty-five years ago
You took my husband from me. Now you take my son.
Agatha: What did I take? nothing that you ever had.
What did I get? thirty years of solitude,
Alone, among women, in a women's college,
Trying not to dislike women. Thirty years in which to think.
Do you suppose that I wanted to return to Wishwood?

Amy: The more rapacious, to take what I never had.
           The more unpardonable, to taunt me with not having it.

The religious element, on the other hand, works less well in all his plays. A spiritual transformation, after all, is an inward happening, and Eliot never found a way of dramatising it externally. *Murder in the Cathedral* illustrates the problem. Becket is visited by four tempters; two of them represent the temptations of returning to favour and power with the king by recovering his former status as a favourite courtier and gifted bureaucrat; the third represents the temptation from the barons to lead them against the king. He disposes of these easily, for they are familiar to him, but he is defeated momentarily by the fourth, who comes in the guise of himself. This is the secret temptation of seeking spiritual glory as a martyr – a merely grander form of egotism. Becket is reduced to an agonised silence, while the four tempters gather round him pouring into his ears inducements to self-contempt, and the Chorus of the Poor Women of Canterbury plead with him to save, for their sake, his spiritual integrity. Whereupon Becket comes out with what is little more than a formula for self-salvation:

> Now is my way clear, now is the meaning plain:
> Temptation shall not come in this kind again
> The last temptation is the greatest treason:
> To do the right thing for the wrong reason.

The anticlimax, after the mounting attacks of the tempters and the agony of the Chorus, is too great: it cripples the play at its most vital point. Similarly, Harry's discovery of the origins of his guilt and fear in *The Family Reunion* is not adequate to explain his recovery of wholeness, even with the aid of the Eumenides (the Furies – but also the Friendly Ones) outside the drawing-room window, a device which Eliot himself ridicules in *Poetry and Drama*. In his later plays, Eliot tried to do with less and less of this sort of device, but his failure to find any more adequate way of dramatising the spiritual predicament made them progressively flatter. If Eliot set out to conquer the London West End stage for poetic drama, one might say that in the end it conquered him.

He was far from being the only dramatist in the thirties to attempt drama in verse. Most notably, Auden and Isherwood made experiments (such as *The Dog Beneath the Skin*) under the influence of Bertolt Brecht, but without Brecht's strength of conviction and savage force; Christopher Fry, with a much better sense of dramatic structure than Eliot's, wrote witty plays which in some ways remind one of verse equivalents of Bernard Shaw. Eliot remains the chief, and it must be remembered that his aims were modest: he declared that the best his generation could hope for was to prepare the way for a renaissance of poetic drama, much as Robert Greene prepared the way for Shakespeare.

All the same, the next tradition of English dramatists, working today – John Osborne, John Arden, Harold Pinter – returned to prose. It seems that the mistake of the poets in supposing that by verse alone could the dignity of the drama be restored was that they underestimated the subtlety, variety and depth achieved by the continental dramatists by their diversification of prose dialogue and their fusion of it with symbol. At all events, the next deeply interesting play in English was to be the prose *Waiting for Godot* (written in French, Englished in 1954) by another Irishman, Samuel Beckett.

Select bibliography

General

Anthologies of poetry

S. Bolt (ed.): *Poetry of the 1920s* (1967)
A. E. Rodway (ed.): *Poetry of the 1930s* (1967)
A. Freer and J. M. Y. Andrews (eds.): *Cambridge Book of English Verse 1900–1939* (1970)
J. Heath-Stubbs and D. Wright (eds.): *Faber Book of Twentieth Century Verse* (1973)
P. Larkin (ed.): *Oxford Book of Twentieth Century Verse* (1973)
Maurice Hussey (ed.): *Poetry of the First World War* (1967)

General history and criticism

B. Ford (ed.): *Pelican Guide to English Literature*, vol. 7: *The Modern Age* (1961)
Q. Bell: *Bloomsbury* (1968)
J. K. Johnstone: *The Bloomsbury Group* (1954)
G. S. Fraser: *The Modern Writer and his World* (1964)
U. Ellis-Fermor: *The Irish Dramatic Movement* (1954)
J. H. Johnstone: *English Poetry of the First World War* (1964)
V. de S. Pinto: *Crisis in English Poetry 1880–1940* (1951)
F. R. Leavis: *New Bearings in English Poetry* (1932; revised 1950)
Edwin Muir: *The Present Age from 1914* (1939)
D. S. Savage: *The Withered Branch: Six Studies in the Modern Novel* (1950)
F. R. Leavis: *The Great Tradition* (on the novel – James and Conrad) (1948)
Walter Allen: *Tradition and Dream: the English and American Novel from the Twenties* (1964)
J. I. M. Stewart: *Oxford History of English Literature,* vol. 12 (on Hardy, James, Shaw, Conrad, Kipling, Yeats, Joyce, Lawrence)

Works on and by principal writers discussed

W. H. Auden

Critical and biographical
R. Hoggart: *Auden; an Introductory Essay* (1951)

183

SELECT BIBLIOGRAPHY

B. Everett: *The Poetry of W. H. Auden* (1964)
J. W. Beach: *The Making of the Auden Canon* (Minneapolis, 1957)
M. K. Spears: *The Poetry of Auden: the Disenchanted Island* (New York, 1963)
J. Replogle: *Auden's Poetry* (1969)
J. Fuller: *A Reader's Guide to W. H. Auden* (1970)
F. Duchene: *The Case of the Helmeted Airman; A Study of Auden's Poetry* (1972)

Poetry and plays

Collected Longer Poems (1968)
Collected Shorter Poems (1969)
Poems (1930; 1933 with six omissions and seven additions)
The Orators: an English Study (1932)
The Dance of Death (1933)
The Dog Beneath the Skin (a play, with Christopher Isherwood) (1936)
Look Stranger! (1936)
The Ascent of F6 (a play, with Christopher Isherwood) (1936)
Spain (1937)
Letters from Iceland (with Louis MacNeice) (1937)
On the Frontier: a Melodrama (with Christopher Isherwood) (1938)
Journey to a War (travel book on China, in verse and prose, with Christopher Isherwood) (1938)
Another Time (1940)
New Year Letter (1941)
For the Time Being (including *The Sea and the Mirror*) (1944)
The Age of Anxiety (1947)
Nones (1951)
Mountains (1954)
The Shield of Achilles (1955)
The Old Man's Road (1956)
About the House (1966)
City Without Walls (1970)
Epistle to a Godson (1972)

Criticism

The Enchafèd Flood, or the Romantic Iconography of the Sea (1951)
Making, Knowing and Judging (Inaugural Lecture as Professor of Poetry at Oxford) (1956)
Secondary Worlds (1967)
The Dyer's Hand and Other Essays (1963)

Ivy Compton-Burnett

Critical and biographical
R. Liddell: *The Novels of I. Compton-Burnett* (1955)

C. Burkhardt (ed.): *The Art of I. Compton-Burnett* (essays by various writers) (1972)

H. Spurling: *Ivy When Young: The Early Life of I. Compton-Burnett* (first volume of a biography) (1974)

Novels

Dolores (uncharacteristic early work) (1911)
Pastors and Masters (1925)
Brothers and Sisters (1929)
Men and Wives (1931)
More Women than Men (1933)
A House and Its Head (1935)
Daughters and Sons (1937)
A Family and a Fortune (1939)
Parents and Children (1941)
Elders and Betters (1944)
Manservant and Maidservant (1947)
Two Worlds and their Ways (1949)
Darkness and Day (1951)
The Present and the Past (1953)
Mother and Son (1955)
A Father and his Fate (1957)
A Heritage and its History (1959)
The Mighty and their Fall (1961)
A God and his Gifts (1963)
The Last and the First (1971)

Joseph Conrad

Critical and biographical

M. C. Bradbrook: *Joseph Conrad: England's Polish Genius* (1941)
F. R. Leavis in *The Great Tradition* (1948)
G. Jean-Aubry: *Joseph Conrad: Life and Letters* (1957)
J. Baines: *Conrad: a Critical Biography* (1960)
E. Mudrick (ed.): *Conrad: a Collection of Critical Essays* (1966)

Novels and stories

Almayer's Folly (1895)
An Outcast of the Islands (1896)
The Nigger of the Narcissus (1897)
Tales of Unrest (1898)
Lord Jim (1900)
The Inheritors (with Ford Madox Hueffer) (1901)
Youth (contains *Youth, Heart of Darkness, The End of the Tether*) (1902)
Typhoon (stories) (1903)
Romance (with Ford Madox Hueffer) (1903)

185

SELECT BIBLIOGRAPHY

Nostromo (1904)
The Secret Agent (1907)
A Set of Six (stories) (1908)
Under Western Eyes (1911)
Twixt Land and Sea (stories) (1912)
Chance (1914)
Victory (1915)
Within the Tides (stories) (1915)
The Shadow-Line (1917)
The Arrow of Gold (1919)
The Rescue (1920)
The Rover (1924)
Suspense (unfinished) (1925)
Tales of Hearsay (1925)

Other work

Conrad's Prefaces (with an Introduction by Edward Garnett, who recommended Conrad's first novel for publication) (1937)
The Mirror of the Sea (1906)
Some Reminiscences (1912)
Last Essays (1926)

T. S. Eliot

Critical and biographical

F. O. Matthiessen: *The Achievement of T. S. Eliot* (1935, enlarged by C. L. Barber 1947)
F. R. Leavis in *Education and the University* (on the later poetry) (1943)
L. Unger (ed.): *T. S. Eliot: a Selected Critique* (a selection from important critical studies) (1948)
H. Gardner: *The Art of T. S. Eliot* (mainly valuable for *Four Quartets*) (1949)
E. Drew: *T. S. Eliot: The Design of his Poetry* (1949)
G. Smith: *Eliot's Poetry and Plays* (1956)
H. Kenner: *The Invisible Poet* (1960)
V. Eliot (ed.): *The Waste Land: a facsimile and transcript of original drafts including the annotations of Ezra Pound* (Introduction by Eliot's widow) (1971)
B. Bergonzi (ed.): *Four Quartets: a Casebook* (studies by various writers) (1969)
S. Sullivan (ed.): *Critics on T. S. Eliot* (1973)

Poems and plays

Complete Poems and Plays (1971)
Prufrock and Other Observations (1917)
Poems (1919)
Ara Vos Prec (includes 'Gerontion') (1920)

The Waste Land (1922)
Poems 1909–1925 (includes 'The Hollow Men') (1925)
In the series 'Ariel Poems': *Journey of the Magi*, 1927; *A Song for Simeon*, 1928; *Animula*, 1929; *Marina*, 1930; *Triumphal March*, 1931.
Ash-Wednesday (1930)
Sweeney Agonistes – Fragments of an Aristophanic Melodrama (1932)
The Rock – A Pageant Play (1934)
Murder in the Cathedral (play) (1935)
The Family Reunion (play) (1939)
Old Possum's Book of Practical Cats (1939)
Four Quartets: 'Burnt Norton' (first printed in *Collected Poems 1909–35*, separately, 1941); 'East Coker', 1940; 'The Dry Salvages', 1941; 'Little Gidding', 1942)
The Cocktail Party (play) (1950)
The Confidential Clerk (play (1954)
The Elder Statesman (play) (1959)

Criticism

The Sacred Wood (1920; enlarged 1928)
Homage to John Dryden (1924)
For Lancelot Andrewes (1928)
Dante (1929)
Thoughts after Lambeth (1931)
Selected Essays (1932; enlarged 1951; includes the five previous prose works)
The Use of Poetry and the Use of Criticism (1933)
After Strange Gods: a Primer of Modern Heresy (1934)
The Idea of a Christian Society (1939)
The Music of Poetry (1942)
Notes towards the Definition of Culture (1948)
Poetry and Drama (1951)
The Three Voices of Poetry (1953)
On Poetry and Poets (1957)
Knowledge and Experience in the Philosophy of F. H. Bradley (1964; a Harvard thesis of 1916)

E. M. Forster

Critical and biographical

L. Trilling: *E. M. Forster: a Study* (1944)
F. R. Leavis in *The Common Pursuit* (1952)
J. K. Johnstone in *The Bloomsbury Group* (1954)
J. McConkey: *The Novels of Forster* (New York, 1957)
K. W. Gransden: *E. M. Forster* (Edinburgh [Writers and Critics series], 1962)
M. Bradbury (ed.): *Forster: A Collection of Critical Essays* (1966)
P. Gardner (ed.): *E. M. Forster; The Critical Heritage* (1973)

SELECT BIBLIOGRAPHY

Novels and stories

Where Angels Fear to Tread (1905)
The Longest Journey (1907)
A Room with a View (1908)
Howards End (1910)
The Celestial Omnibus and Other Stories (1911)
A Passage to India (1924)
The Eternal Moment and Other Stories (1928)
Collected Short Stories (1947)
Maurice (1971)

Other prose

Alexandria – a History and a Guide (1922; enlarged 1938)
Pharos and Pharillon (history) (1923)
Anonymity: an Enquiry (1925)
Aspects of the Novel (1927)
Goldsworthy Lowes Dickinson (biography) (1934)
Abinger Harvest (critical and other essays) (1936)
The Hill of Devi: being Letters from Dewas State Senior (1953)
Two Cheers for Democracy (essays and reviews) (1951)
Marianne Thornton (biography) (1956)

Graham Greene

Critical and biographical

K. Allott and M. Farris: *The Art of Graham Greene* (1951)
M. B. Mesnet: *Graham Greene and The Heart of the Matter* (mainly concerned with the three 'Catholic' novels: *Brighton Rock, The Power and the Glory, The Heart of the Matter*) (1954)
J. A. Atkins: *Graham Greene* (1966)
D. Pryce-Jones: *Graham Greene* (1973)

Novels, stories and plays

Stamboul Train (1932)
It's a Battlefield (1934)
The Basement Room and Other Stories (1935)
England Made Me (1935)
A Gun for Sale (1936)
Brighton Rock (1938)
The Confidential Agent (1939)
The Power and the Glory (1940)
The Ministry of Fear (1943)
Nineteen Stories (including those in *The Basement Room*) (1947)
The Heart of the Matter (1948)
The Third Man and *The Fallen Idol* (1950)
The End of the Affair (1951)

The Living Room (play) (1953)
Loser Takes All (1955)
The Quiet American (1956)
The Potting Shed (play) (1959)
A Burnt-out Case (1961)
A Sense of Reality (1963)
The Comedians (1966)
Travels with my Aunt (1969)
The Honorary Consul (1973)

Criticism and travel

Journey without Maps (travel in Liberia) (1936)
The Lawless Roads (study of religious persecution in Mexico) (1939)
The Lost Childhood and Other Essays (criticism) (1951)
A Sort of Life (autobiography) (1971)

Thomas Hardy

Critical and biographical

L. Johnson: *The Art of Thomas Hardy* (1894; 1923 with new material)
F. E. Hardy: *The Early Life of Hardy, 1840–91* (1928)
    The Later Years, 1892–1928 (1930)
    (a two-volume biography, nominally by his widow, in fact by himself)
D. H. Lawrence in *Phoenix 1: Study of Thomas Hardy* (1936)
C. J. Weber: *Hardy of Wessex* (the standard life) (1940)
D. Brown: *Thomas Hardy* (1954; revised 1961)
R. L. Purdy: *Hardy: a Bibliographical Study* (1954)
J. Holloway in *The Charted Mirror: Hardy's Major Fiction* (1960)
F. B. Pinion: *A Hardy Companion* (a guide to the works and background) (1968)
D. Davie: *Thomas Hardy and British Poetry* (1973)

Poetry

Collected Poems (1930)
Selected Poems ed. John Crowe Ransom (New York, 1961)
Love Poems ed. C. J. Weber (1963)
Wessex Poems (1898)
Poems of the Past and the Present (1901)
The Dynasts (a verse drama on the Napoleonic Wars in three parts) (1903–8)
Time's Laughing Stocks (1909)
Satires of Circumstance (1914)
Moments of Vision (1917)
Late Lyrics and Earlier (1922)
The Famous Tragedy of the Queen of Cornwall (1923)
Human Shows, Far Phantasies (1925)
Winter Words (1928)

SELECT BIBLIOGRAPHY

Novels and stories

(i) *Wessex novels and tales*
Collected Short Stories (1928)
Under the Greenwood Tree (1872)
Far from the Madding Crowd (1873)
The Return of the Native (1878)
The Mayor of Casterbridge (1886)
The Woodlanders (1887)
Wessex Tales (1888)
A Group of Noble Dames (stories) (1891)
Tess of the D'Urbervilles (1891)
Life's Little Ironies (stories) (1894)
Jude the Obscure (1896)
A Changed Man and Other Stories (1913)

(ii) *Other novels*
Desperate Remedies (1871)
A Pair of Blue Eyes (1873)
The Hand of Ethelberta (1876)
The Trumpet-Major (1880)
A Laodicean (1881)
Two on a Tower (1882)
The Well-Beloved (1897)

Other prose

The Dorset Farm Labourer Past and Present (essay) (1884)
Life and Art (New York, 1925)
The Notebooks of Thomas Hardy ed. E. Hardy (1925)

A. E. Housman

Critical and biographical

A. S. F. Gow: *A. E. Housman* (a biographical sketch with a list of his writings including contributions to classical scholarship) (1936)
L. Housman: *A. E. Housman: Some Poems, Some Letters, and a Personal Memoir* (by his brother) (1937)
G. Richards: *Housman 1897–1936* (Oxford, 1941)
G. L. Watson: *Housman: Divided Life* (1957)
C. Ricks (ed.): *A. E. Housman: a Collection of Critical Essays* (1968)

Poetry

A Shropshire Lad (1896)
Last Poems (1922)
More Poems (1936)

Prose

The Name and Nature of Poetry (Cambridge, 1933)
A. E. Housman was a classical scholar who edited a number of Latin texts.

Henry James

Critical and biographical

F. O. Matthiessen: *Henry James: the Major Phase* (1944)
F. W. Dupee (ed.): *The Question of Henry James* (1947; enlarged 1956)
F. R. Leavis in *The Great Tradition* (1948)
Leon Edel: *Henry James (biography)* (1953–   )
D. Krook: *The Ordeal of Consciousness in Henry James* (1962)
L. H. Powers (ed.): *James's Major Novels; Essays in Criticism* (1973)

Plays

Collected Plays ed. L. Edel (1949)

Novels and stories

A Passionate Pilgrim and Other Tales (1875)
Roderick Hudson (1876)
The American (1877)
Watch and Ward (1878)
The Europeans (1878)
Daisy Miller (1879)
The Madonna of the Future and Other Tales (1879)
The Diary of a Man of Fifty and *A Bundle of Letters* (1880)
Washington Square (1881)
The Siege of London (stories) (1883)
The Portrait of a Lady (1881)
Tales of Three Cities (stories) (1884)
Stories Revived (1885)
The Bostonians (1886)
The Princess Casamassima (1886)
The Aspern Papers (1888)
The Reverberator (1888)
A London Life (stories) (1889)
The Tragic Muse (1890)
The Lesson of the Master (stories) (1892)
The Private Life (stories) (1893)
The Real Thing and Other Tales (1893)
Terminations (stories) (1895)
Embarrassments (stories) (1896)
The Other House (1896)
The Spoils of Poynton (1897)
What Maisie Knew (1898)

The Two Magics (stories) (1898)
In the Cage (1898)
The Awkward Age (1899)
The Soft Side (stories) (1900)
The Sacred Fount (1901)
The Wings of the Dove (1902)
The Better Sort (stories) (1903)
The Ambassadors (1903)
The Golden Bowl (1904)
The Ivory Tower (unfinished) (1917)
The Sense of the Past (unfinished) (1917)

Other prose

The Art of the Novel: Critical Prefaces ed. R. P. Blackmur (1934)
Notebooks ed. F. O. Matthiessen and K. B. Murdock (1947)
Letters ed. P. Lubbock (1920)
Selected Letters ed. L. Edel (1956)
James and H. G. Wells: a Record ed. L. Edel and G. N. Ray (1958)
The House of Fiction: Essays on the Novel ed. L. Edel (1957)
Transatlantic Sketches (travel) (1875)
French Poets and Novelists (criticism) (1878)
Hawthorne (criticism) (1879)
Portraits of Places (travel) (1883)
A Little Tour in France (travel) (1885)
Partial Portraits (criticism) (1893)
Essays in London and Elsewhere (1893)
The Question of Our Speech, The Lesson of Balzac (criticism) (1905)
English Hours (1905)
The American Scene (travel) (1907)
Views and Reviews (criticism) (1908)
Italian Hours (travel) (1909)
A Small Boy and Others (autobiography) (1913)
Notes on Novelists (criticism) (1914)
Notes of a Son and Brother (autobiography) (1914)
The Middle Years (autobiography) (1917)
Within the Rim (essays) (1918)

James Joyce

Critical and biographical

S. Gilbert: *Joyce's Ulysses* (1930)
E. Wilson in *Axel's Castle* (essay on *Ulysses*) (1931)
H. S. Gorman: *James Joyce* (biography) (1939)
E. Wilson in *The Wound and the Bow* (essay on *Finnegans Wake*) (1942)
J. Campbell and H. M. Robinson: *Skeleton Key to Finnegans Wake* (1944)

H. Levin: *Joyce: a Critical Introduction* (1941; enlarged 1961)
A. W. Litz: *The Art of James Joyce* (1961; revised 1964)

Works

Letters of James Joyce ed. S. Gilbert (1957)
Chamber Music (poems) (1907)
Dubliners (stories) (1914)
A Portrait of the Artist as a Young Man (1916)
Exiles (play) (1918)
Ulysses (1922)
Pomes Penyeach (poems) (1927)
Finnegans Wake (1939)
Stephen Hero (ed. T. Spencer; the first draft of *A Portrait of the Artist*) (1944)

D. H. Lawrence

Critical and biographical

J. Middleton Murry: *Son of Woman* (biography) (1931)
E. T.: *D. H. Lawrence. A Personal Record* (reminiscences by Jessie Chambers, the 'Miriam' of *Sons and Lovers*) (1935)
F. R. Leavis: *D. H. Lawrence, Novelist* (1955)
H. T. Moore: *The Intelligent Heart* (1955; revised 1961)
H. T. Moore: *Reader's Guide to D. H. Lawrence* (1951; revised 1964)
H. M. Daleski: *The Forked Flame* (1965)
R. P. D. Draper: *D. H. Lawrence: The Critical Heritage* (1970)

Novels, stories, plays, poems

Collected Poems (1932)
Collected Plays (1933)
Collected Tales (1934)
The White Peacock (1911)
The Trespasser (1912)
Love Poems and Others (1913)
Sons and Lovers (1913)
The Widowing of Mrs. Holroyd (play) (1914)
The Prussian Officer and Other Stories (1914)
The Rainbow (1915)
Amores: Poems (1916)
Look! We have come through (poems) (1917)
New Poems (1918)
Bay (poems) (1919)
Touch and Go (play) (1920)
Women in Love (1921)
The Lost Girl (1920)
Tortoises (poems) (1921)
Aaron's Rod (1922)

The Ladybird (stories) (1923)
England My England (stories) (1924)
Kangaroo (1923)
Birds, Beasts and Flowers (poems) (1923)
The Boy in the Bush (with Mary L. Skinner) (1924)
St Mawr and *The Princess* (1925)
The Plumed Serpent (1926)
David (play) (1926)
Glad Ghosts (stories) (1926)
The Woman Who Rode Away (stories) (1928)
Lady Chatterley's Lover (1928)
Pansies (poems) (1929)
Nettles (poems) (1930)
The Virgin and the Gipsy (1930)
The Triumph of the Machine (1930). No. 28 of 'Ariel Poems'
Love Among the Haystacks (stories) (1930)
The Man Who Died (1931) (previously published as *The Escaped Cock*, 1929)
Last Poems (1932)
The Lovely Lady (stories) (1932)
The Ship of Death and Other Poems (1933)
A Collier's Friday Night (play) (1934)
A Modern Lover (stories) (1934)

Other prose

Letters ed. A. Huxley (1932)
Phoenix I ed. E. D. MacDonald (a collection of essays including much of his best criticism) (1936)
Phoenix II ed. H. T. Moore and Warren Roberts (includes previously published work, esp. 'A Propos of *Lady Chatterley's Lover*') (1968)
Twilight in Italy (travel) (1916)
Sea and Sardinia (travel) (1923)
Psychoanalysis and the Unconscious (1923)
Fantasia of the Unconscious (1923)
Studies in Classic American Literature (1924)
Reflections on the Death of a Porcupine and Other Essays (Philadelphia, 1925; London, 1934)
Mornings in Mexico (travel) (1927)
Pornography and Obscenity (1929)
A Propos of Lady Chatterley's Lover (1930)
Apocalypse (Florence, 1931)
Etruscan Places (1932)

F. R. Leavis

V. T. Buckley: *Poetry and Morality: Studies on the Criticism of Matthew Arnold, T. S. Eliot and F. R. Leavis*

Works

A Selection from 'Scrutiny'. Compiled by F. R. Leavis (1968). Includes
    some of his own writings for the review he edited from 1932 till
    1953.
Mass Civilisation and Minority Culture (1930)
New Bearings in English Poetry (1932)
Culture and Environment (with Denys Thompson) (1933)
Revaluation (1936)
Education and the University (1943)
The Great Tradition (1948)
The Common Pursuit (1952)
D. H. Lawrence, Novelist (1955)
Anna Karenina and Other Essays (1967)
Lectures in America (with Q. D. Leavis) (1969)
English Literature in Our Time and the University (1969)
Dickens the Novelist (with Q. D. Leavis) 1970

L. H. Myers

Critical

G. H. Bantock: *L. H. Myers: A Critical Study* (1956)
I. Simon: *The Novels of L. H. Myers* (Brussels, 1956)

Novels
The Orissers (1922)
The 'Clio' (1925)
The Near and the Far (1929)
Prince Jali (1931)
The Root and the Flower (includes the previous two novels with the
    addition of *Rajah Amar*) (1935)
Strange Glory (1936)
The Pool of Vishnu (1940)
The Near and the Far (containing *The Root and the Flower* and *The
    Pool of Vishnu*) (1943)

Sean O'Casey

Critical and biographical

E. Bentley in *The Playwright as Thinker* (New York, 1946)
P. Kavanagh in *The Story of the Abbey Theatre* (New York, 1950)
D. Krause: *Sean O'Casey: The Man and his Work* (1960)
S. Cowasjee: *Sean O'Casey: The Man Behind the Plays* (1964)
S. Cowasjee: *O'Casey* (1966)

Plays

Two Plays (*Juno and the Paycock*; *The Shadow of a Gunman*) (1925)
The Plough and the Stars (1926)

The Silver Tassie (1928)
Within the Gates (1933)
The Star Turns Red (1940)
Purple Dust (1940)
Red Roses For Me (1942)
Oak Leaves and Lavender (1946)
Cock-a-doodle Dandy (1949)
The Bishop's Bonfire (1955)
Five One-act Plays (1958)
The Drums of Father Ned (1960)
Behind the Green Curtains (title play; *Figure in the Night; The Moon Shines on Kylenamoe*) (1961)

Other works

Mirror in my House (New York, 1956; republished London, 1963, under the title *Autobiographies*). Contains six previously published autobiographical volumes

George Orwell

Critical and biographical

L. Brander: *George Orwell* (1954)
Christopher Hollis: *A Study of Orwell* (1956)
Richard Rees: *George Orwell* (1961)
John Wain in *Essays on Literature and Ideas* (1963)
G. Woodcock: *The Crystal Spirit: a Study of George Orwell* (1967)

Works

S. Orwell and I. Angus: *The Collected Essays, Journalism and Letters of George Orwell* (1968)
Down and Out in Paris and London (autobiography) (1933)
Burmese Days (novel) (1934)
A Clergyman's Daughter (novel) (1935)
Keep the Aspidistra Flying (novel) (1936)
The Road to Wigan Pier (social study) (1937)
Homage to Catalonia (history and autobiography) (1938)
Coming up for Air (novel) (1939)
Inside the Whale (essays) (1940)
The Lion and the Unicorn: Socialism and the English Genius (pamphlet) (1941)
Animal Farm: a Fairy Story (satire) (1945)
James Burnham and the Managerial Revolution (pamphlet) (1946)
Critical Essays (1946)
The English People (in *Britain in Pictures*) (1947)
Nineteen Eighty-Four (novel) (1949)
Shooting an Elephant (essays) (1950)
Such, Such were the Joys (autobiography) (New York, 1953)

SELECT BIBLIOGRAPHY

Wilfred Owen

Critical and biographical

Edmund Blunden: Memoir in *Poems* (1931)
D. S. R. Welland: *Owen: a Critical Study* (1960)
Harold Owen: *Journey from Obscurity* (three-volume biography by his
brother) (1963–   )

Works

Poems edited Siegfried Sassoon (1920); new edition with additions ed.
Edmund Blunden (1931); *Collected Poems* ed. C. Day Lewis (1963)
H. Owen and J. Bell: *Collected Letters* (1967)

I. A. Richards

Critical and biographical

J. P. Schiller: *I. A. Richards' Theory of Literature* (1967)
Reuben Brower, Helen Vendler, John Hollander: *I. A. Richards:
Essays in his honour* (1973)

Works

The Foundations of Aesthetics (with C. K. Ogden, James Wood) (1922)
The Meaning of Meaning (with C. K. Ogden) (1923; 1936)
Principles of Literary Criticism (1924; 1926 with two appendices)
Science and Poetry (1926; enlarged 1935; republished as *Poetries and
Sciences* 1970)
Practical Criticism (1929)
Coleridge on Imagination (1934; 1950)
The Philosophy of Rhetoric (1936)
Basic English and its Uses (1943)
Speculative Instruments (1955)
Goodbye Earth and Other Poems (1959)
The Screens and Other Poems (1961)

Isaac Rosenberg

Works

Night and Day (1912)
Youth (1915)
Poems ed. G. Bottomley (1922)
Collected Works: Poetry, Prose and Some Drawings (1937)
Collected Poems (1949). Both collections ed. G. Bottomley and D. W.
Harding

SELECT BIBLIOGRAPHY

George Bernard Shaw

Critical and biographical

G. K. Chesterton: *George Bernard Shaw* (1909; 1935)

A. Henderson: *Shaw: Playboy and Prophet* (detailed biography) (New York, 1932; revised and rewritten 1956)

H. Pearson: *Shaw: His Life and Personality* (1942)

E. Bentley: *Shaw: a Reconsideration* (New York, 1947; 1957)

M. Meisel: *Shaw and the Nineteenth Century Theatre* (Princeton, 1963)

L. Crompton: *Shaw the Dramatist: Intellectual Background of the Major Plays* (1971)

Plays (with Prefaces)

Widowers' Houses (no preface) (1893)

Plays Pleasant and Unpleasant (1898)

(Pleasant: *Arms and the Man, Candida, The Man of Destiny, You Never Can Tell.* Unpleasant: *Widowers' Houses, The Philanderer, Mrs Warren's Profession*)

Three Plays for Puritans (1901)

(*The Devil's Disciple, Caesar and Cleopatra, Captain Brassbound's Conversion*)

Man and Superman (1903)

John Bull's Other Island (1907) with *How He Lied to Her Husband, Major Barbara*

The Doctor's Dilemma (1911)

Misalliance (1914) with *The Dark Lady of the Sonnets, Fanny's First Play*

Androcles and the Lion (1916) with *Overruled, Pygmalion*

Heartbreak House (1919) with *Great Catherine; Playlets for the War*

Back to Methuselah (1921)

Saint Joan (1924)

The Apple Cart (1930)

Too True to be Good (1934) with *Village Wooing, On the Rocks*

The Simpleton of the Unexpected Isles (1936) with *The Six of Calais, The Millionairess*

Geneva (1939)

In Good King Charles's Golden Days (1939)

Buoyant Billions (1950)

Some other works

The Quintessence of Ibsenism (dramatic criticism) (1891)

The Perfect Wagnerite (music criticism) (1898)

Dramatic Opinions and Essays (1907)

The Intelligent Woman's Guide to Socialism and Capitalism (1928)

Major Critical Essays (1930) (*The Quintessence of Ibsenism, The Perfect Wagnerite, The Sanity of Art*)

Our Theatres in the Nineties (theatre criticism 1895–8) (1931)
Music in London (music criticism 1890–4) (1931)
The Adventures of the Black Girl in Her Search for God (1932)
Sixteen Self Sketches (1949)

J. M. Synge

Critical and biographical

W. B. Yeats: *Synge and the Ireland of his Time* (1911)
    The Death of Synge (1928)
D. H. Greene, E. M. Stephens: *J. M. Synge* (biography) (New York, 1959)
A. Price: *Synge and Anglo-Irish Drama* (1961)
R. Skelton: *J. M. Synge and his World* (1971)
    The Writings of J. M. Synge (1971)

Plays

In the Shadow of the Glen (1904)
Riders to the Sea (1905)
The Well of the Saints (1905)
The Playboy of the Western World (1907)
The Tinker's Wedding (1907)
Deirdre of the Sorrows (1910)

Other works

The Aran Islands (1907)
Poems and Translations (1909)
In Wicklow, West Kerry and Connemara (1911)
Collected Works ed. R. Skelton (Oxford, 1962)

Edward Thomas

Critical and biographical

Helen Thomas: *As It Was* (1926)
    World Without End (1931)
    Two biographical studies by his widow
F. R. Leavis in *New Bearings in English Poetry* (1932)
J. Moore: *The Life and Letters of Edward Thomas* (1939)
H. Coombes: *Edward Thomas; a Critical Study* (1956)
W. Cook: *Edward Thomas: a Critical Biography 1878–1917* (1970)

Works

Collected Poems ed. Walter de la Mare (1920; enlarged 1928)
All written 1915–17. Thomas had previously written numerous prose works, of which the following are examples:
Richard Jefferies (criticism) (1909)

The South Country (1909; with introduction by Helen Thomas, 1932)
Algernon Charles Swinburne (criticism) (1912)
Keats (criticism) (1916)

H. G. Wells

Critical and biographical

Van Wyck Brooks: *The World of H. G. Wells* (1915)
P. Braybrook: *Some Aspects of H. G. Wells* (1928)
G. West: *H. G. Wells: a Sketch for a Portrait* (1930)
N. C. Nicholson: *H. G. Wells* (1950)
V. Brome: *H. G. Wells* (biography) (1951)
B. Bergonzi: *The Early Wells* (a study of the science fiction) (1961)
L. Dickson: *H. G. Wells: His Turbulent Life and Times* (1972)
P. Parrinder: *H. G. Wells: the Critical Heritage* (1972)

Novels and stories

The Collected Stories (1927)
The Scientific Romances (1933)
The Time Machine (1895)
The Stolen Bacillus and Other Incidents (1895)
The Island of Dr Moreau (1896)
The Wheels of Chance (1896)
The Plattner Story and Others (1897)
The Invisible Man (1897)
The War of the Worlds (1898)
When the Sleeper Wakes (1899)
Tales of Space and Time (1900)
The First Men in the Moon (1901)
Twelve Stories and a Dream (1903)
The Food of the Gods (1904)
Kipps (1905)
In the Days of the Comet (1906)
The War in the Air (1908)
Tono-Bungay (1909)
Ann Veronica (1909)
The History of Mr Polly (1910)
The Country of the Blind and Other Stories (1911)
The New Machiavelli (1911)
Marriage (1912)
The Passionate Friends (1913)
The Wife of Sir Isaac Harman (1914)
The World Set Free (1914)
Boon (stories) (1915)
The Research Magnificent (1915)
Bealby (1915)
Mr Britling Sees It Through (1916)

The Soul of a Bishop (1917)
Joan and Peter (1918)
The Undying Fire (1919)
The Secret Places of the Heart (1932)
The Dream (1924)
Christina Alberta's Father (1925)
The World of William Clissold (1926)
Meanwhile (1927)
Mr Bletsworthy on Rampole Island (1928)
The Treasure in the Forest (1929)
The Autocracy of Mr Parham (1930)
The Bulpington of Blup (1932)
Brynhild (1973)
A propos of Dolores (1938)
The Holy Terror (1939)

Some other works

A Modern Utopia (1905)
New Worlds for Old (1908)
The Outline of History (1920)
A Short History of the World (1922)
The Work, Wealth and Happiness of Mankind (1932)
The Shape of Things to Come (1933)
Experiment in Autobiography (1934)
The Outlook for Homo Sapiens (1942)
The Mind at the End of its Tether (1945)

Virginia Woolf

Critical and biographical

D. Daiches: *Virginia Woolf* (1942)
J. Bennett: *Virginia Woolf: Her Art as a Novelist* (1945)
B. Blackstone: *Virginia Woolf: a Commentary* (1949)
Dorothy Brewster: *Virginia Woolf* (1963)
Leonard Woolf: *Beginning Again* (a portrait by her widower) (1964)
Quentin Bell: *Virginia Woolf* (biography, two vols.) (1972)

Novels and stories

The Voyage Out (1915)
The Mark on the Wall (story) (1919)
Kew Gardens (story) (1919)
Night and Day (1919)
Monday or Tuesday (stories) (1921)
Jacob's Room (1922)
Mrs Dalloway (1925)
To the Lighthouse (1927)
Orlando (a critical fantasy) (1928)

The Waves (1931)

Flush (biography, about the elopement of Robert Browning with Elizabeth Barrett) (1933)

The Years (1937)

Between the Acts (1941)

Other works

The Common Reader (1st series) (criticism) (1925)

A Room of One's Own (sociological essay) (1929)

The Common Reader (2nd series) (criticism) (1932)

Three Guineas (sociological essay) (1938)

Roger Fry (biography) (1940)

W. B. Yeats

Critical and biographical

L. MacNeice: *The Poetry of Yeats* (Oxford, 1941)

J. M. Hone: *W. B. Yeats* (biography) (1942; revised 1962)

R. Ellmann: *Yeats: the Man and the Masks* (1948)
        The Identity of Yeats (1954)

T. R. Henn: *The Lonely Tower* (1950; revised 1965)

P. Ure: *Yeats the Playwright* (1963)

R. Cowell (ed.): *Critics on W. B. Yeats* (1971)

Poems

Collected Poems (1950)

The Wandering of Oisin (1889)

The Countess Cathleen and Various Legends and Lyrics (1892)

The Celtic Twilight (1893)

The Rose (1893)

Poems (1895)

The Wind Among the Reeds (1899)

The Shadowy Waters (1900)

In the Seven Woods (1903)

Poems 1899–1905 (1906)

The Green Helmet (1910)

Responsibilities (1914)

The Wild Swans at Coole (1919)

Michael Robartes and the Dancer (1921)

The Tower (1928)

Words for Music Perhaps (1932)

The Winding Stair (1933)

A Full Moon in March (1935)

Last Poems (1936–9) (1939)

Plays

Collected Plays (1953)

The Countess Cathleen (1892)
The Land of Heart's Desire (1894)
Cathleen ni Houlihan (1902)
The Pot of Broth (1904)
The King's Threshold (1904)
On Baile's Strand (1904)
Deirdre (1907)
The Unicorn from the Stars (1908)
The Green Helmet (1910)
The Shadowy Waters (1911)
The Hour-Glass (1914)
At the Hawk's Well (1917)
The Only Jealousy of Emer (1919)
The Dreaming of the Bones (1919)
Calvary (1920)
The Player Queen (1922)
The Cat and the Moon (1926)
Sophocles' King Oedipus (1928)
Sophocles' Oedipus at Colonus (1934)
The Resurrection (1913)
The Words upon the Window-Pane (1934)
A Full Moon in March (1935)
The King of the Great Clock-Tower (1935)
The Hern's Egg (1938)
Purgatory (1939)
The Death of Cuchulain (1939)

Some prose

Essays and Introductions (1961)
Explorations (1962)
Autobiographies (1953)
A Vision (1925)
Letters ed. A. Wade (1954)

Index

205

INDEX

Greene, Graham *(cont.)*
  The Power and the Glory 137–42
Gregory, Lady 155, 171
Grenfell, Julian 16

Hardy, Thomas 15, 17, *66–7*, 68, *69*, 70, 71, 77, 189–90
  Drummer Hodge 66–7
  The Self Unseeing 69
Housman, A. E. *65–6*, 70, 71, 77, 83, 190–1
  A Shropshire Lad 65–6
Hugo, Victor 38
Huxley, Aldous 92

Ibsen 6, 93, 165
Imagism 19
Irish Nationalism 20, 77–8, 93, 151, 176
Isherwood, Christopher 128, 130, 181

James, Henry 1–4, 6, 7, 9–10, 12, 13–14, 18, 21, *24–31*, 32, 37, 45, 46, 51, 191–2
  The Ambassadors 24, 26–31
  The Portrait of a Lady 25–6, 31, 175
Joyce, James 91, *92–101*, 122, 192–3
  Dubliners 93, 94–6, 97
  Finnegan's Wake 93, 94, 97, 100, 101
  A Portrait of the Artist as a Young Man 93, 96, 98, 99
  The Sisters 95–6
  Ulysses 91, 93, 94, 96–7, 99–100

Kipling, Rudyard 17

Lawrence, D. H. 10–14, 21, 22–3, 46, *47–64*, 92, 114, 122, 125, 145, 146, 148, 193–4
  Adolf 47–9
  The Fox 54–6
  The Rainbow 49, 56–62, 63
  Sons and Lovers 51–4
  Women in Love 52, 62–3
Leavis, F. R. 28, 125, 146, *147–9*, 150, 183, 193, 194–5
Lewis, C. S. 8
Lewis, Percy Wyndham 91, 123

Macaulay 15
MacNeice, Louis 123, 128, 130
Marxism 123, 128, 149, 170
Masefield, John 124
Metaphysical Poets 19, 83, 85
Middleton, Thomas 85, 88
Mill, J. S. 7
Milton 5, 171
Moore, G. E. 124
Morris, William 14
Murry, John Middleton 47, 49, 150
Myers, L. H. 125, 137, *142–5*, 195
  The Near and the Far (including *The Root and the Flower, Prince Jali, Rajah Amar, The Pool of Vishnu*) 142–5

Newman, Cardinal 86, 89

O'Casey, Sean *176–7*, 195–6
  Juno and the Paycock 176–7
Orwell, George 122, 125, *131–7*, 196
  Animal Farm 135
  Burmese Days 133–5
  Inside the Whale 131, 135
  Nineteen Eighty-Four 134, 136
Owen, Wilfred 16, 71–2, 73, 74, 197
  Anthem for Doomed Youth 71–2

Pater, Arnold 5
Pound, Ezra 16, 18–20, 83, 123

Richards, I. A. *146–8*, 197
  Practical Criticism 147
  Principles of Literary Criticism 146, 147
  Science and Poetry 147
Richardson, Samuel 8, 11
Rosenberg, Isaac 16, *72–4*, 197
  Break of Day in the Trenches 72–3
Rossetti 14
Ruskin 5

Sassoon, Siegfried 16
Scrutiny 148
Shakespeare 5, 6, 17, 85, 157
Shaw, Bernard 6, 22, 78, 114, *164–70*, 198–9
  The Doctor's Dilemma 166–9

INDEX

Shelley 15
Sorley, Charles 16
Spender, Stephen 123, 130
Stephen, Leslie 101–2
Swinburne 14
Symbolists 18, 20, 82, 83, 85
Synge, John Millington 78–9, 80,
  173–6, 177, 199
  *The Playboy of the Western
    World* 78–9, 173–5
  Riders to the Sea 173, 177

Tennyson 14, 19, 85–6
Thomas, Edward 16, 67, *68–70*,
  199
  In Memoriam (Easter 1915) 67
  The New House 69–70
Tolstoy 63

War Poets 16–17
Waugh, Evelyn 92, 123
Wells, H. G. 1–4, 6, 12, 13–14, 22,
  31–7, 45, 46, 50, 92, 114, 124,
  133, 200–1
  Autobiography 3, 32
  The History of Mr Polly 32,
    35–7
  The Island of Dr Moreau 32,
    33–4
  Marriage 3

Wilde, Oscar 5, 78
Woolf, Virginia 91, *101–7*, 111,
  122, 124, 125, 201–2
  A Room of One's Own 101, 102
  To the Lighthouse 91, 103–6
  The Waves 106
Wordsworth 7, 15, 146

Yeats, W. B. 16, 20, *74–80*, 89,
  92, 93, 122, 123, 146, *150–6*,
  170–3, 202–3
  Among School Children 151–3
  Byzantium 154–5
  The Circus Animal's Desertion
    156
  Coole and Ballylee 155
  Deirdre 172
  *The Irish Airman Foresees his
    Death* 75–6
  Purgatory 171–2
  Sailing to Byzantium 154
  The Second Coming 80
  The Tower 150, 151
  The Trembling of the Veil 153
  Vacillation 153–4
  Who Goes with Fergus? 75
  The Wild Swans at Coole 150
  The Winding Stair 150, 153, 154

Zola 9, 100, 133